Tales from Toadsuck

The Adventures of a Young Boy who Lived a
Life Different from Other People His Age

John "J. Dub" Black

iUniverse, Inc.
Bloomington

Tales from Toadsuck

iUniverse books may be ordered through booksellers or by contacting:

iUniverse
1663 Liberty Drive
Bloomington, IN 47403
www.iuniverse.com
1-800-Authors (1-800-288-4677)

ISBN: 978-1-4620-6357-4 (sc)
ISBN: 978-1-4620-6358-1 (hc)
ISBN: 978-1-4620-6359-8 (e)

Library of Congress Control Number: 2011961236

Printed in the United States of America

iUniverse rev. date: 11/16/2011

Contents

Acknowledgments

The stories in Toadsuck are true and took place at several small towns in Arkansas as our family moved about the state. While the events are as I recall them, the names of everyone involved have been changed except for my personal family members.

This book was inspired by my wife, who took the time and patience to convince me that it needed to be written. During three years of writing she was a tireless critic whose thoughts and comments made the book interesting reading. Without my wife, Linda Black, there would not be a book. Thanks, Linda, for challenging me to take the time to get it right.

My editor, Sara Harp, edited the chapters as they were written and challenged me, causing endless rewrites that made the book easier to read. Her talents as an editor were invaluable as we developed our story. Thanks, Sara, for a job well done.

And finally, a special thanks to my good friends at the Culver City Rotary club. They constantly prodded me, insisting that I "pick up the pace" and complete the book because they wanted a copy. Thanks—you were an inspiration!

Prologue
Toadsuck History

Toadsuck isn't a town. It's not even a village. It's a place located on the bank of the Arkansas River. The tale of how Toadsuck came about has been passed down from generation to generation over the years. Several versions of the story exist. This is mine as told to me by my parents when I was a young child living in the area.

Most of the counties in Arkansas are dry. You can't buy anything alcoholic in a dry county, not even beer or wine. The (then) small town of Conway is located in the middle of a dry county.

One of the goals of people living in a dry county is to get to one that's wet. The line that separates the two counties in that area is the Arkansas River. One side of the river is dry, the other wet.

The road that led from Conway to the wet county ended at the bank of the Arkansas River. A ferry had been installed there around 1850 that was large enough to take two wagons and their mules and drivers from one side to the other.

The ferry became more than a way to cross the river. As automobiles became common in the area, taking the ferry developed into a weekend social event. Cars would wait in line for up to two hours for their turn to cross. Men stepped out of their cars to talk about their farms and crops and speculate on the weather. Fishing stories and tall tales could be told as the men gathered in small groups under the shade trees that lined the road beside their parked cars.

The trip across and back could take most of the day. It was weekend entertainment with a stop at the bar located on the wet bank of the river.

The religious people of Conway were highly critical of this activity. They did not smoke or drink and looked down on people who did.

The saying got around that a wild bunch would take the road north till they came to the river, take the ferry across, and sit on a rail fence outside that bar, sucking corn liquor out of jugs till they swelled up like toads.

Over the years, that got reduced down to "Toadsuck."

Some residents in the town of Conway, where I lived, called the name a disgrace. A college professor even suggested that it be changed, but it didn't happen. Today the name and the ferry are a part of the history of the area.

Toadsuck for me was just one stop in the road as I traveled from town to town in Arkansas with my family.

Toadsuck ferry picture taken by Ernie Deane and provided by the Arkansas History Commission

Chapter One
The Men in White

I stood beside the window looking out at the road as an unmarked white van with no windows turned the corner, drifted down the street, and stopped in front of our house. Two men, both over six feet tall and wearing knee-length white smocks with short sleeves, stepped out and slammed their doors. The driver looked at my house and nodded, and they crossed the lawn toward our porch. Dad was in the house but not in the living room. I was watching from the window, and as the men reached the porch, I called, "Dad, some men are coming."

The driver mounted the steps and stopped at our front door. A mop of salted black hair hung below a white hospital cap with a small bill, shading eyes that were too close together and in constant motion. Pockmarked cheeks and thin lips over a wattle neck were imposing, and I released the curtain to avoid being seen.

He stepped to the door, made a fist with his right hand, and pounded hard as Dad came into the room. Frightened by all of this, I moved away from the window to the back of the room. Dad opened the door, and the driver, without smiling, said, "We're from the hospital and have come to pick up Alice Black. Is she here?"

"She's in the back bedroom," Dad answered. "Come on in." He pointed to the hall leading to the back of the house. I didn't know that Dad had called the hospital and arranged to have her committed. She had been acting strange for some time, spending long periods in her bedroom behind her closed door. The screams started several weeks ago and as time passed, increased in volume.

I was ten years old and did not understand the problem but knew that things were not right. Screams from her room were so loud the neighbors complained to the police. After each scream she would yell, "I'm going crazy! I'm going crazy!" It had been going on for several weeks, and the volume increased as Mom groaned at the end of each tirade. According to the police, the neighbors complained that the groans were as loud as her screams.

The men in white crossed the living room, and Dad led them down the hall to the bedroom. I did not understand what was happening and waited for them to return. Mom's screaming grew louder as the men dragged her down the hall, one on each arm so that she could not escape. She looked tiny between them but was kicking and screaming, "Let me go! Let me go!"

As they walked to the door, I shouted, "You let my mom go!" I jumped at the driver, clamping my teeth onto his forearm. The driver yelled, "Ahhhh, I'm just doing my job!" He knocked me into the wall, where I fell to the floor. In a daze, Dad stood behind the men; then he recovered and tried to reach out to me. He had been drinking early in the day and was too slow. I jumped up, ran at the man again, and screamed, "You let her go!" This time the driver was ready with a strong backhand to my ribs that slammed me into the wall again. Light flashed in my eyes, and I couldn't breathe. I fell to the floor, shaking my head in an attempt to catch my breath. The room was spinning, and I could not get up. Dad was beside me, and he lifted me by the arm and said, "Let her go, son. She has to go to the hospital." I squirmed but could not get loose. The men left the room, followed by Dad and me as they walked to the van to place Mom inside. I gulped air and jerked my arm away from Dad. The men opened the rear doors to the van. Inside was a cage with a wire barrier that restricted access to anyone in the front seats. A wooden bench was bolted to one wall. The remainder of the van was empty. The men lifted my mother into the van and pushed her forward as she screamed to let her go, again and again. As she fell to the floor, the driver slammed the doors, produced a key, and locked them shut.

Several neighbors came outside but remained on their porches, watching the events. Dad remained silent as I stood by breathing in gulps as tears ran down my face. My vision blurred with more tears as they drove away with Mom inside. Dad put his arm around my shoulders, pulled me close, and said, "Let's go inside, son."

I remembered that when the screams first started, I could go next door to Mrs. Carlson for help. Her visits seemed to calm my mother down, but it was only a temporary fix. When Mrs. Carlson left, the screaming would start again. After several weeks, she shook her head and refused to visit again, because it wasn't helping. I pleaded with her several more times but finally gave up because she insisted that Mom needed help she could not give. With tears running down my face, I walked home wiping my nose on my shirtsleeve.

I could hear Dad snoring on the couch, drunk again. We needed help, but I had no idea about what to do. I sat in the chair in front of the couch and wiped the tears from my face. I watched as Dad licked his lips, opened his mouth, and continued snoring. About noon, he sat up, rubbed his eyes with both hands, and then stood and walked down the hall to the bathroom and slammed the door. Our house was a "cracker box" that had been built at the end of World War II for families of veterans returning home to civilian life. Houses on both sides of the street were identical, each with a small living room that opened to a dining room, and a kitchen that was crowded by a two-foot circular table surrounded by three metal chairs with cracked vinyl seats. A small window above the table allowed sunlight to enter the room. A hallway at the corner of the living room connected the two bedrooms, one larger than the other. My parents' room had a double bed, two worn end tables, and a chest pressing against the wall beside a closet. My room had a twin bed and a wooden chest of drawers. They were hard to open but worked with a little effort.

When we first moved into the house, Dad built a small garage behind it and began repairing cars for money. With his reputation for good work, customers soon came calling. I became the parts cleaner. It was more fun than making mud pies, and nobody jumped on me for getting dirty.

Success was temporary because of Dad's drinking problem. He would disappear and not return home for days or even a week. During his time at home he kept half-pint bottles of booze hidden in the house and garage. When Mom found one she poured it out, but the supply seemed to be endless.

Dad walked into the room and staggered to his overstuffed chair, turned, and collapsed into the seat. This was common, at least on days when he showed up at all. I sat facing him in a worn chair that was Mom's favorite place to sit. I could tell by the glazed look in Dad's eyes that he had been drinking. We sat quietly as he looked at me, focused, and said, "What are you doing home?"

"It's Saturday," I answered. "There's no school today."

He scratched his unruly mop of gray-streaked hair, rose from the couch, and walked down the hall to his bedroom. He needed a drink, and I suspected that there was a bottle hidden in there somewhere. He would take a drink any time of the day, before daylight in the morning, or late at night. Sometimes he would wake up at three in the morning and take a drink. His body seemed to have a need, and the only solution was another drink. I walked into the bedroom as he reached to the top of the doorsill and removed a pint bottle for a quick drink. I knew the answer but had to ask, "What are you doing?"

"Just a little something to get me through the day," he said as he turned the bottle up, took a long pull, and sat down on the bed, replacing the cap. I knew that the bottle would be stored in one of his hiding places after I left the room.

The stash of bottles was endless, as long as there was enough money to buy more. He was like a squirrel hiding his cache of nuts in preparation for fall and winter. A squirrel never forgets where he hides his nuts, and Dad never forgot where he hid a bottle.

It's common for drunks like my dad to have a talent. It takes only a minute to remember talented people who have had their careers ruined by alcohol. Dad fell into that group, an exceptional mechanical inventor who lost it all to his addiction to anything alcoholic. His ability to repair cars, trucks, tractors, and anything else that had an engine was well known in the community where we lived. And people came to him for help. The key was to catch him when he was sober, but even half-drunk he was better than most other men.

I learned early in life to never trust an alcoholic with money. That's because the alcoholic sees money as an opportunity to purchase more booze. Forget responsibilities such as groceries for the family or a house payment. Go to the liquor store, purchase a bottle, and head out. With a paycheck in hand, Dad would disappear in search of anyone wanting to party. The family was left to suffer in misery, with no money until his return. Of course, when he did return it was because he was broke and had nowhere else to go.

One time Dad had been gone for a week. He walked through the door hungover, unshaven, and in badly wrinkled clothes. Looking through bloodshot eyes, he stated, "I'm sorry." This was Mom's call to battle. The remainder of the morning was so predictable it could have been read from a script. Mom's first question was always the same.

"Where have you been?"

Dad answered, "I was out with Carl."

Mom responded, "For a week?"

"We lost track of time."

With the initial Q and A out of the way, Mom was now ready for the serious part of the battle.

"Where is your paycheck?"

Dad chose not to respond, but Mom already knew the answer. It was gone.

Her next question was, "Do you still have a job, or did you get fired again?"

Dad answered, "I haven't been back. I'll go in Friday, get my tools, and pick up my last check."

Mom was on a mission to break him of his drinking habit. Her call to battle was as strong as Grant's attack on Richmond but as hopeless as Custer's Last Stand. Search and destroy of bottles was a daily ritual, never ending, but Mom had the stamina of a Brahman bull in her mission.

Mom's tirade started. "You're just a no-good drunk. You can't hold a job for more than two weeks. You don't care about your family. How are we going to buy groceries and pay the rent? All you think about is your next bottle." She raised her closed fist to her mouth, extended her thumb, imitating the neck of a bottle, and said, "Suck, suck, suck. That's all you do. Suck on a bottle!" I could see the anger in Dad's eyes, but Mom continued her attack, out of control.

Dad's solid backhand hit her, and she screamed. The force of the blow knocked her into the wall; she collapsed to the floor. I moved between the two, trying to protect Mom, but a young boy had no chance against a two-hundred-pound man, and I was thrown aside. Dad hit Mom again and again while I screamed, "No, no, no!" It did no good. Finally, he left her sprawled on the floor and walked out the front door, slamming it so hard the windows shook. I heard the car start and crunch into gear as he backed down the driveway to the street.

I tried to help Mom, but she could not get to her feet. Tears ran down my face, and I groaned as I sat on the floor, took her in my arms, and held her close. She moaned while I gently rocked her and said, "It'll be all right, Mom. It'll be all right." I realized that her mouth was bloody and blood was dripping from her nose as well. "Try to sit up and lean against the wall while I get you a damp cloth," I said. She was still dazed from the beating but managed to sit while I charged to the bathroom, wet a cloth, and returned. Folding the cloth, I reached down and gently wiped her nose and mouth. The fight was over but would be repeated again and again in the future.

There is no answer to the question of why my mom didn't leave, but she didn't. She stayed and Dad's binges continued, each followed by a fight. She taught second grade at a local school, which did not pay much but provided food when Dad used his paycheck for binges. Our survival was day-to-day. With Dad's disappearances, there were days when we had no food. Mom bought groceries with her pay, but it was never enough to last until her next paycheck. We fell behind on all our monthly bills. The lights and water were cut off for several days, but Mom managed to get them turned back on. Dad was not there and did not help. Pressure on my mother was a load too heavy to bear. She became withdrawn and spent her evenings sitting on a chair in an unlighted room. I could hear her screams as I played in the backyard.

"I'm going crazy! I'm going crazy!" Again and again. Never stopping.

Chapter Two
Early Arkansas Life

Dad was a mechanical genius who could not hold a job. His weakness for anything alcoholic caused most of his problems. Good mechanics were in demand, and Dad had no trouble finding a job even in small Arkansas towns. He believed that the reason for work was to get a paycheck so that the party could begin. When the money held out, he had no interest in returning to work the next day. He would party until the well was empty and then look for a new job.

We moved from town to town in Arkansas, and Mom convinced Dad to move to Memphis so that she could get a job teaching at a private school for boys. We spent a year in Memphis, Tennessee, and then moved back to a small town in central Arkansas.

We had few personal effects and no furniture, so the relocation was made in our 1937 Plymouth sedan. Dad used the money from the sale of the Memphis house to rent a service station just outside of town. It was a small place with two pumps for gas, an outside lift to service cars, and a small café that Mom opened daily for breakfast and lunch. Four bar stools and a small table with two chairs provided the only places to sit.

Mom was not much of a cook, but her chicken and dumplings were delicious. She made them every Wednesday, and it didn't take long for word to get around about a great lunch. Wednesdays were always busy, with local merchants and farmers looking for a good meal.

As business picked up, she needed more tables and decided to use an outside area shaded by several trees. Barrels with plywood on top were used for tables, and folding chairs provided seats. Red-and-white-checkered tablecloths brightened the area, and customers enjoyed eating outside on warm summer days.

Dad's friendly smile and warm handshake were easily accepted in our small town. His ability to repair cars became known, and people came to our station for repairs. Business was good, and the cash register was ringing. Mom prepared a grocery list each day and did the shopping after serving the noon crowd.

One day, Dad finished fueling a car at the pump, checked the oil, added a quart, and said, "Everything looks good." The man handed him the money and drove away.

I was sitting on a stool watching Mom clean the counter when Dad entered the room and said, "There are no more cars to service." The cash register rang when he punched the open key, removed all the bills, and said, "I'm closing the service area and will shop for groceries while you finish the day here."

Mom frowned as Dad put the cash in his pocket, but she nodded and said, "Okay." I had learned that Dad could not be trusted with money, and I saw the concern in Mom's eyes.

I watched from the window as he started the car and headed for town. Mom put both hands to her face and was fighting back tears. She blinked several times and moved her hands to her temples and rubbed them in tight circles while I sat quietly and watched.

A large man perched on a stool at the far end of the counter slurped chili from a bowl and smacked his lips. His deep forehead was shiny with sweat above thick white eyelashes over a nose the size of Arkansas. I stepped behind the counter as he motioned for me to fill his glass with iced tea. He glared at me while I filled his glass to the top and returned the pitcher to its place on the counter. As he raised the glass to his lips and gulped down half, I silently hoped he would finish and leave. With Dad not around, I was worried about a problem.

Two hours later, Mom and I closed the station and walked the few blocks to our new home. It was a small house that sat on concrete blocks with no foundation. The two bedrooms, bathroom, living room, and kitchen were adequate for three people. A tin wood-burning stove was located in the front room to heat the house. When the wind blew, it was an impossible task.

The yard was overgrown with weeds. There was no driveway, but the grass was worn where Dad parked the car at night. A large oak tree stood close to the porch steps with a rope tied to an old tire for a swing.

As the hours passed, Dad did not come home. Mom spent the night alone in the living room waiting for Dad. I stayed in my room but could hear her moan as she rocked back and forth in our ragged upholstered chair. Both arms were torn open, and the seat had a tear with dingy cotton poking through. It was my favorite place to sit because there was no way I could get into trouble for damaging furniture that beat up.

Dawn broke with no sign of Dad. Mom moved to the kitchen to make coffee but did not talk. I pulled a chair back from the table and sat watching her work at the sink. She turned and sat across from me, staring at the floor while tears welled up in her eyes.

With no money, she could not stock and open the station that day. The two dollars in her purse was not enough to buy food for the house. Wesley could be gone for days. They would lose the station to the landlord. The problems swirled in her mind and seemed endless. As tears streamed down her face, she mumbled, "Why has he done this to us?"

I sat quietly in a chair facing her and said, "He'll come back, Mom. He could be back today. It's going to be all right."

She told me to go to school and said she would wait for Dad to come home.

Dad showed up four days later and realized that his wife had to be committed to a mental institution. That move changed my life.

During the Roosevelt years, the Works Progress Administration was very active in Arkansas. Men working for the WPA erected state and county buildings around the state for use by local officials. Many became the center of activity in smaller towns. The town square was more than a gathering place for retired farmers to play checkers. A courthouse, county recorder, sheriff, and other officials occupied the building in the center of the square. Benches and tables were available on the lawn for conversation as well as for an occasional game of checkers. It was a friendly place to visit on a warm, sunny day.

I was too young to spend much time there but did know that most town squares had a pharmacy on one of the streets surrounding the state building that resembled our nation's capitol. And most pharmacies had a soda bar. That was a little piece of heaven if I could just round up enough money for an ice cream or fountain Coke.

It seemed like just about everybody in town needed a shoe shine. Dad bought me a shoe shine box with a footrest on top so I could shine a shoe while its owner rested his foot on the box. For me with the box at my side, the town square became my place of business. I was equipped with black and brown wax polish as well as liquid dye for use on the soles of each shoe. With a good shine, shoes looked almost new. I soon realized that a sales pitch helped to increase business.

"Shoe shine, mister? I have some fresh polish that will make them look mighty good! It will just take a minute, and you will be fixed for the day. How about it?"

The farmer looked down at his dirty shoes and said, "How much you charge for a shine?"

"Fifteen cents. That includes a wax shine, and I put liquid on the soles." I set the box beside his left foot and looked up with a smile.

"All right," he said. "Shine 'em up!"

When the shoes were black, I always used black liquid on the soles. Brown shoes were different. I gave owners of brown shoes the option of either brown or black liquid. That could become a major decision, so I always asked as I started putting shoe polish on the first toe.

"Do you want brown or black on your soles?" I continued.

"Keep shining while I think about it for a minute."

I continued to work and said, "Both look good, but I'm kinda partial to black."

"I believe I'll take black today."

I finished the second toe, tapped his leg, and said, "Another shine by Dub's Deluxe Shoe Shine service."

The farmer chuckled as he dug in his pocket and gave me a quarter. I thanked him and kept the change.

The town pharmacy was owned and operated by Ely Cooper, a thin man, in his midforties, with black hair combed straight back, and rimless glasses resting on a sharp nose over a well-trimmed mustache.

He wore a white pharmacy jacket over a blue shirt and spent most of his day filling prescriptions.

The large building served as a general store and even had a refreshment bar with stools where the customers could sit and enjoy their purchases. Fountain Cokes were the most popular, but Ely would build you a banana split if he was not too busy filling prescriptions.

The long aisles were stocked with just about everything a family would need. Paperback books and magazines lined shelves along one wall, and browsing was permitted.

Ely knew that I had a sweet tooth and had come to expect me and my shoe box on Saturday afternoons. That is, if weather permitted.

"Afternoon. What will it be, son—two scoops of ice cream or a root beer float?"

I had a weakness for both but needed to get back to the town square.

"I'll take a cone with two scoops of strawberry, Mr. Cooper." I watched as he stacked the scoops on a cone and passed it to me.

The key to eating two scoops with no drips is in knowing where to lick. It's even more important on a warm day, and I worked at it while returning to the town square.

The picnic tables were surrounded by men watching checker games. I weaved my way through the crowd, calling, "Shoe shine, fifteen cents. Shine 'em up. I'll make them look good as new." Before dark, I had almost two dollars in change, enough for a treat and a movie.

Dad had trouble holding a job again, and we moved several times in less than a year. I shined shoes in Conway, Hughes, Parkin, Beebe, Earle, and Bald Knob, all in less than a year. I was the shoe-shining version of Johnny Appleseed!

Chapter Three
The Trip to Conway

The annual family picnic was always held in a park near my grandparents' home in Conway, Arkansas. It was a long trip of over one hundred miles, but family attendance was required. If we failed to attend, we would suffer the wrath of Grandma. Mom insisted that we attend, but Dad was not looking forward to the trip.

She was packing two cardboard suitcases as Dad entered the room and grumbled, "We make this trip every year. I don't see why we can't skip this year. It's a long way, and our car is not in very good condition."

Mom replied, "My family only gets together once a year. I need time with my brother and sister. You can tolerate my mother for one night." She frowned and said, "It would be hard to explain to Mother that her mechanic son-in-law can't keep the car running." She chuckled, enjoying her joke.

I watched from across the bed as she packed. Dad stood near the door while she finished and closed the lids. She stepped away from the bed and with both hands on her hips, gave him a sly *you have to do this* grin and said, "These are ready to be loaded in the car." She was ready for an argument, but Dad just nodded and rubbed his chin as he crossed the room. He lifted the cases off the bed and groaned, "Did you load these with bricks? They weigh a ton!"

Mom stepped back with her hands on her hips and answered, "It's everything we will need for the trip. Stop complaining."

I followed Dad outside to the car and stood by while he placed the cases in the trunk. He turned to me and said, "Let's get some tools out of the garage for the trip."

He walked around the car and I followed, expecting to help. As we entered the garage, he said, "Get the tire pump and tube patching kit and put them in the trunk. We may not need them, but it's best to be prepared."

"Yes, sir," I answered. "Is there anything else?"

"No, I'll put what we need in the toolbox, and that should do it."

When the car was loaded, I climbed into the backseat and waited for Dad to start the engine. The trip to Conway would take all day over unpredictable roads, and I settled back and watched the countryside flow past my window.

Our next stop would be at Lena's Barbeque, a small shack beside the road at about the halfway point between towns. Lena's was known to have the best barbeque sandwiches in the area. It could be called a "take-out" place because the small clapboard shack had only one table and two chairs, rarely used by customers. The unpainted shed in back had been built for the sole purpose of smoking meat over a hot charcoal fire. The walls were seasoned and black from years of use in making the only item available, a barbeque sandwich on a fresh bun.

Dad turned our car into the parking area in front of Lena's and beeped his horn twice. Car service was available, and a slender black man dressed in worn jeans and a faded red T-shirt opened the front door to Lena's and slowly walked toward our car. He was over sixty, six feet tall, with rounded shoulders, snow-white hair, a broad nose, thick lips, and alert dark eyes. He looked at Dad, smiled, and said, "Can I help you, sir?"

"Yes," Dad said. "We would like three beef and two pork sandwiches."

"Yes, sir," the man said. "I'll have them for you in just a couple of minutes."

"Thanks. We'll wait," Dad answered as the old man turned and shuffled toward the shack.

Dad leaned forward placing both hands on the steering wheel and said, "That old man has been here for as long as I can remember, and I don't even know his name."

We sat quietly in the car enjoying the barbeque smells. When the man returned, Dad looked at him and said, "I have been buying your sandwiches for years. I never pass here without stopping to pick up some to eat on the road. My wife and son love your sandwiches as much as I do and wouldn't let me go by here without stopping."

Dad stuck out his hand and said, "My name is Wes." He cocked his head toward Mom and continued, "This is my wife, Alice, and my son, Dubbie, is in the backseat."

The old man smiled and said, "My name is Billy. I've been making sandwiches here for over thirty years. My wife and I own the place."

Dad chuckled and said, "You make the best barbeque I've ever eaten. I've been looking forward to some all morning."

The old man nodded and with a smile handed him a paper sack through the open window. Dad thanked him and turned to pass the sack to me with a warning: "We will eat at a stop down the road. In the meantime, stay out of the sack."

"Yes, sir," I said as the delicious barbeque smell wafted through the car. Dad backed, turned, and started down the road. My mouth watered as I looked at the sack knowing better than to touch it.

The road was worn from years of use and neglect. Our speed was less than thirty miles an hour, and Dad dodged the deeper potholes in our path. He concentrated on the road as the car sputtered and bounced through ruts and holes that were unavoidable. Steam rose from the hood and drifted over the windshield. He stopped beside a pasture filled with cows and said, "She's overheating. This is a good time to stop and eat." He walked to the back of the car and removed a vinegar jug of fresh drinking water from the trunk, placed it on the ground beside the car, and looked up to see if Mom was watching.

I stepped out of the car, shut the door, and watched as he ducked inside the trunk and lifted a small bottle to his lips and took several gulps. He returned the bottle to his hiding spot inside the trunk and whispered to me, "Don't tell your mother. I just needed a little something to perk me up."

The hollow feeling in the pit of my stomach was what I always felt before a fight started. I lowered my head, nodded, and turned away. Mom was opening her door but did not see Dad drinking. I watched thinking, *Good, another fight avoided.*

She opened the paper sack and gave us our sandwiches. I took mine, removed the paper, took a large bite, and sat on the fender of the car. Mom returned to her seat, and Dad ate standing beside me. She looked at me and said, "Go get the bottle of water. I've got some glasses by my seat." She reached beneath the seat and removed three glasses from a brown paper bag. I returned with the bottle, unscrewed the cap, and poured water into the glasses, resting on the fender. Dad continued to eat when I set the bottle on the ground and passed a glass to Mom. She remained in her seat as I continued to enjoy my sandwich.

When we finished eating, Dad said, "Open the hood, but don't touch the radiator. It's still hot, and you could get burned." He walked to the back of the car and reached into the trunk to get a water can to fill the radiator with.

Using a shop rag, he turned the radiator cap and jerked his hand away as steam hissed around the loose opening. I watched as the hissing slowly stopped and Dad removed the cap, shielded his hand with a rag, and began adding water. He stopped when the radiator overflowed and then replaced the cap. I returned the can to the trunk while Dad closed the hood and moved to his seat behind the wheel. I watched while he turned the key and pressed the starter button. The engine turned over but failed to start. Dad mumbled, "Damn car." He stopped cranking and switched off the key. "Let's give it a minute," he said, "and I'll try it again."

Mom turned to Dad and said, "You never work on your own car, always someone else's. If you spent some time fixin' this one, we wouldn't be sittin' here on the side of the road." Dad glared at her and said, "Shut up! I don't need you to tell me what to do."

A shouting match was under way, and I opened my door and stepped out of the car. I was an expert on my parents' fights, and this didn't sound serious.

"Someone has to," Mom answered as she opened her door. She stepped around the car and stood beside Dad, and then leaned in to sniff his breath.

"Have you been drinking?" she asked. "Do you have a bottle hidden in the car?" She turned and walked to the back of the car to inspect the trunk. Dad got out and followed her, shouting, "You stay out of the trunk. There is nothing there but tools."

The trunk lid was open, and Mom stuck her head inside to move tools around in her search for a bottle. She continued to dig inside the trunk as Dad glared at her and moaned, his mouth hanging open. I knew she would find the bottle; her specialty was finding bottles hidden around the house. The fight that always followed was a daily routine that I hated but had come to expect. I stepped between them in a futile attempt to prevent a roadside fight. Dad grabbed my arm and threw me to the ground without taking his eyes away from the trunk. I sat up and looked down the road at an approaching car, coming in my direction. An older couple sitting in the front seat stared at us while their vehicle moved closer. I placed both hands on the ground in front of me and jumped to my feet to get out of the way. The car passed, and they continued to stare but did not stop. I stood beside the road and watched as it backfired and disappeared around a curve into the woods.

Mom backed away from the trunk with a bottle in her hand, shook it at Dad, and screamed, "I knew it! I knew it! You've been drinking all morning!" Dad groaned and watched as Mom turned and threw the bottle against a tree. It exploded, and he leaped at Mom, grabbing her shoulders with both hands. She tried to pull back while Dad held her by her dress and backhanded her with his right hand. She fell to the ground crying hysterically with both hands covering her head. I stood frozen while she rolled on her stomach and tried to crawl away. I fell to the ground beside her, screaming, "No! No! No!" Dad ignored me and stood over us, glaring. I looked up at Dad and held up my hand, begging him to stop. "Don't hit her again! Please don't hit her again."

Mom groaned and rubbed her cheek, crying. I could see the fear in her eyes as she looked at Dad and said just above a whisper, "Please don't hit me again!"

He stood over her with his fists clenched and an evil grin on his face and shouted, "I told you to stay out of the trunk."

Time seemed to stop. Several minutes passed in silence. Dad was breathing in gulps, and I could smell the alcohol as his breath reached me. Finally, he rose to his full height and turned to the front of the car.

I stood and helped Mom to her feet while she continued to rub her cheek. "Are you okay?" I asked. Her face was starting to swell, and it was a bad bruise. She looked at me and made an unsuccessful attempt to smile. I moved beside her and placed my arm around her shoulder while she staggered and braced herself on the car to avoid falling. She was only five feet tall, but my head barely reached her shoulder.

Dad opened the car door and slipped into his seat as if nothing had happened. That was how the fights always ended. It was like a thunderstorm that blew through and was forgotten the minute it left. Mom was on the other side of the car, and he could not see her unstable condition. I held her close as she crept slowly beside the car.

I looked into her eyes and said, "Easy, Mom. I've got you. We're almost there."

The door was open, and I held her arm as she settled on the corner of the seat and mumbled her thanks and gave me a grateful look. I lifted her legs and moved them inside the car so that the door would close and then walked to the back of the car in an attempt to escape this craziness. It didn't work. I could not think of anything to do that would help. Frustrated, I gave the trunk lid a hard slam.

Dad continued to ignore Mom as he stared out the window and mumbled, "She should be ready. If it doesn't start this time, I'm going to have to work on the engine." The engine turned over several times, coughed, fired, sputtered, shook, and settled into a smooth idle. He cocked his head to listen to the sound of the motor and said, "It's a little rough but hitting on all cylinders. It should be okay." The engine backfired and revved as he pressed on the gas pedal, and then let it settle back to an idle. "We're fine," he said.

Mom sat in her seat and quietly sobbed as she patted her eyes with a hanky.

Stunned by what had happened, I stood behind the car with both hands in my hip pockets.

Dad stuck his head out of the window and shouted, "Get in the car. We're leaving." Afraid of being left behind, I jerked my door open and jumped inside, landing on the floor in front of the seat. The gears in the transmission ground as Dad pulled the floor shift into low and let the clutch out. The car jerked forward, slamming my door shut behind me. Still upset about the fight, I took a deep breath and scrambled into my seat as the car continued to jerk while moving down the road. I listened to the throb of the engine and stared at the front seat as my breathing slowed.

The trees passed by my window while I thought about what had just happened. Why did my dad drink every day? If he would just stop, maybe my mom and dad would stop fighting. Other families didn't fight all the time. I wanted a normal life with a happy family. Tears ran down my face. I rubbed my eyes with my fists and tried to swallow the lump in my throat as I watched the trees pass by my window. I leaned back, closed my eyes, and thought about the day when I would be big enough to protect my mom. I knew that day would come and dreamed about how I would beat Dad to the ground if he tried to attack my mom. I settled back in my seat listening to the purr of the engine and soon fell fast asleep.

Chapter Four
The Family Picnic

As we turned off the road into the park, I could see Grandpa standing beside a picnic table. Several boys my age were in a circle playing catch with a softball. My cousins Tommy and Billy waved and continued playing with two boys I didn't know.

Grandpa looked up as our car came to a stop and I waved. With both hands holding an ice cream freezer, he could only smile and nod his head.

I jumped out of the car, ran over, and said, "Hi, Grandpa. What'cha doin'?"

He laughed and said, "I'm gettin' ready to make some ice cream. Do you want to help?"

"Sure," I said. "Can I turn the crank?"

"This is a big ice cream maker, and it's full. It will take about an hour of cranking to get good, hard ice cream. You can start." He continued, "I'll get some of the other boys to take a turn." He waved his arm and shouted, "Billy, Tommy, come over here and help us make some ice cream."

They stopped playing catch and joined us beside the picnic table. I smiled and said, "Hi." They nodded, smiled back, and watched Grandpa position the ice cream maker at the end of the table. Ice had to be packed around the metal container inside the bucket before we could crank. Grandpa opened a cooler beside the table and, using his hands, scooped ice to place inside the bucket. I reached into the cold ice water and, using both hands, scooped ice and packed it around the container.

Grandpa walked to his car for more rock salt, leaving the cooler unguarded. Billy reached into the cooler for a small piece of ice, laughed, and threw it at Tommy, who lunged for the cooler and splashed water in response. I yelled at Billy to duck and stepped back to keep from getting wet. Billy looked in my direction and threw a piece of ice that I sidestepped. Everyone laughed as Grandpa returned to the table and continued packing the bucket with ice; then he sprinkled rock salt on top and checked the crank to make sure it was free.

I grabbed the handle and started to crank. It was easy and fun. The boys formed around me while I continued to crank. They knew I would get tired and were waiting their turn.

The ice cream started to freeze, and cranking became harder. I looked at Tommy standing beside the handle and said, "It's getting harder. Do you want to do it?"

He was older than me, and he took the handle and said, "I'm strong enough to crank till it's done."

Grandpa smiled and said, "When the crank gets so stiff it will hardly turn, the ice cream is done. That's going to take a while. We want good, hard ice cream. All of you will have a chance to crank before it's done."

I stepped back from the ice cream bucket and surveyed the park. Bleachers at the back of the park had been built beside a baseball diamond. It had been neglected, and high grass was growing in the infield. Several wooden picnic tables were scattered around, but most were not being used. Two boys pedaled bikes across the field and disappeared into the woods.

The table beside ours was stacked with trays and dishes of food. My favorite food, deviled eggs, sat on one end and looked too good to resist. When no one was watching I sneaked over, picked one up, and stuffed it into my mouth. It was delicious! A second one was a must. I picked it up, eating half in one bite.

Mom caught me sneaking food and said, "Get away from the table. We're going to eat in just a few minutes. You can wait." She smiled and gave me a gentle swat on the back of my head.

I went back to the ice cream maker. Billy was cranking and struggled with each turn. I asked, "Is it getting harder?"

"Yes," he said. "It's almost done."

I picked up the ball that was on the ground beside the table and asked, "Anyone want to play catch?"

Tommy stepped toward the open field and said, "Throw it to me."

My pitch was high and he jumped, catching it in his right hand. Several of my new friends walked to the field, and we passed the ball around. A bat was produced, and we went to the diamond to select sides and start a game. I knew how to hit the ball but was weak on running the bases. At my turn to bat, the pitcher lobbed a slow ball over the plate and I hit a fly to left field and ran toward first. The left fielder missed the fly and turned to chase the ball as I rounded first and started to second. When I was halfway there the boy on second caught the ball, and I slid to a stop, turned, and sprinted back toward first. The first baseman caught the ball, laughing, and ran toward me. I slid to a stop, turned, and started back toward second. The ball went over my head to the second baseman, who was laughing as he said, "Unless you've got a base in your back pocket, you're dead." I knew it was over and tried a slide but was tagged out, and everybody laughed as I jumped up and dusted off my pants.

The play was over when Grandpa looked at us and shouted, "Dinner is ready—come and get it!"

Mom had prepared my plate, making sure I had enough vegetables. I had a big appetite; my plate was piled high with chicken, sweet potatoes, carrots, green beans, salad, and a deviled egg, with a wedge of warm cornbread resting on the salad. I settled at a nearby table across from Tommy and Billy where they were enjoying their meal. Inserting the lone deviled egg in my mouth, I looked at Tommy and mumbled, "Maybe a good meal will help me to run faster."

Tommy laughed and said, "If you want to get to second, you are going to have to hit the ball farther." I groaned at the thought and took a big bite of my cornbread.

The adults sat at a separate table with Grandma in a chair at one end. This was her day to hold court. She was tall and slender with a full head of gray hair that had a slight purple tint. Her large, floppy hat shielded a face covered with cheap cosmetics to conceal the blemishes of age, a sharp nose, and a mouth that seldom smiled. A faded long-sleeve blue-and-white print dress reached the top of her laced shoes. Her steel-gray eyes were in a constant squint that could look right through you, and her false teeth seemed to always be clenched but clicked when she talked. The stuffy old gal ran the family, and Grandpa, with an iron hand. She was treated with great respect, feared and tolerated by all. She finished eating and moved to a nearby park bench, which was shaded by a flowering magnolia tree.

I made it a point to stay clear of her, but that did not always work. She looked at me and said, "Dubbie, come here and sit beside me. I want to talk to you."

I looked down at my feet wishing I was somewhere else, but I knew I had to sit beside her on what I believed bordered on death row. Thinking, *Let's get this over with,* I walked to the bench and sat as far away from her as possible.

She looked at me without smiling and said, "You are a nice-looking young man."

"Thank you, Grandma."

"Do you know what you want to be when you grow up?"

"Yes, ma'am, I do."

"What is it?"

This was the first time anyone had asked me that question. As I sat on the bench next to Grandma, I thought of that beautiful bright orange garbage truck with me behind the wheel. Me, in a blue uniform with a cap and telling my helpers what to do, driving the truck slowly down the street. I would blow my powerful air horn often so that everyone would know I was coming. My ambition was to be the person in charge.

I might as well give Grandma the good news. Looking directly at her for the first time, I said, "Grandma, when I grow up I want to drive a garbage truck."

She appeared to choke, and then coughed and said, "What?"

Maybe she didn't understand that it was a bright orange truck with chrome wheels and an air horn. Feeling confident about my career decision, I set about to help her understand and said, "It's a city garbage truck. Bright orange with chrome wheels and an air horn." *There, that should do it.*

Her eyes glazed over as she held a handkerchief to her mouth and gasped for breath.

I waited but was beginning to expect the worst. Could it be that she didn't like bright orange?

Taking a deep breath, she exhaled and said, "What? What? Did you say a garbage truck?"

"Yes, ma'am!" I answered. She was beginning to get it, and I said, "All the garbage trucks in town are orange and look beautiful."

Her face paled as she gasped for breath. She slumped forward with her head on her chest. Mom rushed to her side and began patting her back, looking daggers in my direction. Grandpa appeared at her side with a wet towel and placed it on her forehead, while Mom continued to gently pat her back. Not understanding the problem, I stood and stepped back from my seat and watched Mom and Grandpa trying to help her.

Things were not going well. I knew I was in trouble. When Grandma was on the road to recovery, Mom grabbed me by the arm, and off we went to the other side of the park. It was time for a talk.

"What on earth made you say you want to drive a garbage truck?"

Silence. The only way to go in this mess.

"When anyone asks you what you want to be when you grow up, tell them you want to be a lawyer or doctor. That's the answer—do you understand?"

I looked down at my shoes and said, "Yes, ma'am."

We returned to the picnic. I made a point of steering clear of Grandma. That worked. She did not call me over a second time.

The following morning we loaded the car for the drive home. I sat in the backseat and watched the countryside pass by. I still wanted to drive a garbage truck, but without telling Grandma.

Chapter Five
A Plantation Visit

Dad walked into the living room, looked at me, and said, "Your uncle Jed has asked us to come to the plantation for a visit. I'll have to do some work on our car, but we should be able to go this weekend."

I leaped out of my chair and said, "Can I help you work on the car?"

"Sure," Dad answered. "I'll pick up some parts this afternoon, and we can start tomorrow."

Mom walked in from the kitchen and said, "I can have us packed and ready to go Saturday morning. If we leave early, we can be there before dark."

Dad spent most of the next day under the hood of our old Plymouth sedan. A worn and rusted three-foot-long red toolbox filled with wrenches sat on the ground beside the fender. I waited in front of the box to place tools in his hand as he worked. It was a fun job as long as I passed the right tool.

Dad continued to work under the hood, stuck his hand out behind his back, and said, "I need a half-inch box-end wrench."

I opened the third drawer, found the wrench, and placed it in his hand. The tool disappeared under the hood briefly but was returned as he shouted, "You gave me an open-end wrench; I said a box-end. Put that back and give me the right wrench!"

I took the wrench and searched the drawers for the right tool, found it, and placed it in his hand. My eyes welled up with tears, but I wiped them away quickly so Dad wouldn't see.

We finished the work and tested the engine in time for Mom's call to supper. The engine ran fine, but the radiator had a slight leak. Dad turned the key to off and said, "There's a can of Stop Leak in the bottom drawer of the toolbox. Dump the entire thing in the radiator. That should stop it."

Excited about the trip, I was up before dawn the next morning. A long ride in a car was an adventure, and I was ready for the challenge. Dad carried two bulging suitcases through the front door and stacked them in the trunk beside a five-gallon water can, jack, lug wrench, pump, tire patch kit, and tools for emergency repairs. The trip from Toadsuck to the plantation would take most of the day.

The car bounced down the road as I fell asleep in the backseat. After an hour, the radiator overheated and steam drifted from the hood over the windshield.

I sat up as Dad stopped the car, checked the engine, and said, "As usual, old Betsy has overheated and we have to wait for the engine to cool."

An hour later, Dad filled the radiator, started the engine, and we were on our way. The dirt road had deep potholes and rocks that slowed our progress. Dad dodged as many as possible, but some were unavoidable. Steering around a tree stump near the side of the road, he said, "They say an Arkansas road is a stretch of land where the stumps don't exceed two feet in height, and I'm starting to believe it!"

The dirt road wound through the woods past several farmhouses and ended at a two-lane gravel road. As we turned right, the car began to vibrate, forcing Dad to stop. The left front tire was almost flat and needed patching. Dad looked at me and said, "Get the jack out of the trunk, and let's jack it up so we can take the wheel off and patch the tube."

We arrived in the late afternoon. After a glass of cool well water, we were shown to our rooms to rest. Visitors were always given an opportunity to recuperate from their journey. Our trip had enough trauma to justify a nap, but I was ready to explore the farm. Mom knew that I was too excited to take a nap and said, "Go on and have fun. Stay near the house. Don't go farther than the barn."

"Yes, ma'am," I said and walked toward the barn. Several mules stood idly in a pen beside the barn watching my approach. One walked to the gate and snorted, looking at me curiously. I opened the gate, stepped inside, and patted his neck. He nuzzled my shoulder, and I reached up to scratch his ears as I breathed the animal smells in the pen.

Days on a plantation start well before daylight. The women believed that breakfast was an important meal and cooked for a variety of appetites. I joined everyone at the table, ate half a biscuit, a piece of bacon, and most of my milk. No matter how much you eat, mothers always want you to eat more.

"Just take a few more bites," mom said, handing me a well-buttered biscuit.

You're kidding. I want to go outside, I thought and mumbled, "I'm full."

"They are starving in China, and you have to eat your food."

"Okay, anything to help the Chinese, whoever they are," I mumbled to myself. I reached for the biscuit, opened it with my thumbs, and placed molasses inside. Since I was required to eat more, it might as well be something good. While I worked on the biscuit, three men left the table and a fourth arrived, poured a cup of coffee, and left with it in his hand. I felt trapped and stuffed the remains of the biscuit in my mouth, gulped some milk, and started for the dairy barn. Milking had top priority, followed by plowing, and chopping or picking cotton, depending on the time of year. The early morning routine is all business, the air is electric, and each person has an assigned job that must be started on time and completed on schedule. With little or no conversation, everyone moved at a steady pace taking care of what was needed. That's plantation life.

The dairy barn was a long, narrow building beside an open field just to the right of the main barn. Windows lined the front wall and could be opened for ventilation. The back of the building was open, the roof supported by oak posts. Milk cows were trained to walk directly into their stalls to eat their morning hay while being milked. Several people sat on small stools beside cows and squirted milk into buckets resting just below their full udders. A barnyard cat stood behind Jim as he milked the cow closest to the side door. Jim squirted milk at the cat, and it opened its mouth to catch as much as possible from the brief shot. Laughing, I asked, "Does he do that every day?"

Jim answered, "He's a barnyard cat. He lives here and keeps mice out of the building. I give him a little milk every day."

The cat ignored me and went on his way. Everyone was busy milking, and I decided to walk to the main barn. My dad was there talking to Uncle Jed. They walked around the barnyard with me close behind.

Uncle Jed was a big man, well over six feet tall. A stained straw hat covered a full head of gray-streaked black hair. His face was lined and weather-worn. A full mustache shielded a large mouth that was turned down and seldom smiled. Steel-blue eyes and a booming voice left no doubt about who was in charge. High-top work boots, well-worn jeans, and a print shirt were standard dress for him every day. On cooler days, he added a denim jacket. The loose clothes concealed a strongly built two-hundred-and-ten-pound frame.

There was talk about the animals as we moved along the fence beside the barn. I followed along but was not paying attention to the conversation. Everyone stopped at the pigpen. The smell was strong and foul. The pen looked as large as a football field but was only about thirty by thirty feet in size. A wire fence that was supported by oak posts contained the hogs. The ground inside was muddy, with several large holes full of dirty water. One hog wallowed in the water, but several others moved toward us in search of food. A wooden trough inside the pen was used for their feedings. Their grunting sounds were frightening, and one had his mouth open, showing sharp teeth. Frozen, I stood watching.

My uncle looked down at me and said, "Boy, if you aren't good today, I am gonna put you in a feed sack and throw you in this hog pen."

Uncle Jed had my undivided attention. I was so scared that I would not talk to anyone for the remainder of the day. I believed what he said and wanted to make sure not to do anything that would cause him to throw me in the pen.

The best place to hide on a plantation is the loft of a barn. Bales of hay are perfect for building your own secret room. The hay is fun to play in and comfortable when a nap becomes the order of the day. I climbed the ladder to the loft with thoughts of building my own secret room.

Bales of hay stacked five high lined the back wall, with loose straw piled in front. Several sparrows fluttered about in the rafters. I selected several bales in front of the stack for building my private room, pulled them in line around the straw, and lifted several to make a second layer. My hideaway was complete, and I jumped into the pile of straw to enjoy the peaceful quiet of the loft. A sparrow flew from one beam to another in the ceiling and chirped while I lay back on the soft hay to watch. I fell asleep and woke up after dark to voices that were near the ladder leading to the loft.

"Has anyone seen the boy? He seems to have disappeared," Jim asked.

"Nope. Not around here," Marty answered. "We'll help you look for him."

After they left the barn, I climbed down the ladder and headed for the house. At first everyone was glad to see me, but then they were irritated that I had been gone so long. Mom had lots of questions, but being shy was my strong suit.

"Where have you been?" she asked.

I stood in front of her looking down at my shoes and waited for her to continue.

"You know better than to go off like that. Were you in the woods?"

Silence was the answer, and with my head bowed, I continued to look at the floor as I scraped my shoe back and forth.

Mom placed her hands on her hips as she glared at me and said, "You tell me the next time you head out like that!"

"Yes, ma'am," I answered. It worked, and I headed for the front porch.

Visiting Uncle Jed and Aunt Mabel in Mississippi was an exciting time because country life has so many interesting things to do. Uncle Jed managed a large plantation with several hundred acres of land used mostly for planting cotton. The center of activity was a sprawling log cabin home occupied by Mort and Olive, the plantation owners.

Storytelling was at its best in front of a fire. Mom and Aunt Mabel were moving about the kitchen and clearing the table. Dishes rattled in the kitchen as Mort reached for the poker, stirred the fire, tossed in another log, and settled in his rocking chair. Dad and Uncle Jed carried their chairs closer to the fire to enjoy the heat. Storytelling was about to start, a part of the day that was always past my bedtime. Trying not to attract attention, I moved to a wood crate near the stone fireplace to listen to them talk.

Uncle Jed said, "Did you hear what that crazy red mule did to Bill today? He was plowing with him and had the reins tied and over his back so they could come out under his arms. Something must have spooked Red, because he took off. Drug Bill over five hundred yards before anyone could get him stopped."

"Was Bill hurt?" Mort asked.

"Nope. But he was a little beat-up and mad as hell at the mule. I don't expect he will ever put the reins under his arms again!" Jed laughed.

Mort grinned and said, "No better way to learn than that." He went to the fireplace, added another log, and used the poker to move it on top of the burning pile. The fire hissed and popped as sparks flew up the chimney and heat warmed the room.

Returning to his seat, he said, "That electric fence we put in around the barnyard is really doing the trick. I saw one of the horses touch it with his nose, and he must have jumped back six feet when it bit him." Mort laughed and continued, "The charge is reduced by an amplifier so that the shock won't hurt an animal, but it is just enough to keep the livestock from trying to break out."

Uncle Jed watched the flames in the fireplace and said, "Jim Howell was over last week and decided to put an electric wire around the pen he has his prize bull in. Beautiful bull but mean as hell! Up until now no pen could keep him in for more than a few days. Jim said he was sick and tired of chasing him in the middle of the night and an electric fence might be just the answer. After he installed it, he plugged it in and took down the old barbed wire because it would no longer be needed. The problem was that Jim didn't think that he needed a condenser because of the size of the bull. He waited outside the fence with his son, Jimmy, as the bull wandered over and then touched the wire with his nose. One hundred and ten volts knocked that bull flat on his ass."

Uncle Jed laughed and continued, "Jimmy yelled, 'Daddy, Daddy, we've killed our bull! He's dead!' That fifteen-hundred-pound bull was sprawled on the ground without moving. Foam dribbled out his mouth, and his eyes showed only white. Jim sprang to his feet, ran toward the bull, and yelled, 'He ain't dead. Cut a sapling. I'm gonna beat on him until he wakes up and gets on his feet.' The farmhands stopped working to watch the show. It was a sight to see! Jim must have beat on that bull for a good ten minutes while everybody watching fell down laughing. The bull finally came out of it and sat up. After a few minutes, he wobbled to his feet and walked away. Jim headed for the barn to unplug the fence."

Mort snorted, and Dad laughed so hard he almost fell out of his chair. The story called for a taste of white lightning, and the jug was passed around.

"Did anyone find that runaway cow that was up in the north pasture?"

"Nope. We looked all over, but she was nowhere to be found. Must have gotten out somehow."

Mort wrinkled his brow and said, "I'll tell Bill to get a couple of men to look in the brush down by the creek. She probably went that direction looking for water."

There was a long pause while men gazed at the fire and took turns with the lightnin' jug. Bill came in to join in with the storytelling. I sat quietly on my crate hoping that no one would notice that it was past my bedtime.

"How's the cotton look?" Mort asked.

"Looks good. I think it's about ready," Bill said. "I looked at the back field today, and it's in full bloom."

"Do you think we ought to start pickin' tomorrow?" Mort asked.

"Yep," Uncle Jed answered. "Let's start with a full crew in the north field tomorrow morning."

Mort continued to watch the fire as he answered, "I'll tell the foremen tonight before we go to bed, and they will put the word out for an early start."

A day in the cotton field was always exciting, and I decided to get to bed for a good night's sleep. The hardwood floor was cool on my feet as I slipped out of my clothes and crawled under a soft wool blanket. The bed was cool but would soon be warm from my body heat. I pulled the blanket around my head and drifted off to sleep.

An outhouse was located two hundred feet to the rear of the main building. It was built in the southern tradition with a wooden door and a sloped roof that was of real value when it rained. A handle secured the door from the inside to provide some privacy. The Sears catalog resting next to the seat was the only paper available. It was believed that the catalog helped its user to build a strong constitution. It made good reading material along with a page or two for satisfying a personal need. A sack of lye sat on the floor with a cup resting inside. The lye was to be sprinkled in the toilet hole when we finished. It kept the smell down and the flies away. Another modern convenience of the twentieth century!

I soon learned that an outhouse is for daytime use only. It was located well away from the main house at the end of an unlighted path. Finding the small structure was difficult without a flashlight. In the winter, the seat was cold and if someone left the door open it could even frost over. Believe me, parking your butt on a frosted toilet seat is something you will let happen only once. I know and am now a member of the "daytime only" club.

The ringing of the breakfast bell woke me up. My featherbed was warm and comfortable, but I knew that the wood floor would be cold on my feet. When the morning's activities could no longer be ignored, I threw the covers back and stood beside the bed. Dressing quickly, I gathered up my shoes and socks and headed for the fireplace. Warm again, I waited for breakfast.

Food on a plantation is plentiful and delicious. Most men take in more calories for breakfast than Jenny Craig recommends in an entire week. They don't get fat, because plantation work is a grueling daily routine.

Hot biscuits were always on the table, and fresh-churned butter made them delicious. Sausage, eggs, home-fried potatoes, and strong coffee made for a hearty meal. Mom fixed a plate for me along with a glass of milk. I ate up hoping to avoid hearing about the starving people in China this morning. Cotton was in full bloom, and I wanted to spend the day in the fields.

When the coast was clear, I slipped out of my seat and moved to the porch. Several mule-drawn wagons were idle in front of the barn. Men were loading equipment needed for the day's picking. The mules stood quietly while their tails swished to keep flies away.

As the field workers boarded wagons, I trotted across the yard. A foreman ran each wagon. I was looking for Nate because I knew he would let me ride up front and pick cotton with his crew. He was in front of the barn loading sacks into the back of a wagon. At six and a half feet tall and well over two hundred pounds, with reddish-brown skin, a bald head, and muscular arms, he towered over me as I approached. I looked up and said, "Hi, Nate. Can I ride with you?"

He turned, smiled down at me, and said, "Sure! Are you gonna do some pickin' with my crew?"

"I know how to pick. Have you got a bag for me?"

"Our bags are a little large for a boy your size. Work with one of the men, and you can put your cotton in his bag. Is that okay?"

"Yes, sir. Can I ride up front with you?"

"Sure. Climb up. We'll be leaving in just a minute."

The good thing about riding on a cotton wagon is that you sit up high. You can see all over. The cotton crop was good, and the fields were solid white as far as you could see.

As the sun came up, men and women adjusted the shoulder straps on their bags and began picking cotton. The long bags trailed behind them as they moved down their rows. Swift hands moved from stalk to stalk plucking cotton to deposit in their bags. The field was silent, and the only sound was made by a crow cawing in the distance. A hawk high above made lazy circles as it searched below for food.

As bags were filled, each was weighed and recorded in the picker's name. Weighing a full bag is the time for a drink of water. The water barrel attached to the side of the wagon was cool even in the day's heat. Picking continued nonstop with only a short break for lunch. Most of the field hands carried a can of dog food as their only nourishment for the day. Red Heart was their favorite because it was pure horse meat and had the best taste.

A full wagon meant a trip to the cotton gin, and I planned to ride along. The gin was noisy and buzzing with activity. Several wagons were in line to have their cotton weighed and then sucked into the gin with a large vacuum tube. While waiting their turns, drivers climbed off their wagons to talk with friends from other plantations. It was a social time as they traded stories on the progress in each field. I looked down from my seat as several men gathered beside the wagon and began to talk.

"What does your crop look like this year?" Nate asked as he watched their faces for a reaction.

"It's good! The best I have seen since the flood," Gilbert said. "It must be good all over. Look at the wagons in line. All are full to the top. It's going to be a good year."

"Do you have enough pickers at your place?" Nate asked.

"We could use another fifteen, but there are no more around this year. Everybody has found work because the crop is so good."

We pulled forward under the suction pipe that would eventually empty our wagon. I jumped down from my seat and walked to the back of the wagon to watch it being emptied.

A man from the mill climbed into the back, reached up, and pulled the pipe down to begin sucking cotton into the mill. I watched as he worked from the front to the rear, cleaning out the wagon. Nate returned to his seat, and it was time to leave. Using the wagon wheel for a step I climbed up, sat beside him, and was ready to go. We returned to the field to join our crew for the second load of the day.

The picking continued as the sun began to sink below the trees and the white cotton turned gray. Our wagon was almost full as Nate climbed up to his seat and said, "We have to drop this load at the gin before we go to the barn. Do you want to come along?"

"Yes, sir," I said as I climbed into my seat. Nate slapped the reins on the rumps of his mules and in a commanding voice said, "Get up!" The mules jerked the wagon forward, and we were on our way. I looked back at our wagon loaded to the top with soft white cotton and jumped from my seat into the middle of the pile. The soft cotton felt good, and I decided to ride the rest of the way right there.

The line at the gin was longer this time but more relaxed. It was the last stop of the day, and the drivers gathered behind the lead wagon to talk.

"It looks like we're gonna make a good living off the crop this year," the front driver said. "Might even have enough money left over to visit Sally's this fall."

Several men laughed as one said, "Be careful. You can catch something visiting Sally's."

One driver grinned and said, "Yep, but it could be worth the trip."

The lead driver snorted, climbed onto his wagon, and said, "I'm empty. Got to go. I'll see you guys tomorrow." He pulled away from the cotton gin and started down the road toward his farm.

Nate pulled forward, and I walked knee-deep through the cotton to my seat so that the wagon could be emptied. Nate and I watched as the gin operator climbed into our wagon and pulled down the vacuum pipe and sucked up our load.

The mules walked faster after we left the gin and started home. Nate laughed and said, "The team knows we are goin' home, and they're ready to get out of their harness. It's been a long day. Are you hungry?"

"I sure am!" I said as I rubbed my stomach and heard it growl.

"We'll be there in a few minutes, and I suspect supper will be ready."

Mules are patient animals that are easy to work with in the fields. They seem to know what is happening and will stand quietly while the wagon is being loaded and made ready for the gin. Their pace between the gin and the cotton field is always the same. That changes at the end of the day when they seem to know they are headed for the barn. The pace picks up and the team will, on its own, break into a trot as we move out of the field toward the barn. Long shadows stretched across the road while I held on to my seat with both hands and the mules trotted home to end the day.

That evening, everyone gathered outside on the porch to talk about the day and tell more tall stories. Aunt Mabel made room for me on the swing. After a full day in the cotton field, I was ready to relax. My legs did not reach the floor, so she moved the swing slowly back and forth. As the men talked, I watched the pulsating glow of lightning bugs moving about in the front yard.

In the quiet, peaceful night I leaned against Aunt Mabel and soon fell asleep. I slept soundly beside my aunt until my dad picked me up and carried me to bed. I was so tired that I did not remember much about undressing, but I do know that Dad helped and threw back the covers so I could crawl inside.

Chapter Six
Saturday Night in Town

The trip from the plantation into town was a weekly event that always happened on Saturday. By mid-afternoon, the livestock had been tended to and the farmhands had returned to the lodge for weekly baths and preparation for their night in town. Water was warmed in buckets on the kitchen stove and poured into metal tubs located in the washroom. After a week of work in the fields, a bath was an enjoyable event. That is, if the water was warm enough.

The tub was half-full as I stepped into the water. It was cool, which for me meant hurry up. I grabbed the bar of soap and rubbed it under both arms and between my legs. Mom stepped into the room with a bucket of warm water and said, "Look down. I'm going to pour this over your head." I closed my eyes, ducked my head, took a deep breath, and waited for the water. She poured the entire bucket over my head and said, "Wash your hair. Your ears need a good scrubbing. Get them good."

I rubbed the bar between my hands to work up lather, let it fall into the water, and began scrubbing my hair. Mom always checked my ears, which made soaping and rinsing that area important. With my eyes closed, I continued to wash my hair and slipped under the water for a quick rinse. That done, I stepped out of the tub, did a spot dry with the towel, pulled on my jeans, gathered my shirt and shoes, and headed for the fireplace. I sat on the hearth with the fire warming my back while I put on my socks and shoes.

. Mom stood in front of the fireplace watching me dress and said, "I'm not going into town tonight. Your dad left at around noon, and I'm going to wait here until he comes back." I nodded as I finished tying my shoes and said, "I'll ride in with everybody else and stay in town until the wagon starts back."

A cotton wagon drawn by two mules would be our trip into town. The trip lasted about a half hour and carried a load of excited people that made for lively conversation

I stepped down from the porch as Mike stood beside the wagon looking in my direction. I crossed the yard as he turned, and using the wagon wheel for a step, I climbed into the seat. Picking up the reins, he looked back and asked, "Is everyone here? Are we ready to go?" I climbed in back and sat with my feet dangling over at the end of the wagon bed.

Bill nodded and said, "Everyone's here." Mike slapped the mules' rumps with the reins and shouted, "Get up!" The mules started their slow walk toward the road. Mike slapped their rumps again, urging them to move faster.

"Is anyone here going to the movie?" Nate asked. "I hear it's a western with lots of action."

"Not me!" Bill answered. "After we pick up some lightnin', I'm going down to the barbershop. There is always something going on there. How about you, Jed?"

"The first thing I'm gonna do is walk around town and try to find me a girl to talk to. Women are a lot more interesting than the barbershop."

Bill agreed. "Yep, but finding a lady is a lot harder than going to the barbershop." He chuckled. "That is, unless you go down to Cora's, but she charges." Mike looked back from his seat and said, "Right, and she could give you something you could take with you when you leave."

Everyone in the wagon roared with laughter. I listened but was not sure what he meant. Jed was sitting next to me and said, "Cover your ears, Dubbie. You're not supposed to listen to this." I knew this was about girls and gave him a sly grin but did not cover my ears.

Two men snickered as Chuck looked at Jed and said in a whisper, "And that could bring about a trip to Doc Wilson's office."

Jed grinned as he tugged at his ear and said, "I guess I should go to the barbershop."

Several men nodded as Mike said, "I'm not going by Cora's tonight. You guys are on your own."

I knew enough about girls to know they were a problem. I did not know how to talk to them, and my attempts at conversation usually ended badly. They always giggled while I tried to talk, making me blush. I could feel the heat on my face, and things got worse. I guess that "tongue-tied" applies to me, because around girls I could hardly talk at all. Playing kick-the-can was more fun.

I did not understand what they were saying about Cora, but I knew it didn't sound good. Visit Cora and then go to the doctor? I planned to remember this when I grew up, and I intended to stay away from Cora.

The sun dropped behind the trees, and shadows stretched across the road as the wagon bumped slowly toward its first stop, a stump at the edge of the woods that lined the dirt road. The county was dry, and everyone knew that making and selling whiskey was illegal. There were no bars or liquor stores in the county, and you had to drive to the county line to buy a six-pack of beer.

Teetotaling, born-again Christians believed that drinking was a sin and had voted in elected officials who supported their position. The peer pressure was so strong that even people who enjoyed an occasional drink voted to keep the county "dry." The issue had been settled years ago at the polls and was no longer considered to be a problem. The rigid citizens in the county could hold their heads high and profess to shun the evil of drink even though many enjoyed a nip now and then on their Saturday night in town.

A still less than a mile from town was hidden in a thickly wooded area that lined the road into town. The woods around the still were a dangerous place that the townsfolk avoided. Everyone knew that you could get yourself shot just walking in the woods near the still and steered clear of the area, but you could purchase whiskey using a system set up by the still owner.

Sam Robinson owned the farm that included the wooded area that concealed the still. His farming talents were questionable, but his reputation for making fine whiskey was known throughout Mississippi. Sam was over six feet tall and thin as a rail, with shaggy hair covered by a tattered and stained straw hat. His bulbous nose and unkempt mustache covered crooked yellow teeth stained from years of chewing tobacco. High cheekbones covered by pockmarks and a two-day-old beard gave him an imposing look. But Sam was shy and rarely seen in town. He ran the still alone and was happy making whiskey.

Even the sheriff knew about it, but the need for an occasional drink had brought peaceful coexistence to the area. That is, until the "born-again" group complained enough, forcing him to make a halfhearted attempt to locate the still. The sheriff and several deputies would enter the woods, making enough noise to be heard for miles around and announcing their approach. A gunfight soon developed, but both sides used shotguns that were harmless except at close range. Everyone fired their guns and there was shouting and yelling, but no one got hurt. The sheriff's halfhearted efforts at locating the still were appreciated by the town's residents, but the still was never found. Peace and quiet returned once again to the wooded area beside the road.

Just about anyone in town could obtain directions to the still. . Sam, however, was a cautious man. It was impossible to tell if he was watching from the woods, but most suspected that he was. I watched from my seat at the back of the wagon as we approached the tree stump.

Bill stopped the wagon and said, "Did any of you bring bottles for the stump?"

Three men nodded and jumped down as Nate answered, "I brought mine." He pulled a pint bottle from his rear pocket. Two men removed bottles that were sitting on the wagon floor behind the driver. "Remember," Nate stated as they walked toward the stump, "Sam does not make change, so you have to put the exact amount of money under your jug."

I jumped down from my seat at the rear of the wagon to watch what they were doing but knew better than to ask questions. This was for the grown-ups, and kids were expected to stay quietly aside while the transactions took place.

The two-foot-high tree stump was the only way to communicate with Sam. The process was simple and totally reliable. Place the money for your purchase on the stump along with an empty jug, drive out of sight, and return in fifteen minutes. The money will be gone, but your jug will contain what was known as the finest whiskey in the county.

Mike climbed up to the driver's seat, picked up the reins, and shouted to the mules, "Get up." Our wagon creaked and one mule snorted as we started to move out of sight of the stump. Nate sat at the back of the wagon with his legs dangling over the side and crossed them at his ankles. He looked over his shoulder and said, "This takes about fifteen minutes, but it's sure worth it." Several men nodded as the wagon stopped out of sight of the stump so that Sam could complete the transaction.

It was a good time to plan the evening. "Does anyone know who is in the movie tonight?" Mike asked. "Last week it was Whip Wilson."

I looked around and said, "The poster in front of the movie house last week said it would be Lash Larue. He uses a whip and always wins his fights."

"I like Tom Mix better," Mike answered. "He uses a gun and never misses."

Nate chuckled and said with a smile, "Right, at least in the movies. We can check the front of the theater on our way to the general store."

I sat beside Nate, swinging my feet as the wagon moved slowly down the dirt road. He turned around to comment, "They have westerns just about every week, but last month they had an Esther Williams movie. That's one beautiful woman, and can she swim. My tongue was hanging out by the time it ended, and I walked out of there with a limp."

Everyone laughed, and when they stopped Mike looked at Nate and said, "Are you carrying enough hardware to make you limp, Nate?" The wagon roared with laughter as Nate flushed but was slow to respond.

I turned to Mike and asked, "What's hardware?"

He looked at me and answered, "Ask me that again, kid, in a few years."

I jumped down from the back of the wagon and picked up a small rock beside the road to toss at a tree. Missing the tree and becoming bored, I began a search for another rock that was the right size.

After some thought, Nate answered, "I know a lady in town that can give you a good answer!"

Mike gave Nate a sly smile and said, "That being the case, she couldn't be a lady! Have you got an open account at Cora's?"

Several men laughed and one snorted while Nate sat quietly, hoping the conversation would die if he did not say any more.

"You guys can sit around daydreaming about women all you want," Mike shouted. "I'm going to the barbershop to find out what's goin' on in this county. Anyone that wants to go with me is welcome."

Enough time had passed, and the driver pulled the wagon around to the stump. Three men jumped down to collect their newly filled bottles. I watched but thought about candy at the general store. Red licorice was my favorite, and I intended to buy some to eat at the barbershop.

The wagon drifted slowly past the general store as I jumped out of the back and joined the crowd on the wooden sidewalk. Spending Saturday night in town was a weekly ritual followed by most of the farmers in the area. The walkways and streets were crowded with people enjoying the evening. Two men sitting on a bench in front of the store talked about cotton, and I stopped to listen as one said, "Have you seen the cotton bales stacked on the dock beside the gin?"

"Nope," the other man answered. "I haven't had a chance to get down there."

"There are so many bales it's impossible to take a count," the first man answered. "This has got to be our best crop in years."

The gin was located three blocks away beside the railroad tracks. I decided to walk down and take a look. The bales were taller than my head and broader than my outstretched arms. Three-inch-wide metal bands held the compact cotton securely in place. The bales were stacked two high, but one lone bale sat by itself in front of the pile. I leaned against it, but it did not move. The compressed cotton had to weigh several hundred pounds.

I jumped down from the dock and saw two boys my age sitting on the ground beside the railroad tracks, and I recognized Tommy. He looked up as I approached and said, "Hi, what'cha doin'?"

Tommy smiled and said, "We're having ourselves a cigarette."

"Have you ever smoked before?" I asked.

"Yes," he answered, "but my folks don't know about it. Me and Wendell hide when we do it."

Wendell nodded and said, "My folks would thrash me good if they caught me smoking. I keep the cigarettes hidden in the tack room at the barn." He laughed, took a drag, inhaled, and coughed.

I laughed and said, "You guys have never smoked. You are bullshittin' me while you try to learn how."

Tommy was two years older than me and a head taller. He stood, glared at me, and said, "Do you want to fight about it?" Both his hands were balled into fists, and he took practice swings in the air while stepping in my direction. I had learned to stay out of a fight you can't win, and this one was hopeless. I stepped back and said, "Hey, I was just kidding." He dropped his arms and unclenched his fists as I backed away. I took a deep breath, relaxed to blow it out, and asked, "Can I have a puff? I know how to smoke."

Tommy looked at me and said, "If you know how to smoke, how come you don't have some cigarettes?"

"I don't have any place to hide them, but I have smoked before," I lied.

"Okay," Tommy answered, "but only one puff, 'cause we can't stay here all night."

I reached out as he handed me the lit cigarette. With the cigarette in my right hand, I looked down and placed the damp paper to my lips. Tommy and his friend watched as I tried to look like I knew what to do, but actually, I had no idea. I sucked in, and the smoke burned my throat and filled my lungs. It hurt, and I jerked the cigarette away as I bent over and coughed out of control. Both boys roared with laughter while I held my stomach and continued to cough. Everything started to spin and I staggered back, tripping over my feet. I tried to sit as Tommy stood over me laughing and said, "Now who's bullshittin' who? Admit this is the first puff you've ever had."

I continued to cough and answered with a nod, turning away. Tommy moved in front of me and with a sly grin, said, "You don't know how to smoke, do you? This is your first try, isn't it? Admit it."

I coughed again, cleared my throat, and said, "It's my first time, and I don't want to learn how." I decided to leave them puffing away and walk back into town. I walked away as Tommy screamed, "Beat it, wimpy!"

The barbershop was busy with men waiting on the bench beside the door. I settled on the steps as Mike started to tell one of his stories. Several men were smoking, and he saw this as an opportunity to have some fun. He looked over at two men puffing away and commented, "Smoking will kill you, but the cigarette companies will never admit it."

He waited, giving them a chance to nod in agreement, and continued, "They found the answer. It was an eighty-five-year-old farmer living south of here that had smoked his entire life—over two packs a day. The man from the cigarette company went to him and asked him if it was true that he had smoked Camels all of his life. The farmer said he started smoking when he was eleven and never stopped.

The cigarette man asked him if he would be willing to make a commercial about how long he had smoked. The farmer said he would be happy to, as he took a drag from his cigarette. The cigarette guy said to come to his office at nine the next morning to be filmed having a smoke and telling his story. The farmer said he couldn't do it then. The man said, 'Okay, how about ten o'clock?' Nope, not then either. The cigarette feller said, 'All right, let's do it at one o'clock. Is that all right?'".

All conversation had stopped. Mike had everyone's attention and was ready for his punch line. He leaned forward and said, "The farmer looked at the man and said, 'You don't understand. I don't stop coughing until three in the afternoon.'"

Everyone roared with laughter while the two men who were smoking snuffed out their cigarettes.

Laughter continued as several men shook their heads and pulled pint bottles from their hip pockets. I watched as the bottles were passed around, with men taking drinks and breathing out loudly to reduce the burn in their mouths. I looked away and thought of the last fight my dad had had with Mom. He came home drunk and in a foul mood. Mom yelled at him, and the fight was on. I wasn't big enough to stop it, but I tried, and Dad grabbed me by the arm and threw me into the wall.

The man sitting beside me on the steps saw the sad look on my face and asked, "Son, are you okay? You look like something is bothering you."

I turned to him, managed a weak smile, and said, "Thank you for asking. I was just thinking about something I need to do."

He nodded and rejoined the conversation on the porch.

The sun had set, and quiet time came to the barbershop porch. Two men in rocking chairs talked quietly, keeping the conversation to themselves. I thought about the smoking story as I walked to the general store to buy a little more licorice. After my problem at the cotton gin, I decided that smoking was not something I intended to do when I grew up.

I crossed the street holding my brown paper bag of licorice and read the marquee about the movie. It was a shoot-'em- up with John Wayne. My favorite. John Wayne always wore a white hat and beat up the bad guys. It was easy to tell who the bad guys were because they always wore black hats. The theater was packed, and I took a seat up front so I could enjoy all the action. The movie was great. John Wayne gave the rustlers a lickin', and he didn't even lose his hat. My kind of movie!

I left the theater and walked toward the wagon, knowing that we always left after the movie ended. Mike was not there, but several men stood close by talking as I climbed in back and leaned against the sideboard. The trip home was always quiet, and I began to daydream about wearing a white hat and beating up on the bad guys.

Chapter Seven
A Plantation Funeral

Bo was born in a shanty house on my family's plantation. Most black plantation workers had little or no classroom schooling, and Bo was no exception. He could read some but had never been given the opportunity to learn how to write. The challenges of plantation work did not require the use of either skill. Bo was good at planting, picking, and chopping cotton, which was all that was required.

He was twenty years old, six feet tall, with a thirty-inch waist, broad shoulders, and a wiry athletic frame. His mosquito-bitten arms were moist with sweat as he worked picking cotton in the fields. A thin print shirt offered some protection with a worn sweat-stained straw hat shielding his face and neck from the hot delta sun. His calloused bare feet looked overly large below ragged jeans that were too short. A quick temper and willingness to fight were the reasons for several scars on his face, the largest just above his left eye. His dark eyes were those of a troubled young man.

As dawn began to break, the field-workers lifted their long cotton bags from the back of the wagon. Each bag had a shoulder strap so that both hands were free for picking. The long bags dragged on the ground as they moved down the rows pulling cotton for their daily earnings.

As the sun rose over the distant trees, the fields were white as far as you could see. It was a good year, and the cotton was in full bloom and ready. While the men concentrated on picking, the quiet in the field was interrupted by the call of a crow flying overhead. Faster pickers with full bags returned to the wagon to deposit their loads.

The foreman stood at the rear of the wagon and waited for his crew to return to deposit their cotton. A hook dangled from a scale attached to a post on the wagon to weigh each bag before it was emptied. The weight would be entered on a board alongside the picker's name. At the end of the day, the weights would be tallied and each person paid in cash. Bo slipped the strap over his right shoulder and started down his row with the bag moving along the ground at his side. The sun was up, and the day started to warm. He would pick until the bag was full and then return to the wagon, and weigh and deposit his load.

I jumped down from my seat on the wagon and walked with shirtless cotton pickers as they entered the field and began filling their sacks. Bo was beside me, and I listened as he talked.

"I'm going to leave this place one of these days," Bo said to his friend in the next row. "There is more to life than pickin' cotton."

"There is nothing wrong with pickin' cotton," came the response. "We been doing it all our lives. No reason to change."

"I know life can be better than this, and I intend to find out," Bo stated. "I'm gonna talk to Mr. Jed about a better job so I can save me some money."

"All you gonna do is make Mr. Jed mad. He gets mean when he is mad. If I was you, I would leave that man alone."

"I'm not gonna let him beat me up," Bo fumed. "I'm gonna take along a club to protect myself."

The bag filled as he neared the end of the row. It was time to return to the wagon. Bo lifted the bag and placed it on the hook while the foreman watched, noted the weight, frowned, and entered it on his clipboard.

"Your bag is light, Bo," the foreman said. "You're moving slow out there. Everybody else has already weighed their first bag, and all of them are heavier than yours. You are not going to make much money today unless you pick it up."

Bo looked down, avoiding the piercing eyes of his boss, and moved toward the water barrel. "It's hot out there today," he said. "Can I have a drink of water?"

"Sure, the barrel is over half-full."

As he walked to the barrel, he deposited a small stone in his right pocket. Each time a bag was weighed, another stone would be added.

It was an easy way to track the number of bags turned in by the end of the day. The dipper hung from a hook beside the barrel. Bo opened the lid, sunk the dipper in the cool water, and started to drink. The foreman looked his way and said, "Hurry it up, Bo. You are behind everyone else and need to catch up."

Bo emptied the dipper on the ground and answered, "I'm working, captain. Don't push me."

The foreman glared at Bo, stepped forward to the water barrel, and said, "Don't give me no lip. Get back to work now, or you are off for the day."

The foreman was four inches taller than Bo and had a reputation as a fighter. Bo's temper flared, but this was not a fight he wanted. Avoiding eye contact and irritated, he reached for his bag, returned to the field, and continued to pick down his row. Mad and brooding, he continued to work while planning his meeting with Jed that night.

The sun started to drop below the trees, and shadows extended across the edge of the cotton patch. The foreman rang the bell calling his crew to the wagon. Picking ended for the day, and it was time to tally the work and return to the barn so that the crew could be paid. The crew piled in the wagon for the trip, but Bo remained behind, crossed the road, and walked into the woods to search for a piece of wood that could be used as a club. An oak tree split by lightning had several branches about the size he wanted. A branch three inches in diameter was on the ground unattached. Bo stripped off the smaller branches, laid it over a log, and broke off a piece two feet in length so that it could be concealed behind his back.

Jed pulled his chair away from the table, sat, and waited for his wife to bring a glass of iced tea. Mabel placed two glasses on the table beside a small bowl of lemon and sat beside her husband as he spooned in sugar and began to stir. Ice tinkled in the glass as he said, "I need to inspect the fields before dark. We have a good crop this year, and I want to get it picked before more rain comes."

"I'll plan supper a little late tonight to give you enough time," she said.

Jed stood, finished his tea, gave his wife a brief kiss, and walked to the door. With the pickup in use, he planned to drive the dusty Ford sedan parked beside the porch. The six-cylinder engine started easily and settled into a smooth idle. Jed placed a pad and pencil on the seat beside him, put the car in gear, and started down the road.

He inspected the cotton on Friday of each week, driving over dirt roads from field to field, stopping at each to make notes for next week's work schedule. Cotton ready for harvest would have workers assigned the following Monday. His inspection would continue until well after dark. He carried no money and was not concerned about problems, but he believed in being prepared. A 357-Magnum pistol, snug in its holster, was within reach between his legs, just under the seat.

He began his inspection of the south fifty-acre plot as the sun settled over the hills, turning the cotton from white to gray. It was ready to be picked, and he wanted it done before the next rain. Stopping the car on the dirt road, he made a note on his pad to schedule a crew to start work Monday.

Bo was sitting on a tractor left in the field for use the following Monday As the car stopped, he jumped down from his seat and called to the man.

"Captain, can I speak with you?" Bo said as he walked toward the car.

Jed, irritated at the interruption, glared out his open car window and said, "What do you want, boy?"

"I'm tired of picking cotton. I want to make more money. I need a better job."

"If you want to make more money, you need to pick more cotton," Jed replied. "I've heard that you've been moving a little slow out there."

"That ain't so. I been doing the work. What I need is a better job."

The anger in Bo's eyes and voice made Jed stiffen in his seat. This was about to be a problem, and he wanted to be ready. Bo could not see his right hand as he slowly moved it toward the gun.

"Pickin' cotton is all we have to do around here," Jed said. "You ought to be happy doing just that."

"I'm not pickin' cotton all my life. I'm gonna get a better job and get off this farm." His eyes blazed as he breathed in gulps. He moved closer to the car door and tightened his grip on the club, his right hand clenched into a tight fist.

Jed could see the fight coming and intended to meet Bo head-on. He reached for his gun while opening the door to face Bo at eye level.

Jed's eyes seemed to bore into Bo as he eased from the car to a standing position.

Bo could see the gun, and his anger quickly turned to panic. Jed was mean and with a gun, dangerous. Bo swung his club, striking Jed's neck just below the ear. Jed stumbled and fired his gun into the ground.

Bo grabbed for the gun while Jed, dazed from the blow, was unable to resist. Both men grappled for the gun. Bo was stronger and twisted the weapon away from his body toward Jed. The struggle continued, and the gun exploded between them. The bullet went into Jed's chest directly below his heart. Breathing out a puff of air, he groaned as his knees collapsed. The gun fell to the ground as Bo pushed him against the side of the car. He stepped back as Jed fell to the ground but did not move.

Breathing rapidly, Bo stood above the bleeding body of the man who had been his boss. The car door stood open with the motor running. He decided to put the body back in the car behind the wheel. The limp body weighed over two hundred pounds and was difficult to move. As Bo worked to ease Jed into the car, his hands and shirt became covered with blood.

Standing beside the car, he realized that he was in serious trouble. With no place to hide, the only answer was to run. As panic set in, he ran across the cotton field into a large wooded area. Once in the trees, he considered what to do. His chest hurt, breathing was difficult, and sweat blurred his vision. Gasping for air, he collapsed on a log and leaned against a limb beside his seat. There were no options. He could not go home. He had no money and no place to hide.

Mabel placed a dish of corn on the table, picked up a pitcher, and moved around the chairs, filling glasses with tea. Jed was expected soon, and she intended to be ready. Two men sat by the fireplace, and three foremen talked quietly on the porch, waiting for Jed to arrive and call them inside for supper.

Mabel frowned and paced the room after an hour passed with no sign of her husband. She called the lead foreman in from the porch and said, "When Jed left, he said he was going to inspect the fields for next week's schedule. He's probably still out there. Take the pickup and tell him that dinner's getting cold and to get in here so we can eat."

"Yes, ma'am," Adam said. He crossed the room, opened the screen door, and bounded down the steps into the yard. As his eyes adjusted to the darkness, he could see the pickup parked in front of the barn. The old truck was used every day but was on its last leg. There was no window on the driver's side, and the door was hard to open because the handle was broken. He jerked open the door, climbed in, and gave it a hard slam, causing a cloud of dust. The engine coughed, started, and settled into a rough idle, causing a noisy vibration under the dash. He pressed the clutch, pulled the gearshift into low, revved the engine, and was on his way.

The access roads around the first two fields were empty. Two field hands walking down one road stood aside and waved as he drove by with the truck lights on bright. Jed's car sat idling at the entrance to the third field. Adam could see the open car door with no one around. The truck rolled to a stop behind the car, and Adam stepped out calling, "Jed, where are you?" Receiving no answer, he called again. "Jed, dinner's ready. Can you hear me?"

The uneven throb of the truck engine broke the silence. Adam stood quietly waiting for Jed to answer. He had to be close, as his car door was open and the engine was running. Adam walked forward, looked inside, and saw Jed sprawled across the front seat. There was blood on the seat, the floor, and the ground beside the car. He stepped back and moved around the car to the passenger door to see if Jed could possibly be alive. The smell made him choke. Jed's eyes were open, but he was dead. With a choking cough, Adam ran to the truck and drove to the house for help.

Several men were sitting on the steps of the porch watching as Adam drove the pickup across the yard, skidded to a stop, and jumped out, leaving the door standing open.

Running toward the steps, he said, "Jed's dead. Somebody's killed him. In his car. There's blood all over the place. In the car. On the ground. Jed's lying in the front seat, dead."

"Where's his car?" someone said as Adam gasped for breath, and then answered, "At the entrance road to field three."

Olive, the plantation owner's wife, opened the screen door, stuck her head out, and said, "What?"

"Someone has killed Jed," Adam said. "In his car. There is blood all over the place. I checked and he was not breathing. No pulse. He was just lying in the front seat."

Olive, looking stunned, slowly crossed the porch and sat on the swing. Everyone waited as she sat glassy-eyed, looking across the yard. Minutes passed, and a foreman walked up the steps, sat on the swing beside her, and just above a whisper said, "Miss Olive, Miss Olive."

She turned and looked at him, still dazed. "Yes?" she said.

"Tell us what to do, Miss Olive."

"Go get the sheriff and tell him to bring the coroner," she said. "Show him the way to field three." She looked at Adam and said, "Take a man with you, and go back to the car. Wait there until the sheriff shows up."

Three foremen were quietly talking at the end of the porch. . Cal, the oldest, clenched his jaw and said, "We have to find the son of a bitch that did this." The two men nodded, and one said, "He can't be far if he's on foot. If we leave now, we should be able to chase him down." The other foreman said, "If he is on foot, we need to take my two hounds to track him."

Cal looked at Olive and said, "We are going to find the man who killed Jed."

They agreed to meet at the barn in fifteen minutes to saddle horses and go after the killer.

In less than an hour, they were at Jed's car with two bloodhounds straining at their leashes. The car door was still open. The seat and floor were bloody, but Jed's body had been removed. The club Bo had used was on the ground by the door. The dogs sniffed the club and began following the tracks left by Bo during his panicked departure. They were on their way, with three men on horseback close behind.

Bo could hear the dogs' howling barks as they followed his trail. Trapped, with no place to go, he tried to hide in the branches of a tree. The dogs followed the scent to the tree, and the riders knew they had found their quarry.

"Get down out of that tree," one rider shouted as he stepped down from his horse with a pistol in his right hand.

Bo, hands shaking and eyes wide with fear, begged for mercy as he fell to the ground. "I didn't mean to hurt Mr. Jed. He had a gun, and it went off. Please. I didn't mean to hurt him. The gun just went off."

A twelve-foot leather whip was coiled on the saddle horn between Cal's legs. With the handle in his right hand, it uncoiled and dangled on the ground beside his horse. He spurred the horse forward and flicked the whip at Bo's head. The split tip wrapped around his head and split his right ear. Bo screamed in pain. Cal lashed out again and again. Bo, still screaming, tried to run but staggered and fell. The blows kept coming, each one opening a new wound.

A second man stepped off his horse while the first knotted a rope, threw it over a tree branch, and shouted, "You killed Jed, and we are going to hang you."

Tears ran down Bo's face as he gulped breaths of air and pleaded, "Please. I didn't mean to hurt him. It was an accident. The gun just went off." His eyes blurred with blood and sweat as he rolled, tried to stand, and was kicked in the ribs. Unable to breathe, he fell back to the ground. One man was at each arm, and they lifted him to his feet, slipped a rope over his head, and tied his hands behind his back.

He continued to scream, "Please. It was an accident! It was an accident! The gun just went off. It was an accident!"

Cal guided his horse to the rope, looped it around his saddle horn, and backed away from the tree, pulling Bo four feet off the ground. Kicking his feet and squirming with a gurgling sound, he jerked back and forth as his life ended. When death came, the rope was tied off so that he remained hanging for all to see.

The men returned to the barn and unsaddled their sweat-covered horses. The riders dried them with towels and gave them a good brushing, and then they placed them in stalls and gave each a pail of grain. It was time to return to the house and talk with the family. As they mounted the steps, Olive sat on the swing with Mabel at her side. Olive's eyes were red and tears stained her face as she gazed across the porch to the lawn. Several neighbors sat quietly on the steps trying to provide comfort but not knowing what to do.

The three men crossed the porch to Mort. Cal said, "We took care of it. He won't ever hurt anyone else." Mort nodded his approval as the men returned to the steps and joined the neighbors. One had a bottle of Jim Beam, and each took a drink and passed it to the next man. It was going to be a long night.

Three short rings of the telephone meant the call was for our house. There were two other phones on the line, and they could listen in as we talked. Calls were not common, and people in the other houses enjoyed listening to the conversations. Both ends of the line were hooked to party lines, and calling was difficult with lots of static. Yelling was required, but it could be done.

Dad was asleep on the couch and I was sitting in our badly worn chair reading a superman comic book. Most of our furniture was beyond repair but we made it work. Mom was in the kitchen washing dishes when the phone rang.

Dad stepped to the wall, reached for the earpiece, and said, "Hello?"

"Mr. Black?" the earpiece hissed.

"Yes?" Dad answered loudly.

"Mr. Black, I'm calling for Mabel. Jed has been shot and didn't make it. He passed away last night. He was shot by one of the field hands. Mabel asked me to call you."

Dad sucked in a deep breath, pausing to absorb what he had heard. "We will be there as soon as we can," he said as he hung up the phone, turned, and spoke to Mom. "My brother has been killed by one of the workers. We have to go there for the funeral." He sat on the couch with his elbows on his knees, leaned forward, covered his face with both hands, and began to sob. Mom sat beside him with her arm around his shoulders. I remained frozen in the chair facing the couch until Dad stood with tears in his eyes and took a deep breath. He breathed out and said, "We have to leave as soon as possible. Let's get ready to go."

We packed and began the long trip over roads that were challenging during the day, but even more difficult at night. Our 1937 Plymouth was not built for this, but Dad was a good mechanic and had tools for the occasion.

"Give me a pair of pliers, some wire, and a crescent wrench, and I can fix anything on a car," he would say.

We arrived as dawn was breaking over the trees. Cars were parked at odd angles in the yard around the main house. The porch was full of men talking in hushed voices about what had happened. From pieces of conversation, I learned that several men had chased down the man who shot Uncle Jed and hung him from a tree. He was a black man, and the comment was, "That's the way it's done here in Mississippi."

Inside the house, women were cooking enough food to feed a small army. Some brought large dishes, while others brought the makings for cooking on location. It was the start of a southern funeral and lots of food was a requirement.

The next day, people returned around mid-morning to continue doing whatever they could to ease our family's pain. I sat on the porch steps and listened to the men talking among themselves.

"Jed never had a chance to get out of his car," Adam continued.

Cal sat on the steps, stretched his legs, and nodded. "He was killed with his own gun. He kept it under his front seat."

"That's probably why he lost the fight," Adam said. "He couldn't get out of the car to defend himself."

The sheriff delivered Jed's car, and everyone gathered around for a look. There was blood on the seat, dash, steering wheel, and floor. The sheriff said that Jed was dead in his car when they found him. I knew the blood was Uncle Jed's, and it scared me.

Later that day, a pickup truck arrived with a casket. Men moved off the porch to carry it inside, where it would remain until the burial. The casket rested on sawhorses to the right of the fireplace. It remained closed with flowers on the lid.

The men returned to the porch. Small bottles of white lightning were produced, and talk continued. The conversation was low and moved to other subjects. I was seven years old and knew that if I kept quiet, they would let me stay and listen.

"How's your cotton look this year?" Adam asked.

Mort grinned and said, "Good, so far. If the weather holds, it's going to be a good year."

"I hear that you bought a new Plymouth."

"Yep, it's a four-door with a six-cylinder engine. Runs good."

Adam was curious. "What kind of mileage do you get?"

"Eight miles to the gallon on the road. I probably could do a little better if I worked at it."

"Do you remember that pet squirrel that the Corley's kept over at their house?" Cal asked.

"Yep. He spent most of his time on the roof of the front porch, didn't he?"

"That's the one. Old man Corley taught him to jump on his head and ride to the fence gate. That worked fine until last week. The preacher came calling, and he's bald. As he left Corley's house, the squirrel jumped from the roof of the front porch onto his head. With no hair to hold on to, the squirrel scratched him up real good. I heard that he had to go to the doctor for some stitches."

Both men laughed quietly.

"That had to be something to see! I wish I could have been there. What did Corley do with the squirrel?" Adam asked.

"He took him out in the woods and let him go," Cal said. "Had to, after what he did to the preacher."

The burial took place three days later. We sang hymns, and the preacher gave a talk while everyone listened quietly. Most southern Baptist preachers know how to give a "hellfire and brimstone" talk that is suited to any occasion. Ours was one of the best, and he gave a rousing sermon that ranged from birth to life, death, and beyond. With that motivation, we returned to our car for the long drive home.

Chapter Eight
Peaceful Valley

Dad disappeared the day the men in white came and took my mon. I was ten years old and living alone in our house. I knew that dad was not coming back and I could not continue to live in our house.

As dawn broke, I slipped out of bed, dressed, and walked into the kitchen. There was no food in the refrigerator or cabinets. I drank a glass of water and searched the cabinets for something to tie my pillowcase to the bike handlebars. The toaster cord would have to do. I stepped outside as dawn was breaking, placed the pillowcase on the front fender of the bike, and tied it to the handlebars.

It was time to leave. As the sun came up, I mounted my bike for the long ride to what I hoped would be my new home. My stomach growled as I crossed the empty town square and started down the road leading out of town. I had to leave this place before the men in the white van came to take me away. The sun rose over the trees, the day warmed, and I began to sweat.

The road was narrow with almost no traffic. Thick woods shielded farmhouses, and none could be seen from the road. The woods were quiet, and I could hear any car coming well before it came into view. As other roads crossed my road, I became unsure of my route. Feeling lost, I continued to pedal as I looked for a farm near the road.

As I pedaled up a gently sloping hill, the road snaked alongside a fenced pasture with cows and several horses. A narrow dirt road looking well used wound into the woods beside the pasture. A white two-story farmhouse sat at the edge of the pasture in front of a red barn inside an enclosed slat fence that had been whitewashed. Three horses stood quietly inside the corral, and watched as I turned off the road and pedaled up a dirt path to the house. I stepped off my bike, laid it on the ground, and walked to the screen porch that ran the width of the building. Mounting the steps to the porch, I called out, "Hello! Is anyone home?" No answer. I called again, "Is anyone home?"

A voice from inside the screen door answered, "What do you want, young man?"

"I am going to my uncle's farm. Its not far from North Little Rock but I'm not sure of the way. Do you know how to get to Peaceful Valley?"

"Never heard of it. No such place around here."

"I think that's the name of the farm. I know it's next to the road that comes out of North Little Rock. Can you tell me how to get there from here?"

The tall gray-haired man behind the screen looked at me and said, "Come on in for a glass of water, and I'll tell you how to get to the road near here that comes out of North Little Rock. That should help."

I crossed the porch and stepped into a large room with a musty farmhouse odor. Smoke drifted from burning wood inside a stone fireplace mounted in the center of the back wall. An overstuffed couch sat in front of the fireplace looking comfortable and well used. Two straight-back wooden chairs beside the couch were tattered from years of use. The oak floor was solid but scarred and needed refinishing. A drop-leaf wood table rested against the wall opposite the fireplace with matching chairs at each end.

I followed the farmer as he crossed the room and called to his wife, "Martha, there's a young man here in need of a drink. Can you draw him a glass of water?"

A plump, gray-haired lady wearing a blue print dress approached the kitchen door and smiled as our eyes met.

I looked down at the floor and said, "Hi."

She continued to smile and said, "What brings you way out here? We are the only farm in these parts."

"I'm on my way to my uncle's farm," I answered. "It's in Peaceful Valley, but I'm not sure how to get there."

56

Martha looked at her husband and said, "Earl, have you ever heard of Peaceful Valley? I've never heard the name."

Earl rubbed his chin and hesitated before answering, "There's no Peaceful Valley around here."

Martha could see the sad look on my face and wanted to help. "That's probably the name of the farm. Do you know what road it's on?"

I looked up and brushed the hair out of my eyes. Martha had disappeared into the kitchen, leaving me to talk to Earl. I spoke louder so that she could hear. "I know that it's on a road that comes out of North Little Rock."

The hand pump squeaked as Martha worked the handle and water flowed from the spout into the sink. She continued to pump, filled two glasses, and returned to the living room. Handing one to me, she said, "Here, you look like you could use a drink."

"Thank you," I said, taking a big gulp. "I've been riding all morning. Your well water tastes really good."

"Thank you," Earl said. "The road that leads to North Little Rock is several miles away. Stay on this road until it dead-ends into another road. If you turn left, it will take you into town. Your uncle's farm will probably be to the right. You have a long ride ahead of you."

After listening to his directions, I finished the water and said, "Thank you for the drink."

Martha reached for the glass and said, "I wish we could help you, but our truck is broken down. We have ordered the parts, and they should be here any day."

"That's okay," I said, disappointed. "Thanks again for the drink. I'll be going now."

I mounted my bike and gave them a wave as I pedaled toward the road. Martha looked upset as she stood beside Earl, but she attempted a smile as she waved back.

I had not thought it through, but now I realized that the trip would take most of the day. As the sun reached its peak, my shirt became soaked with sweat. I had not eaten since yesterday, but tried not to think about it. My stomach growled, and I felt weak and slowed but did not stop. The flat road in front of me wound through oak trees, but there were no houses in sight. The sun reached its peak, and sweat dripped into my eyes, making it hard to see. A crow landed in the center of the road and began picking at the remains of a squirrel. As I approached, it cawed a protest and flew into the woods to wait for me to pass.

I heard a truck approaching from behind and moved to the side of the road so that it could pass. As the truck reached me, it screeched to a halt. A man who looked as big as a mountain was behind the wheel of the green pickup. Tattered coveralls, white socks, and high-top shoes left no doubt that he was a farmer. The straw hat on his melon head was weather-beaten and appeared to be on its final days. Light brown hair from under the hat reached his shoulders. Bright blue eyes, and a square chin with an unkempt mustache and three-day-old beard gave him an imposing look. His smile showed crooked teeth, and he said with a laugh, "Where you going, boy? There's not much around here, so you have to be a long way from home."

"Yes, sir! I'm on my way to my uncle's farm. It's called Peaceful Valley. Do you know where it is?"

"I sure do. It's a good ten miles from here. Do you plan on pedaling that bike all the way there?"

"Yes, sir. I need to get there today."

He stepped out of the truck, slammed the door, walked back to the tailgate, and said, "Let's put your bike in the back, and I'll take you there."

"Thanks," I said as he loaded the bike in the truck bed and shut the tailgate. I climbed into the cab next to the driver. As the truck pulled away, he said, "They call me B.J. What's your name?"

"Everyone calls me Dubbie, but that's not my real name."

"What's your real name?"

"John, but nobody calls me that."

"Okay, Dubbie it is. How come you are going to your uncle's farm?"

"My mom is in the hospital," I said. "I don't know where my dad is, but he didn't come home, and after several days I decided to ride my bike to my uncle's farm."

"Do they know you are coming?"

"No, sir, they don't," I said. "I couldn't stay at my house any longer and don't have anyplace else to go."

He frowned and chewed at his upper lip in thought. I sat quietly looking out the window as he said, "Are you running away from home?"

"No, sir," I answered. "My mom and dad are both gone, and I couldn't stay there by myself. I heard the neighbors talking about calling the social workers to have me picked up and placed in a home, and I decided to leave early the next morning. I'm hoping my aunt and uncle will let me stay with them."

"Have you been riding that bike all day?" he asked.

"Yes, sir," I answered. "I left before daylight but didn't think it would take this long."

He looked at my thin frame and said, "Have you had anything to eat today?"

I looked down at the floor of the truck and said, "No, sir, I haven't."

B.J. looked at me with a sad grin and asked, "Are you hungry?"

I looked up and said, "I'm hungry enough to eat the bark off an oak tree."

He stroked his mustache and said, "I have a piece of a Spam and cheese sandwich that might taste better than tree bark. You can have that if you want. It's inside the brown sack here on the seat."

I thanked him and reached inside the soiled bag for a sandwich wrapped in wrinkled paper. The bread was stale, but I munched away thinking it was the best thing I had ever tasted. It felt good on my stomach.

The truck chugged along at a speed not much faster than I had been going on my bike. The engine sputtered and backfired, and the truck jerked. I watched as he shifted gears, looked at me, and said, "It's running a little rough but should be okay. We use it around the farm, but it's not very good on the road."

It took over a half hour to reach my uncle's farm. B.J. stopped the truck beside several mailboxes attached to a rail that was waist-high, for easy use by the mailman servicing the area. As he unloaded my bike, he said, "There you go. Do you know how to reach the house from here?"

"Yes, sir. Thank you for the ride."

"No problem. Good luck, kid," he said with a grin as we shook hands. I mounted the bike and started down the narrow gravel road leading to my uncle's house.

Aunt Ona Belle and Uncle Joe lived in a house that was little more than a shack. There was a living room, small kitchen, one bedroom, and a covered porch that ran alongside the structure. The roof of the house was corrugated tin, as well as the sides of the building. From a distance, it resembled a utility shed a farmer would use to store tools. Tall poles had been mounted in the ground to become the corners of the building. The wood floor was supported with concrete blocks that kept it stable. The front room was both a living room and a kitchen separated by a table and chairs. The matching couch and chair in the living area were worn from years of use but were comfortable for sitting. A small chest against the wall across from the table was the only other piece of furniture. A wood-burning cookstove sat along the back wall of the kitchen with a flue that extended up through the roof. The handle halfway up the pipe was used to control the fire so that the top of the stove could be used for cooking. The counter along the back wall was the width of the kitchen with a hand pump beside the sink so that water could be brought up from the well below.

A potbelly wood-burning stove sat beside the door to the porch and warmed the house during winter. There was no heat in the back room. The curtain that hung across the door between the kitchen and bedroom had been pulled aside so that heat would drift to the back of the building. The bedroom had a bed, chair, and chest of drawers alongside a makeshift closet with a hanging curtain that had been pushed aside. The back wall had a small window that looked out on the chicken pen and barnyard.

The open porch had steps leading to a yard where Aunt Ona Belle hung her wash on several lines that had been strung between T-shaped poles. A well-beaten path led to an outhouse and continued on to the barn. A six-foot-long doghouse with a sloped roof sat to the left of the path. Two small rooms inside the doghouse had separate entrances and were filled with straw to provide warmth on cool winter nights.

An oak barrel at the back of the house was filled to the brim with cool, sweet rainwater that was enjoyable to drink on a hot summer day. The fenced area behind the house contained several dozen chickens and a large tom turkey. A chicken coop at one end of the pen had several straw nests so that the hens could lay their eggs. The turkey didn't seem to do anything, but he looked like he owned the place.

The barn was small with a horse stall at each end facing out to a covered area that ran the length of the building. The area between the stalls was an enclosed storage room that contained hay, feed for the animals, and farm equipment. The area around the barn was fenced so that the farm animals could move about. It was a well-organized working farm.

As I rode my bike toward the house, I began to realize the magnitude of my situation. I was ten years old, Dad had disappeared, Mother was in a hospital, and I had no place to live or call home. I pedaled and fought back the tears that began to well up in my eyes. I hardly knew the aunt and uncle that I hoped would take me in. Filled with doubt, I stopped the bike beside the porch and called out, "Hello. Is anyone here? Aunt Ona Belle, are you here?"

The screen door creaked open, and a tall, thin lady wearing jeans, a print shirt, and high-top shoes stepped out. Her large mouth and slender nose were characteristic of the family. Streaks of gray in her brown hair and a deeply tanned face made her look older than her years. She looked at me, and her blue eyes sparkled. She smiled and in an astonished tone, said, "Goodness sakes alive, Dubbie! What are you doing here?"

"I came to see you because I don't have any place to stay."

"Get off your bike and come on inside. You look like you could use a glass of water and something to eat." She gave me a concerned look and then turned away.

I leaned my bike against the porch and climbed the steps to the kitchen. As my aunt poured water from a pitcher, she spoke again.

"Did you ride your bike all the way from your house in Jacksonville?"

"Yes, ma'am, but a man with a pickup gave me a ride part of the way. It sure helped, 'cause my legs were really tired when he came along."

While we talked, she placed bread on a plate and began slicing ham from a roast on the counter. My mouth watered as I watched. She slathered mayonnaise on two slices of bread, and then stacked on several cuts of ham, freshly sliced tomatoes, and lettuce. After cutting the sandwich in half, she placed it in front of me and said, "Would you like some water?"

"Yes, ma'am," I answered, and then I took a huge bite and began to chew. The sandwich seemed to take my mind off everything that was happening. My aunt pulled her chair away from the table and sat across from me while I continued to eat.

I knew she wanted to know why I was there, but things had happened so fast during the last week that I did not know where to start. I finished half the sandwich and looked into her eyes as she smiled and said, "I want you to tell me what has happened to you and your mother and father."

Chapter Nine
My New Home

I sat at the kitchen table while Aunt Ona Belle asked questions about my mother and father. I answered as best I could, but she seemed flustered when I was unable to give her the information she wanted. She pulled back a chair and sat in front of me as we talked.

"Where is your mother?" she asked.

"Some men in a white van came to our house and took her away," I answered. "She didn't come back, and I don't know where she is."

She leaned both elbows on the table and covered her face with her hands. I sat quietly while she moaned and waited for her to stop. She sat back, took a deep breath, blew it out, and asked, "Was your dad there when the men came and took your mother?"

"Yes, ma'am," I answered. "He took them to the bedroom to get Mom. She fought them and I tried to help, but it didn't do any good. They put her in the back of their van and drove off."

My aunt looked away as I leaned over my plate and took large bite out of the sandwich she had made for me. I chewed, thinking that it was much better than the one given to me by the farmer driving the pickup, but I appreciated both.

Aunt Ona Belle turned back to me and said, "Do you know where Wesley is now?"

I swallowed a mouthful of food and answered, "He left several days ago and never came back."

"Were you living in the house by yourself?"

"Yes, ma'am," I answered. "But I could not buy anything to eat after Dad took my paper route money out of the jar in my drawer."

"Did he take all your money?"

"Yes, ma'am," I answered. "The jar was empty when the paper man came to make his weekly collection. He got mad and said that I couldn't deliver newspapers anymore. After he left, I knew that I couldn't stay there any longer and decided to leave early the next morning and come here on my bike."

"That was a long ride," she said. "You were lucky that man came along in his pickup and gave you a lift." She smiled as I finished the last bite of bread on my plate, and then asked, "Did you enjoy your sandwich?"

"Yes, ma'am," I answered. "It was great!"

She carried my plate to the sink, rinsed off the crumbs, and dried it with a towel while I sat at the table and watched. Minutes passed as she leaned on the sink with both hands and looked out the window. The noise of my chair sliding back from the table broke her gaze, and she turned to look at me. I took a deep breath, looked at the floor, and quietly shuffled my feet.

She used a dish towel to wipe her eyes and said, "Joe will be along in about an hour. Why don't you go outside and play with the dogs until he gets here. Sandy will keep you company, and he is good at retrieving a stick."

I slipped out of the chair and said, "The sandwich was really good. Thanks."

She smiled and said, "You go on outside and play. It's going to be all right."

I crossed the porch as Sandy and Star watched from the yard hoping for some attention. My stomach was full for the first time in days, and it felt good. I gave Sandy a pat while Star stood by my leg wiggling her stump of a tail. The little cocker's long blond ears almost touched the ground.

My two new friends followed along as I walked toward the barn. The dogs were dancing in circles as we moved along, but my mind drifted to what could happen when Uncle Joe came home. If they did not want me, Aunt Ona Belle would call the foster home people and they would send someone to take me away. I thought of running, but where to? I had no place to go. There was no one else that would take me in. I had no friends, and my aunt and uncle were the only relatives in the area. I walked around the barnyard and found a stick for Sandy to chase. The big setter was ready to play and barked several times because I had a stick in my hand. Each time I tossed the stick, Sandy would chase it and return to drop it at my feet. I continued to throw the stick while watching the house for my uncle's arrival. Star sat by my left foot and looked up expecting a pat on the head. She was a dog that wanted to be loved.

I wanted my aunt and uncle to know that I would work hard if they let me stay with them. My stomach tightened, and my breath came in fast gulps. *I was scared.* I did not want to go to a foster home and live with strangers. I had to avoid that and would tell my relatives that I would be good and work hard.

A tattered old Plymouth turned off the main road and stopped in our drive just off the road. I watched as Uncle Joe stepped out, retrieved his lunch box, and slammed the door. The car was black but so rusted it was hard to tell. The front bumper was missing, but the headlights were in place on the fenders. He was a railroad switchman and usually worked the evening or night shift at a switchyard in North Little Rock. He worked those shifts so he could devote his days to farming, his first love.

I remained out of sight behind the hay mower as he walked toward the house swinging his lunch box. He crossed the porch, opened the kitchen door, and stepped inside.

I knew that their conversation would be about me, so I walked to the house and took a seat on the porch chair just outside the kitchen door. I had to know what they intended to do and was too nervous to wait at the barn. I could hear them talk as I sat quietly beside the door. I held my breath and moved closer to the door so that I could see them through the crack. I leaned forward and thought, *If they do not want me, I don't what I will do. I just know that I am not going to a foster home.*

Aunt Ona Belle turned as Uncle Joe crossed the room and said, "Hi. Would you like a glass of tea?"

He smiled as she motioned to the pitcher sitting on the table and said, "I'll cut some slices of lemon. We need to talk."

He pulled his chair away from the table, slipped into the seat, and said, "Is everything okay?"

"No, it's not," she answered. "Things have blown apart over at Jacksonville. Alice has had a breakdown and been taken to the hospital. She is probably in the state mental institution, but I don't know for sure. That place is an asylum, and she could be in there for a long time."

"When did it happen?" Uncle Joe asked.

"About a week ago, and then things got worse. Wesley took off on one of his drinking binges, but before he left, he stole all of Dubbie's paper route money and left him alone in the house with no money for food. There ought to be a law against abandoning a kid like that. He's my brother and I hate to say it, but he is one useless bastard."

"Are you serious?" Uncle Joe groaned. "He took off and left the boy there by himself?" He stopped stirring his tea and looked to her for an answer.

"Yes," she said. "And Dubbie stayed there alone for several days until he overheard the neighbors talking about calling social services to have him picked up and placed in a home."

He frowned, rolled his eyes, and said, "I'm almost afraid to ask. Then what happened?"

"Dubbie got on his bike this morning and pedaled it all the way here." She said, "He might not have made it, but a farmer with a pickup truck saw him struggling up a hill and gave him a ride for the last ten miles."

"He did?" Uncle Joe asked. "Is he here now?"

"Yes," she answered. "I think he is down at the barn. He looked really upset. The boy is desperate. Has no place to live. He asked me if he could live with us. What do you think?"

Uncle Joe sipped his tea and stirred in a slice of lemon as he considered the situation.

My chest tightened, and I held my breath waiting for an answer. I was so scared I wanted to run but sat frozen to my seat. My legs refused to move. Minutes passed that seemed like hours.

I could see my uncle through the crack in the door as he rubbed his chin, swallowed, and said, "We don't have a bedroom for him. I don't know how we can take on a kid right now. We don't even have a place for him to sleep. I guess we can put him on the couch for the night."

With a lump in my throat, I continued to watch through the crack and thought, *Please let me stay! I'll be good. I'll work hard. I won't let you down.*

"We can't turn him in to the state," she answered. "They will put him in a foster home, and he doesn't deserve that."

"You're right. I just don't know what to do," Uncle Joe said as he ran his right hand through his hair and then took a swallow of tea. "Do you think we can afford the expense of a boy living with us?"

Aunt Ona Belle stood in the center of the kitchen looking down at the floor and said, "We don't have any choice. He's not just any kid. He is a member of the family. We have to help." She sighed as she leaned against the kitchen counter, pursed her lips, and said, "Don't you have a bunk bed stored in the barn?" She shifted her position and continued, "We can set that up on the porch. It's not enclosed, but there will be a roof over his head. With some extra blankets, he will be comfortable at night. With our mild winters, there should be no problem. After what he has been through, sleeping on the porch should be a piece of cake."

Uncle Joe paused and stared at his tea in thought. Aunt Ona Belle waited, giving him time to make a decision.

I tried to sit back in the chair and managed to take a deep breath. The feeling came back to my chest as I puffed out the air.

Uncle Joe nodded and said, "A bunk bed on an open porch isn't much, but I guess it's better than a foster home. It will have to do. Put him on the couch tonight, and we can set him up on the porch tomorrow." Lifting the glass and finishing the tea, he stood and said, "I have to feed the livestock and say hello to Dubbie."

I stood, crept quietly across the porch, and then ran to the barn.

I stood beside the barn tossing a stick that Sandy retrieved, tail wagging, as he waited for the next throw. While we played, I watched the house expecting my uncle to come to the barn where I waited. I wanted to talk with him and tell him that I would work hard and not be a problem. It seemed like hours, but I knew he would come along. Finally, the screen door to the house opened and Uncle Joe stepped out. I watched as he crossed the porch and started down the path to the barn. My hands trembled and my heart pounded as I sat on the seat of the hay baler and waited for our first meeting.

As he opened the gate, he looked at me and said, "I hear that you had a full day. Are you all right?"

"Yes, sir," I answered.

"Do you want to help me with the feeding?"

I jumped down from the baler and said, "Yes, sir." We headed for the barn. I knew it was going to be all right; I had a new place to live.

He opened the feed room door, filled the pail with grain, and said, "Put this in Cricket's feed box, and bring the pail back so I can give you Mike's grain."

"Yes, sir." I took the pail and walked toward Cricket's stall. The big mare was waiting inside as I approached. My hands shook, but my breathing was returning to normal. I stepped into the stall. *I have a place to live!* I wanted to scream as tears welled in my eyes. *No foster home for me!* I thought as I stepped to the feed trough and dumped in the grain. Cricket began to eat while I stroked her neck.

Uncle Joe could see that I was upset and wanted to make me feel better. Handing me a pail of grain for Jack, he said, "You can sleep on the couch tonight. I'll fix you up with a bed tomorrow."

I smiled and blinked my eyes to hide the tears as I took the pail. The lump in my throat made it impossible to talk, and I could only nod as I turned toward the stall.

I returned to the feed bin as Uncle Joe stepped to the water trough and started to add water. I watched as he said, "It's important that our livestock have fresh water every day. When you feed them at night, always add water to the trough."

My voice had returned, and I answered, "Yes, sir. I'll remember."

We finished at the barn, and I walked beside my uncle as we started toward the house. The sun was dropping behind the trees, leaving long shadows across the yard. Sandy and Star followed close by knowing that is was about time for their food.

Uncle Joe closed the barnyard gate and walked with me down the path to the house. I wanted him to know how much I cared and took his hand as we walked together. He looked down at me with a smile, and I wanted to thank him, but my throat was so tight I could not talk. I looked up with moist eyes and smiled back. *It was going to be all right!*

We crossed the porch and stepped into the kitchen as Aunt Ona Belle placed food on the table and said, "You two wash up at the sink, and let's have supper."

After several days with almost nothing to eat, I enjoyed every bite of the meal, and Uncle Joe passed a platter to me so I could have another helping of mashed potatoes.

I finished and carried my plate to the sink and started clearing the table. Aunt Ona Belle washed the dishes while I stood beside her and dried them with a dish towel. The day had been overpowering, and my stomach and throat were raw from emotion. I wiped a dish as she looked at me and said, "You don't have to worry about a foster home. We want you to live with us."

She continued to wash dishes as I turned to look in her eyes and said, "I'll be good and work hard." I wiped my eyes trying not to show that I was starting to cry.

"I know you will," she answered, and she turned toward the sink to look out the window. Using a cloth in her pocket, she dabbed at her eyes while I continued to wipe and stack dishes. Time seemed to stop as she continued to gaze out the window, but finally she turned to look at me. I rushed to her, threw my arms around her waist, and collapsed on her shoulder. She wrapped her arms around me as I whispered in her ear, "Thank you, thank you. I won't let you down." We were both crying, and I could not let her go.

Later that evening, she brought blankets and a pillow to make a bed on the couch. As I climbed into my new bed, the farm smells came through the open windows along with a gentle breeze that cooled the room. Feeling warm and safe in my new bed, I closed my eyes and thanked God for his help and asked him to bless my new home. I drifted off to sleep listening to an owl in a nearby tree and the whip-poor-will's calling down by the creek.

Chapter Ten
Life on the Farm

Hearing movement in the kitchen, I got up and quickly dressed. Dawn was breaking, and Uncle Joe had started a fire in the wood-burning kitchen stove. It was still dark out, but daylight was peeking over the trees. I walked into the kitchen and saw that a fire crackled in the stove, sparks shot up the flue, and flames roared as the room began to warm. I watched as Uncle Joe stepped to the sink, filled the coffeepot with water, inserted the basket, filled it with coffee, replaced the lid, and set it on the cast-iron top. I waited as the pot hissed and the coffee started to perk. Uncle Joe had already dressed in coveralls, high-top shoes, a flannel shirt, and a waist-length jeans jacket. Wearing his straw hat, he went over to the perking coffeepot, picked it up, and poured two cups. A cup was required before we started the day's chores.

Uncle Joe came over to the table where I was sitting, with a cup containing coffee, milk, and two heaping spoons of sugar. My first coffee, and it tasted good. I warmed my hands as I drank. Uncle Joe sat at the table and sipped his coffee from a spoon. I sat on the chair beside the stove and pulled on my socks as he said, "It's still dark out. We have time to finish our coffee before going to the barn to feed the animals."

I sipped my coffee and waited for him to finish so that we could leave the warmth of the kitchen. The cool night air on the porch made the crackling fire even more enjoyable, and I settled back in the chair and moved my feet closer to the stove. They were warm as toast, and I slipped them inside my high-top shoes.

Uncle Joe walked to the sink, rinsed his cup, and placed it on the counter. I joined him, rinsed my cup, and placed it beside his.

Uncle Joe looked at me and said, "Slip your jacket on, and let's go."

The screen door creaked as he went out, and I crossed the room to follow him. We walked down the path leading to the barn.

Several weeks had passed, and I had learned how to feed the livestock each morning before catching the bus to school. With my uncle's help, the feeding went fast and I arrived at the bus stop early. I waited with several other kids as we listened to the honking school bus telling us it was less than a mile away. When the bus arrived, Sandy watched beside the road as we loaded and drove away.

When the bus returned to our mailbox in the afternoon, Sandy was waiting, tail wagging. We crossed the yard as I looked at the big dog and yelled, "Go get the paper, boy. Go get it!"

Sandy ran across the yard, scooped the paper up with his mouth. and started for the porch. I ran for the porch with my books dangling from a belt that held them together. It was a close race but one that the dog almost always won. He dropped the newspaper by the kitchen door and looked at me with an expression that said, "I beat'cha again."

I left my books on the bed and rounded the porch to the chicken pen, which was located behind the house, just in front of the barnyard. Sandy followed but stopped at the gate and rested on the grass, placing his head between his paws.

Chickens milled about inside, and our tom turkey gobbled a protest as I entered with a pan of grain. The big bird flapped his wings and gobbled again but remained at the far side of the pen, clearly irritated at the intrusion.

Uncle Joe had built a fifteen-foot-long chicken house at the back of the pen. It was five feet high in the front with a sloping roof that reduced the height to four feet at the back. The lower half of the shed had been enclosed with wood, the top half with chicken wire to allow ventilation during hot summer days. Overheated chickens don't lay eggs, which made ventilation in the shed important. Nests with straw beds lined the back wall, there for hens to lay their eggs. They were separated by thin wood dividers but were open in front so that the chickens could step inside. As they climbed out of the nest, they always clucked loudly and scratched the earth.

The best way to feed chickens is to spread the grain around the pen. It's done a handful at a time, by throwing the grain across the yard. As the chickens approached, I took a handful of grain and tossed it in their direction. The birds pecked at the grain while I continued to spread feed around the yard. The big turkey pecked at the grain between gobbles that told me I was not welcome in his territory. When my grain bucket was empty, I gathered the eggs and started for the house.

The yard was smooth dirt, surrounded by chicken wire attached to wood posts that were ten feet apart. The five-foot-high fence kept the chickens inside, but occasionally one would escape and wander around the yard in search of food.

Sandy considered any chicken outside the pen to be fair game. The good news was that he didn't want to kill the chicken; he just enjoyed the chase. It was a game, and he loved it. The chicken, on the other hand, was not so inclined. A chicken was out, and the game was on! Running, flapping its wings, and clucking loudly, the chicken dodged to avoid Sandy's approach. The barking dog missed his mark, and slipped by with feet scrambling to stop the overshot and return to the chase.

The racket soon had the attention of everyone in the house. I stepped off the porch into the yard and realized that we had a chicken on the loose, with my dog in hot pursuit.

Sandy and the chicken ran in circles in the yard as I yelled, "Sandy, Sandy, come here!" He ignored me as he barked and ran after the bird. I joined the chase, trying to catch Sandy while the chicken screeched and ran in circles with its wings flapping.

The terrorized chicken, running erratically while trying to escape capture, was appearing to tire. I could not catch the chicken but did catch Sandy, grabbed his collar, and brought him to a stop with the command "sit." The exhausted chicken also stopped and sat, appearing thankful for the break. Sandy, now in control of his emotions, quivered with excitement as I slowly approached the chicken. I came within six feet; the chicken spread its wings and ran.

This was too much for Sandy, and the game was on again. I soon realized that I was the slowest one in the race. The chicken had the best moves, dodging left and right. Sandy was fastest but could not make the quick turns, and I was breathing hard bringing up the rear. After a long chase, the chicken gave up and squatted, and I made a leaping dive to grab its body with both hands. I held the chicken out of reach of

Sandy as it pecked at the back of my hand. The chase was over. Sandy was at my side as I walked around the house to return the bird to its pen. I opened the gate and gave the bird a gentle toss as Sandy stood outside wagging his tail.

As the days passed, I could see that the tom turkey was the "ruler of the roost," the one in charge. Turkeys tend to strut, but this one took it to extremes. Weighing over thirty pounds with a six-foot wingspan plus an irritated outlook on life, he was impossible to ignore. He didn't like me on day one, and things went downhill from there. This was a bird with attitude, and I was the target of his wrath. Feeding is an easy job; that is, unless the pen has an oversized turkey claiming ownership of the area you have violated.

On my very first feeding, old Tom let me know that my presence was not appreciated. As time passed, he became even more aggressive. With wings spread, he strutted to let me know this was his pen and I was an intruder. I decided to stay close to the gate to allow a fast exit if he made a serious attack. I stepped inside the pen and closed the gate, with Sandy watching my every move through the chicken wire.

While I spread grain, Tom strutted and gobbled, trotting within a few feet of me and then backing off. This was old Tom's call to battle. He extended his long neck, spread his wings, and gobbled his irritation as I backed to the far side of the pen. This was not my best move. Tom was between the gate and me. I continued to move around the pen spreading grain while Tom strutted and planned his next attack. I attempted to sidestep as he raced toward me with wings spread, gobbling all the way. Since I had no escape, I backed off and threw grain at his feet. The big bird stopped to eat, giving me time to escape through the gate.

I needed help with how to deal with this bird. Rif Jones owned a farm about two miles down the road and raised several hundred turkeys every year for Thanksgiving. I mounted my bike and started down the road for a visit with him. A man who raises hundreds of turkeys every year surely would know how to deal with a mean bird like ours.

Rif and his wife, Eva, lived in a small clapboard house in the woods just off the main road. If it had ever been painted, it was so long ago you couldn't tell. The yard was overgrown and cluttered with leaves from the surrounding oak trees.

The fenced area behind the house was fifty yards long and equally as wide, with a sea of white turkeys clustered in one corner gobbling and pecking at the ground.

I rode my bike to the back of the house and yelled, "Hello. Is anyone here?"

Rif opened the kitchen door and eased his six-foot-four-inch frame through the opening onto the porch. His sun-reddened face was deeply lined under a mop of thick snowy-white hair. Soiled farmer coveralls were held in place by straps across his broad shoulders. Thick white eyelashes shielded brown eyes, and he had a red bulbous nose that made you smile. It gave him a humorous look.

Rif had the dense muscle of a man who had worked a farm all his life. He rubbed his jaw with a callused hand, gave me a befuddled look, and said, "Hi, Dubbie. What brings you around here?"

We shook hands as I looked across the yard and said, "You sure do have a lot of turkeys. I was hoping you could help me with a problem I'm having. Do you have any mean turkeys in that pen?"

"Stupid is more like it," Rif answered. "I believe that the turkey is the dumbest bird that God ever created. They've got a brain about the size of a pea and don't even use that." He grinned at his attempt at humor.

I laughed at his remark and said, "I've got a big tom turkey in our chicken yard with a pea brain. He's not just dumb, but mean. I feed him, and he still chases me out of the pen."

"There's nothing that a turkey can do that surprises me. I have been raising them for years, and they constantly come up with ways to hurt themselves."

He continued, "Last year, we had a heavy summer rain and a bunch of my birds stood in the middle of the yard with their beaks turned up until they swallowed so much water they drowned. I lost almost two dozen birds in that storm." He frowned and shook his head, as if thinking about what had happened.

"Now," he said, "every time it rains I have to run out there with a hoe handle and stir them up so they won't just stand there and drown." He chuckled and continued, "I sure hope no one sees me out there in the rain thrashing around with a damn hoe handle. It looks so crazy, they'll want to have me picked up and placed in a padded room."

I grinned and covered my mouth with my hand because I was laughing so hard.

Rif's mouth turned down as he kicked the dirt with his boot and bit his lower lip in thought. Time passed while we looked out at the pen. The turkeys were flocked together, and he looked at me and said, "Do you see how they are all bunched up in one corner of the pen?"

"Yes, sir," I answered. "Is there a reason for that?"

"None that I know of," Rif said. "They do it all the time, but the problem is what happens next. One of the turkeys will leave the flock and work his way to the empty side of the pen. That shouldn't be a problem, but in the clouded minds of turkeys, it is. A little time will pass, and the turkeys in the flock will start looking at the lone bird on the other side of the pen. I guess they think he is doing something special, because they stampede and hundreds of turkeys run across the pen in a panic to get to the other side. No reason for that; it just happens. Depending on the size of the stampede, several of the birds will fall and be trampled. Sometimes they just get hurt, but they can get killed. I lose birds like that all the time."

"Wow," I said, trying to show sympathy for Rif's turkey problems.

He grimaced and said, "The turkey trick of the year was last year's self-inflicted suicide. A turkey would stick his head through the chicken wire fence, get hung up, and cut itself trying to get its head back out and then bleed to death." Rif shook his head, frowned, and continued, "I had to buy finer-meshed wire and rewire the entire pen that year to get it stopped."

Listening to all these problems prompted me to ask, "With all this going on, how come you still raise turkeys?"

He looked down at me and then out across the pen, and answered, "Probably because I'm about as dumb as they are." We both laughed, and he continued, "It's a living, and I know a lot about turkeys. I guess that's the real reason."

My brain was racing as we walked toward the pen. Rif knew just about everything there was to know about turkeys. I wanted to ask him about how to deal with old Tom, but he appeared upset from talking about his problems.

We stopped beside the fence and watched the cluster of white birds on the far side of the pen. He placed his hand on top of the post and said, "I guess the good news is that they are not strong enough to knock down the fence." He grinned and tested the post to be sure it was sturdy.

I decided it was time to talk some serious turkey. "Mr. Jones," I said, "this old tom of mine is so big and strong I'm afraid he's going to attack me. He struts, spreads his wings, and then runs at me. So far, he has stopped, but I'm afraid that one of these days he's going to jump on me."

Rif continued to look across the yard and said, "A bird that big has feet that can cause some damage. His feet are more dangerous than his beak."

"That's what I thought," I said. "What can I do to get this bird to back off and leave me alone?"

Rif looked at me and answered, "Tom thinks he is stronger and in charge. Each time he chases you out of the pen, he is going to be even more aggressive. An attack is sure to come unless you deal with it."

"How do I deal with it?" I asked.

"Get yourself a stick. Always have it with you when you go into the pen. When Tom runs at you, hit his body with the stick. You can hit his wing, but I recommend that you stay away from his head. You don't want to kill the bird; you just want his respect. You don't have to hit him that hard to make him respect you and your stick. A few days of that, and your problem should be solved."

I thanked Rif for his help and thought about a plan as I pedaled my bike on the road toward home. I intended to be ready for old Tom at the feeding this afternoon.

Each day, the feeding had become more difficult. Old Tom had taken up the challenge of keeping me outside his pen. There were days when he would be near the gate at feeding time and I could not enter. I waited beside the gate until he moved away before stepping inside to feed the chickens. It was time for me to show Tom who was in charge of the pen at feeding time. My plan was to hit Tom as he attacked. That should teach him to leave me alone.

At feeding time that afternoon, I entered the pen with my left arm around the feed basket and a stick firmly in my right fist. Tom, with wings spread, strutted back and forth gobbling to announce his intentions. His war dance was something to watch, and I stood there waiting for the usual charge. Tom turned and with wings spread, came at me in a fast trot. This was worse than I expected, but I waited until he was within range of my stick, dropped the grain bucket, and swung my stick at his body. My swing was high, and I struck him on the neck just below his head. He dropped to the ground and did not move.

I looked down at him, and my mouth dropped open as I thought, *I've killed old Tom! What will everyone think?! I have killed our only turkey.* My heart raced and I breathed in gulps as I dropped to the ground and rubbed his neck and head, hoping that would help. Finally, he opened his eyes and eventually sat up. Several minutes passed, and he finally stood and wobbled to the other side of the pen.

I knew the next day would be a test, but I decided to enter the pen without my stick. I wanted old Tom to leave me alone but did not want to kill the bird. As I moved through the gate, several chickens ran to my feet expecting grain. Old Tom remained at the far side of the pen, gobbling several times to protest my presence. There was no strutting, and the gobbles seemed friendlier. Several days passed, and I decided to cross the pen and spread grain in front of Tom and wait for his reaction. The big bird gobbled and pecked at the food as I stood close by and watched. I looked down at the turkey and whispered to him, "I'm the new king of the roost around here, you turkey! Mess with me, and I'll go get my stick and give you another lesson."

Carrying the eggs I had collected from the henhouse, I rounded the corner of the building to find Uncle Joe sitting on the steps of the porch. I placed my pail of eggs on the top step, looked at him, and said, "I've had a problem with our turkey, but it looks like we are okay now. I hit him with a stick, and he leaves me alone when I feed the chickens."

Uncle Joe grinned and said, "Big birds like that strut around and gobble to show off but usually are not harmful. They can hurt you with the claws on their feet unless you show them who is in charge."

I turned and sat on the bottom step and answered, "I think he was picking on me because I'm new and just a kid. I was fair game, and he was trying to show me that he was in charge of the pen."

We sat quietly looking out at the field of tall, green corn growing just beyond our yard, and Uncle Joe finally said, "The corn looks like it's ripe and ready to eat. Why don't you pick us about eight ears, and we'll clean them for dinner?"

"Yes, sir," I said while slipping off the step and tucking in my shirt.

My uncle looked at me and said, "You have done a good job of feeding the chickens. Do you think you can handle feeding the livestock?"

Surprised by the question, I looked down, smiled, and said, "Yes, sir."

"It's a big job," he said. "You'll have to feed at dawn and again just before dark, but I think you know what needs to be done. When you get home from school, the chickens have to be fed and eggs gathered. Can you do all that?"

"Yes, sir," I answered. I had a strange feeling in the pit of my stomach. Uncle Joe trusted me, and I wanted to do a good job.

"Starting tomorrow morning, it's your job."

My throat tightened as I looked at my shoes, but I managed to say, "Thanks. I won't let you down."

"I know you won't," he answered. "If you have any problems, let me know so I can help."

The stalks of corn were over six feet tall with brown tassels topping each stalk. I moved slowly down a row and selected a stalk with two large ears wrapped tightly with green leaves. Both ears had tassels on top indicating their maturity. I pulled back the leaves on one ear and popped a kernel with my thumbnail to be sure it was not overly ripe. The milky juice squirted out, and I knew the corn would be perfect for dinner. I gathered eight ears and held them against my chest with my left arm as I crossed the field toward our house. After stacking them on the cleaning table beside the house, I bounded up the porch steps to my makeshift bedroom beside the kitchen door.

I was happy in my new home and liked sleeping on the open porch. The bottom half of the bunk bed and mattress rested against the wall, with several blankets folded and stacked at one end. All were needed on cool nights and felt good when I snuggled inside and pulled the covers around my ears.

Aunt Ona Belle opened the kitchen door, looked at me, and said, "If you clean those ears now, I'll cook them for dinner. My meat loaf will be ready in about a half hour."

"I'll have them ready for you in just a few minutes," I answered, crossing the porch to return to the table.

The meat loaf and corn were great, and a tall glass of iced tea made them perfect. Uncle Joe and I competed over who could do the best job of eating an ear of corn, and he won. I left a few grains on the cob, and his ear was completely clean. He laughed while I tried to clean up my mess.

I carried the dishes to the sink, and while my aunt washed, I dried and put them away. The evening had started to cool, and Uncle Joe tinkered with the fire in our potbelly stove, warming the room. With the chores done, we settled around the stove to enjoy the warmth and listen to the radio.

Warm and comfortable, I looked at my new family and said, "I'm going to bed. I need to be up early in the morning to feed the livestock."

Uncle Joe nodded while my aunt smiled and said, "Sleep tight, and don't let the bedbugs bite."

I laughed and said, "I don't have bedbugs!" I stepped through the door to the porch. I spread the blankets on the bed, unlaced my shoes, laid my jacket, shirt, and jeans on a straight-back wooden chair, and slipped under the covers. Warm and cozy, I listened to whip-poor-wills calling in a hollow near the stream that ran through our property. Things were going to be okay. I had a place to live and a comfortable bed. My uncle had given me a job, and I was determined to do it right and not let him down. I could see my breath in the cool night air as I drifted off to sleep thinking about my new job.

Awake well before dawn, I sat on the edge of my bed and placed both feet on the cold wood floor. The cast-iron door to our potbelly stove clanged shut, and I knew that Uncle Joe had built a fire. I picked up my clothes and slipped into the kitchen to enjoy the warmth. My shoes were warming beside the stove as I pulled on my jeans and slipped into my shirt. Both were cool, and I pulled the chair closer to the fire.

The morning was cool, and dawn was just starting to break. I slipped into my shoes, stood, and noticed a plate of biscuits on the table, next to the stove. They looked too good to resist, so I grabbed one, took a bite, and headed for the barnyard. As I passed the doghouse, I was joined by Star and Sandy, tails wagging. Sandy rubbed my leg, and I gently patted his head, stroked his back, and reached for Star, who loved everybody. Star wanted attention but clearly had her eye on the biscuit in my right hand. Breaking it in half, I looked at her as she stood on her hind legs and whined.

"Here you go," I said and threw a piece of the biscuit in her direction. She jumped and caught it in midair. Sandy sat in front of me patiently waiting for his treat. I held out the piece of biscuit that was left, and he gently took it from my hand. As the dogs enjoyed their treat, I walked toward the barnyard gate.

Cricket, a Clydesdale mare with hooves larger than a plate, long legs, a broad chest, dark auburn coat, swishing tail, and gentle brown eyes, met me at the gate. Primarily a plow horse, she also pulled wagons, balers, and a mower, all in concert with Mike, a tall, graceful red Missouri mule with a white nose and large floppy ears. The two were inseparable. Jack, a black mule, had a long black tail and mane and was the grandfatherly type. He was older and gentle in nature, and almost nothing excited Jack.

The three waited at the gate as I entered, and then they turned and followed close behind me as I walked to the barn. They had individual stalls and knew where to go for their meals. Opening the tack room door, I stepped inside and searched for the pail used to measure the grain I had to give to each animal. No pail was in sight, so I searched the barn. It wasn't in any of the stalls, so I made a quick check of the loft; nothing there but hay. I finally found the tipped-over pail beside the water trough next to the barn door. Gathering it up, I returned to the feed room to complete the morning chores.

Inside individual stalls, each animal waited for the morning grain. I opened the feed room door, filled the pail, and walked to Cricket's stall with her breakfast. I gently rubbed her nose, and then dumped the grain into the feed trough. As she munched away, I returned to refill the pail and feed Jack. Gentle Jack waited at the stall door as I entered. Lowering his head to eye level was a request to have his ears scratched; I shifted the pail to one side and scratched his right ear, saying, "Good morning, Jack. Does that feel good, old boy?" I moved to the back of the stall to place the grain in his feed trough.

Mike waited in his stall, watching as I walked to the feed bin for his grain. "I'm coming, Mike," I said while walking toward his stall. This was a mule with a sense of humor. I knew to expect the unexpected. As I entered the stall, Mike turned to face his trough as I walked alongside, bucket in hand. As I reached his midsection, he sidestepped, pinning me to the wall. I knew he would hold me there because I guess he thought this was funny.

"Move over, Mike."

He didn't move, and I was still pinned. The stall was unlighted and dark; I had no choice but to wait him out.

"Come on, Mike! Move over!" I slapped his stomach with my free hand, but he didn't move.

Still pinned, I made a third plea, trying to sound in charge. I shouted, "Get over, Mike! Come on, move!"

Finally, there was some action. He sidestepped to the right, releasing me from his grip. The path was clear, so I stepped to the trough, poured the grain, and waited for Mike to begin eating. Stroking his neck, I said, "You need to find another way to have fun, big guy. What are you going to do when I grow up? You won't be able to pin me then!"

He continued eating, and I returned the pail to the feed bin, closed the door, and crossed the barnyard to the house. My aunt heard me on the porch and announced, "Breakfast is ready. Come and get it!"

The biscuits were hot, and there were scrambled eggs and soft fried potatoes. I gulped my milk, buttered a biscuit, and piled on scrambled eggs as Aunt Ona Belle said, "I think I heard the bus, so you'd better hurry."

With the biscuit in hand, I returned to the porch, gathered my books, and started to the bus stop. Sandy joined me and wagged his tail as a request for a bite of my food. We moved across the yard while I ate; then I reached down and handed him the last bite.

The big yellow bus screeched to a stop as I trotted past the mailboxes to board it and begin another day at school. As I climbed the steps to the bus, Sandy stood quietly by the road with a sad look on his face. I looked back knowing that he would be waiting for me when I returned and said, "Go home, boy. I'll be back after school." Our driver, Mr. Todd, closed the door and put the engine in gear, and we were on our way.

Chapter Eleven
Barbershop Talk

A stop at the general store was required, but a small part of the evening. The wagon emptied as it reached the store; its passengers were on their way to an enjoyable night with friends from other farms. The small town was alive with people. It was a warm night, and social activity would be outside.

I stepped inside the store and breathed in its unique smell. Farm implements lined the left wall. Ten-foot-long rectangular tables in the center of the room were piled high with clothing, boxed shoes, and round bolts of cloth in every color imaginable. A seven-foot-high cast-iron potbelly stove rested in the center of the back wall and was surrounded by chairs and wood crates sitting at odd angles. The counter on the right wall stopped at a glass display case filled with candy. I walked to the case and gawked at the rainbow of colors in search of my selection. The store clerk gave me time to look and then said, "Can I help you, son?"

"Yes, sir," I answered. "I would like to buy some red licorice."

"How much money do you have?" the clerk asked.

"Fifteen cents."

"Okay, fifteen cents' worth of licorice it'll be," he said, while opening the back of the case to count out the correct number of pieces. I placed my fifteen cents on the counter as he folded the sticks in half and slipped them into a small paper sack. I went outside and decided to enjoy my first taste of the candy.

Several men sat on the steps in front of the store talking. Others gathered in groups on the street, in front of stores and in the town square. Checkers was the game at the square. While some men played, others gathered in groups talking quietly as the sun slipped behind the buildings and the evening began.

I found a can to kick and with my right foot launched it toward the barbershop. Two kicks later, I found a seat on the front steps so that I could see inside the shop.

Several men sat on the steps and in chairs outside the open door. Men waiting their turn for a haircut occupied chairs inside the shop. I was in a good position to listen to everyone talk and knew better than to try to participate. The barbershop was for "men only," but young boys were allowed to attend as observers—but start talking, and they would send you on your way. As long as I sat quietly, the adults did not seem to mind my being there.

Pimento, the shop's owner, was almost six feet tall and slight of build with a ruddy complexion. A full head of gray-streaked black hair was combed straight back and smoothed with rose hair oil. His brown eyes were hidden behind thick reading glasses perched on a red nose. He always wore a knee-length white pharmacy coat over his cotton shirt and jeans while he was cutting hair.

If he had a last name, no one seemed to know. He owned the town's only barbershop, a one-man operation with enough room to accommodate ten or more visitors. The two wooden rocking chairs on the front porch were always occupied in the early evening. Several straight-back wooden chairs with vinyl seats sat at odd angles near the rocking chairs. Steps ran the length of the porch and were a comfortable place to sit if you were suited to the hard wood. The barber pole mounted at the end of the building was the shop's only advertisement. The front door was always open so that men on the porch could hear, and join, the conversation.

Inside, old but comfortable chairs lined one wall facing the direction of the barber chair. A shelf behind the barber chair was littered with cutting instruments, aftershave lotions, and hair treatments. A wall-length mirror above the shelf allowed customers to see the room while getting a haircut. The lingering fragrance of lotions combined with cigar and pipe smoke gave the room its unique barbershop smell.

It was known for good haircuts as well as for local area gossip. Pimento was a showman, and the shop was his stage. This was the nerve center of town, and he was equipped with an endless supply of stories to tell while cutting hair. Watching haircuts on Saturday night was good entertainment and always drew a crowd. Men with pints in their hip pockets gathered on the porch to watch the sunset and talk farming, hunting, and fishing with their friends. The conversation was lively, and all the men participated. It was a comfortable place with men talking among themselves while others sat back and enjoyed the stories.

Pimento said, "Jim's bull got out again this week. That's one mean bull. It took them half a day to catch him."

From the porch, a farmer said, "Was anyone hurt?"

Pimento answered, "One guy got knocked down and stepped on, but nothing was broken. The bull tore down a holding pen. Wasn't strong enough, I guess. A bull that big has to be in a strong pen." He continued, "Then, on top of that, his son Jimmy got suspended for a week at school on Tuesday. He called that old Ford he was driving the *Mayflower*. Said he named it that because so many girls had come across in it. The principal found out and suspended him. Told him he couldn't come back until he got the name off the car."

From the porch, someone said, "Sounds to me like I need to borrow the car." Laughter echoed from inside the shop.

When the stories were good, the shop remained open late on Saturday night. Pimento never seemed to tire of cutting hair and would stay open as long as needed. The crowd would overflow onto the porch and pass around the white lightning as they listened to the tales.

Pimento believed that God created Wednesday for fishing, and the shop was always closed that day. Catfish were plentiful in the river, and Pimento owned a flat-bottom fishing boat that he kept at a dock located not far from town. He usually fished alone but knew I loved to fish and would occasionally let me join him for the day.

As dawn broke, he parked his rusted pickup, collected his gear, and started down the dock to the boat. The small cooler in his right hand contained a six-pack of beer and a glass vinegar jug filled with drinking water. I lifted my cane pole, a coffee can half-full of dirt and worms, and a sandwich bag out of the truck. I turned and trotted to catch up to his fast pace. As we reached the dock, I looked at him and asked, "Where are we going to fish today?"

"We'll go upriver to a spot I have fished that is in a cove on the far bank. I've caught fish there before, and it should be pretty good."

I nodded and said, "I dug some worms last night and have plenty for both of us."

He grinned and said, "I brought some rotten catfish bait. We'll try both and see which one they like. It should be a good day."

The small outboard motor started with the second pull and purred at an idle while I released the boat from the dock. The motor clunked as Pimento shifted to reverse and backed away from the dock. We moved into the current as he clunked into forward and spun the small aluminum boat around and turned the throttle wide open. The boat lurched forward as I placed my hands on the seat to balance against the quick start. The sun was peeking through the trees, and the river was smooth. It was going to be a good day.

As the spot came into view, we approached a low overhanging tree branch and I secured the boat with a line coiled in the bow. As the boat swung gently around with its stern pointed downstream, Pimento opened his fishing box and began tying his rig. After slipping a weight on the line, he tied on a swivel snap followed with a three-foot leader and hook. A float was attached to the line three feet above the weight. He put some foul-smelling catfish bait on the hook and dropped the line into the water. The bobber floated gently on the surface while Pimento settled down to enjoy his morning.

My fishing line was tied to the tip of my six-foot-long cane pole with the float and hook already in place. I stirred the coffee can with my finger, found a worm, placed it on my hook, and raised my pole to drop the rig into the water.

As mid-morning approached, only one fish had struck the bait, causing Pimento's float to dip under the water and making ripples on the surface. As he attempted to set the hook, the fish slipped away. The fish had ignored my bait, and I settled back to enjoy the warm summer day. A crow called from a nearby tree as Pimento moved to the center of the boat and opened his cooler to retrieve a cold beer from under the ice. The can hissed as he popped it open and returned to his seat in front of the motor. "It looks like the fish are not biting," he said between sips of beer. "There is a Coke in the cooler when you want one."

"Thanks," I said. "I'll save it for later in the day."

We sat quietly watching our stagnant lines until Pimento said, "I know there are fish in this river. They just don't happen to be where we are."

I nodded and said, "Where do you think they might be?" Pimento was the best fisherman in our town, and I believed everything he said about fishing.

"I wish I knew," he answered. "We will fish here a little longer, and if nothing happens, we'll move to another spot."

Several hours passed with no strikes, not even a nibble. Pimento gazed across the river and said, "I have had some luck fishing while the boat drifted down the river, but it's a lot of work and more trouble than it's worth. It's hard to manage the boat, fishing rod, and line with everything in motion. Even with two of us, it's not fun." He pursed his lips as he reached for a drink of water from his vinegar jug. After several gulps of water, he smacked his lips and said, "It would be a lot easier if we could just let the rig float unattached."

I thought about that and said, "If you let it drift down the river, wouldn't you need a big float? One that the fish could not pull under and just take off?"

Pimento held the vinegar jug with both hands as he looked at me and said, "It would have to be about the size of this bottle." As he screwed the cap on the jug, he grinned and continued, "In fact, this jug would probably make a good float. It's large enough and has a loop on the neck that we could use to tie our line. Empty it, screw the cap on tight, turn it upside down, and it's unsinkable, no matter how large the fish."

I watched as he returned to his seat and set the bottle in an upright position between his shoes. He continued to look at the bottle and said, "The weight would have to be heavy enough to slow the jug as it drifted downriver. All we would have to do is follow the jug until a fish takes the bait, chase down the bottle, and pull it in."

"It sounds easy," I thought out loud. "Chasing a jug with a fish on it would be a lot more fun than sitting here staring at our bobbers."

Pimento emptied the jug and screwed the lid on so that it would be airtight. Using line from his fishing box, he tied a leader to the finger hole on the neck of the bottle. Three feet down the line, he attached the heaviest weight in his box so that the bottle would sit upright as it floated down the river. A four-foot leader line was next, with two hooks about a foot apart to complete the rig.

As he tied the last hook on the line, he looked at me and said, "Nothing happening here. Let's move into the current and give our bottle a test."

I nodded and stood to untie our line from the tree branch. The boat slowly drifted down the river as Pimento placed bait on the hooks and gently slipped the bottle over the side into the water. He started the motor and left it in idle as the bottle floated away.

Two hundred yards downstream, the bottle dipped halfway under water and bobbed toward a downed tree resting at the river's bank. A fish was on, and Pimento revved the engine to give chase. As the boat reached the bottle, I leaned over and pulled it into the boat, followed by a four-pound catfish on the hook at the end of the line.

We laughed as I shouted, "What a way to catch fish. This is fun!"

Pimento chuckled and with a grin said, "A new way to fish!"

The steady but gentle flow of the river was perfect for the sport of "jug fishing." The challenge and the fun were to keep track of your jug. This was a story to be told at the barbershop. Saturday was the busiest day of the week, at least at the barbershop. Pimento planned to share his idea with the crowd he expected that afternoon. Chairs along the wall were full of men waiting their turn for a haircut. Several men sat in chairs on the porch smoking and telling stories. Two farmers in overalls occupied the rocking chairs and listened to the tales. I sat close by on the porch steps, which was close enough for me to hear the conversation.

Pimento talked as he continued to cut a farmers hair. "Have any of you boys heard of jug fishing?"

After a long pause, one of the men said, "What's that?"

Pimento said, "That's where you hook your line to an upside-down vinegar jug and let the entire rig float down the river. When the fish hits, the jug bobs and you go after it with your boat. Pull your jug in, and you've got the fish."

There was laughter from the porch. Someone said, "Whoever thought up a crazy idea like that?"

A heavyset farmer sitting in a rocking chair on the porch said, "I ain't chasing no vinegar jug around the river in a boat."

I grinned but sat quietly. These guys didn't know how much fun you could have chasing a catfish that was pulling your jug around the river. The belly laughs on the porch could be heard inside the shop. Pimento was now ready for his punch line.

"Would you chase the jug if it had a twenty-pound catfish on the other end?" he asked.

From the barber chair, a farmer said, "I would chase a jug from here to hell and back for a twenty-pound catfish."

Pimento said, "Well, that's what you are likely to get, because a floating rig gets exposed to so many other areas. A floating rig is likely to catch more fish, and that usually amounts to some big ones."

A thin man wearing jeans and a flannel shirt listened to the conversation from his position on the steps and shook his head in disbelief. He removed his straw hat, wiped his brow with a handkerchief, and said, "Have you ever done any jug fishin'?"

"I took Dubbie with me last Wednesday, and when we weren't getting any bites on our lines, I decided to rig a jug and give it a try." He looked at me on the porch and continued, "We caught fish, didn't we, Dubbie?"

Knowing that kids were rarely allowed in barbershop conversations, I looked at him, smiled, and proudly said, "Yes, sir, we did."

"Chasing that jug with a fish on it was a hell of a lot of fun," Pimento said. "I'm going jug fishing next Wednesday. If any of you want to follow me, you're welcome to come along." He continued to cut hair but looked out the front door and shouted, "Dubbie, I'm gonna need someone to work the bow. Do you want to go with me on Wednesday?"

Excited by the thought, I screeched at the top of my voice, "Yes, sir!"

That was the day that jug fishing was born. It was a fun sport made even better on a hot summer day with an ice cooler full of beer and pop in the bow of the boat. But fishermen are competitive, and jug-fishing contests soon developed. Why use one jug when several increased your chances for a big fish? Some boats carried ten or more jugs and would launch all at the same time for the trip downriver. The jugs moved with the current and rarely at the same speed.

River fishing required a light boat that was easy to handle and stable so that a man could stand up and move about as he fought the fish to a successful catch. The most popular boat was a twelve-foot-long flat-bottom aluminum boat with three board seats. One was mounted in front of the motor, with one in the middle of the boat and one at the bow. The seats were stable, but a cushion was needed for a comfortable day of fishing. A small motor was all that was needed, but some men preferred a larger outboard for additional speed and maneuverability. Boats with big motors could reach a bobbing jug quicker and usually caught more fish.

Competition was strong as farmers followed their jugs trying to catch the biggest fish of the day. Confusion developed as boats crisscrossed the river trying to follow the jugs moving downstream.

Once, a jug bobbed off toward the riverbank as two boats gave chase. The lead boat had a bigger motor and was winning the race while being screamed at from the bow of the losing boat. "That's my bottle! You git away from it!"

The driver of the faster boat roared with laughter and said, "If you can't keep up, you don't deserve a fish!" He reached the bottle and pulled in a five-pound catfish.

Not one to be denied, the slower boat caught up and rammed the first boat, knocking one man into the water. Byron, the driver, bellowed, "You jackass. You knocked Billy into the water!" The bow of the slow boat rested on top of the boat it had just rammed. There was no damage to either boat, and Eddie, the driver of the second boat, laughed and said, "That'll teach you to mess with one of my bottles. If you don't give me that fish, I may just hit you again!"

Byron stood in the back of his boat, laughed, and said, "I'll give it to you tomorrow. I'm eating it for dinner tonight!" He roared at his joke while other men joined in. Pimento stopped our boat to watch. I sat on the bow seat watching the screaming match, with my mouth hanging open.

Three boats stopped to watch the battle while the swimmer made an unsuccessful try at climbing back into his boat. His partner shut off the engine and stepped forward to give him a hand. With the fish inside the boat, the fight was over, but the arguing continued until Byron noticed two other bottles bobbing in different directions. Looking down at his partner holding onto the side of the boat, he shouted, "Two bottles out there are getting away with fish on. Get in the damn boat! Now!"

Billy, his partner, threw one leg over the side of the boat and attempted to pull his body into the boat with one hand. Halfway there, he slipped back into the water as Byron reached down to help. Billy's

250-pound body was too much for Byron to lift out of the water, and he fell overboard beside his partner.

The men in two boats close by roared with laughter as one man said, "You guys don't need a jug; just wrap the fishing line around your wrist and jump in!" One man laughed so hard that he started coughing out of control.

Both men remained in the water holding onto the boat when Byron said, "You go first, Billy, and I'll push you up and into the boat." Al, the front man in a boat less than ten feet away, snorted and said in a loud voice, "To lift a man the size of Billy, you are gonna need a crane. Do you want me to pull up and help?"

"We've got enough going on here and don't need a smart-ass!" Billy shouted.

Byron answered, "I would appreciate it." As the boat pulled alongside and Al reached down to grab the back of Billy's shirt, Bryon pushed, and with Al's help, Billy rolled over the side and landed on his back in the bottom of their boat. Byron slipped back into the boat easily and returned to his seat in front of the motor. Several motors started, and boats moved in different directions as Byron asked, "Do you see any of our bottles farther down the river?"

Billy scanned the river and answered, "I think I see one farther down near the left bank."

The game was on, with no two boats going the same direction as they chased bobbing vinegar jugs.

The bottles continued down the river, with some caught in eddies, while others moved faster and became mixed with other bottles traveling a similar path. It became impossible for the owners to track the bottles they had floated earlier in the day. Any bottle with a fish on the line became fair game. An orderly day of fishing had become a demolition derby as boats bumped into each other, and men hooted with laughter as they beat another boat to a bobbing bottle and pulled in a fish.

Five miles downstream, the men called it a day and began rounding up bottles for the return trip to their dock. When all the bottles were recovered, they turned their boats into the current and began the trip upstream to their camp. The bottles were stacked on the dock so that everyone could inspect their lines and recover those they had floated at the start of the day.

Pimento picked up three jugs and I carried two as we walked to his truck while talking about the day.

"This is the most fun I've ever had fishing," Pimento said.

"Me, too." I nodded. "I laughed so hard when those guys were in the water, I almost fell overboard."

"We are going to have a jug-fishing contest next Sunday," he said. "Do you want to fish with me that day?"

"You bet!" I answered. "I will be at your house early and load our equipment in the back of your truck."

As we bounced down the dirt road to his house, Pimento was quiet for several miles and then said, "We need to figure out a way to identify our jugs in the water as they float downstream. The jugs all look the same, and it's impossible to tell which one is yours. Several guys were upset because another boat took a fish off their hookup."

It was dark as he drove his truck inside the garage, which was also a storage area for tools and yard equipment. The truck lights illuminated the back wall of the garage, where a gallon can of red paint stood out on the shelf directly in front of his hood. "That's the answer." He looked at me and said, "I'm gonna paint the bottom of my jugs red."

"I like red. It's easy to see and will set us apart from all the other jugs," I commented as we began unloading the back of the truck.

Pimento thought and said, "I'm gonna get everybody to paint their jugs their favorite color. Some may want to paint an X or an O on the bottom of their jugs, and that will work too."

I thanked him for taking me fishing and mounted my bike for the ride home.

The following afternoon, the barbershop was busy, with several men waiting for their turn in the chair. I arrived as the sun slipped below the stores and shadows stretched across the unpaved street. Sitting quietly on the steps, I listened to the men talk.

The front door was open, and two men sat in chairs on the porch and talked quietly. Pimento continued to cut hair as two more men arrived and sat on the edge of the porch beside the steps. A farmer in grease-stained coveralls sat on the steps making a hand-rolled cigarette with a small sack of tobacco. Pulling the string on the sack and returning it to his shirt pocket, he placed the wrinkled paper between his lips and lit it with a match. Blowing out smoke, he said, "I heard that everybody had a real good time jug fishing yesterday. Were any of you guys there?"

Cy rocked gently in his chair on the porch and said, "I was there and can't remember when I've had so much fun. I laughed so hard my ribs hurt."

It was the opening that Pimento wanted, and he said, "We're going to have a contest next Sunday. The jugs got mixed up drifting down the river yesterday, but I have figured out how to fix that. I have painted the bottom of my jugs red."

Cy asked, "Red? What good is that gonna do?"

"My red jugs are going to stand out as they drift down the river." Pimento continued, "Everyone that's fishing should pick out a paint and color their jugs so they can spot them going down the river."

Two men nodded their approval as Cy said, "That sounds like a good idea. I think I'll paint a white X on the bottom of my jugs so that they will be different from everything in the water."

Pimento arrived at the boat dock Sunday morning as dawn began to break over the trees across the river. Ten teams had committed to the contest, and several were already there preparing for an active day. A fire crackled in the stone pit near the dock, and several men warmed their hands near the flames. The morning was cool but would warm up when the sun lifted over the trees.

Pimento parked the truck near the fire pit, and we stepped out to warm up before starting the day. I turned my back to the fire and felt the heat through my shirt as Pimento stepped close and rubbed his hands together near the flames. The fire crackled and popped while we stood quietly enjoying the heat. Pimento turned to warm his back as Sammy looked at him and said, "How many jugs are you fishing with this morning?"

Using both hands, Pimento rubbed the back of his legs and felt the warmth of the fire on his pants. His lips moved slowly as he tried to remember the number of jugs in the back of his truck. Finishing his count, he said, "Five. I painted the bottom of my jugs red so that we can see them better in the water. Dubbie is fishing with me, and the two of us should be able to track five bottles without any trouble."

Sammy smiled and said, "Sounds like you have a plan, but there's no way to know what the current will do as we move downstream."

Pimento nodded and said, "That's what makes a contest like this fun."

The day warmed as the sun peeked over the trees, and Pimento left the fire to begin loading his boat. I joined in and made several trips, making sure nothing was left behind.

I stepped down into the boat and sat on the front seat to organize the equipment, while Pimento mounted the outboard motor and hooked up the red gas tank sitting in front of the engine. The engine started with the first pull and settled to a quiet idle as we released the lines to the dock and pushed the boat away. The boat drifted away from the dock as Pimento counted seven boats at the dock with two more moving into the current to begin their trip upstream. An oak tree about a mile away marked the starting point for the contest.

The boats formed a line across the river where they intended to deposit their jugs for the trip downstream. While his outboard idled at neutral, Pimento slipped his five jugs into the water. The jugs and the boat drifted lazily down the river. The two-mile trip down the river would take most of the day and end with a fish fry over an open fire at the dock just before sunset.

Over fifty jugs moved slowly down the river, followed by the fishermen in their boats. All knew that the action was about to begin.

A jug bounced on the water and moved toward the bank as Don said, "We've got a hit on the blue jug, and it's going off to the left. Better get on it quick while it's still hooked up!"

Cy yelled, "Blue is my color. That's one of my jugs!"

Both Sammy and Cy chased after the jug, but Sammy was faster. He was trying to reach the bouncing jug as the two boats bumped, knocking Sammy off balance and into the water.

Cy shouted, "That ought to teach you to leave my jugs alone!"

Sammy reached for the side of his boat and sputtered, "Damn, you didn't have to knock me into the water. I was just trying to help."

"The hell you were!" Cy shouted. "You wanted my fish. That's why I bumped your boat." The jug continued to move away as Cy chased it and pulled in a catfish that weighed about ten pounds. Standing in the middle of his boat with the fish above his head, he laughed and shouted, "This is the standard, boys. Try to keep up!" One man gave him a one-finger salute while several others laughed.

Jimmy, in the bow of the lead boat, shouted, "There's a hit on the white bottle, and from the way it's taking off, should be a good-size fish. Bill, pull your boat up and see if you can grab the jug."

Bill pointed his boat toward the jug, opened up his engine, and bellowed, "Move out of the way up there. I'm coming through!"

Several other hits followed, with jugs moving in all directions around the boats. The orderly movement down the river fell apart as boats bumped together and cut across each other's paths in their pursuit of a bouncing jug.

Pimento saw one of his jugs take off and screamed, "I've got a big one on! Look at that jug take off. Out of my way, boys. I'm about to pull in the biggest fish of the day!"

I screamed, "Eeehaaa!" Pimento moved to the seat in front of the engine, opened the throttle to full, and turned the boat toward the bobbing bottle. The bottle was moving toward the far bank as Pimento bumped a boat in his path and yelled, "Move over, Jim! Look at that bottle move. It's getting away!" Jim pushed away from Pimento's boat as it continued toward the bottle. Two other boats followed to watch the chase, but Pimento's boat was faster and began to pull away. I moved to the floor of the boat on my knees and rested my elbows on the bow seat, staring at the moving bottle.

Closing the distance, Pimento laughed and crooned, "I'm comin' for you. You can't get away from me." The jug bounced in circles as the boat slipped by and made a U-turn for the next attempt. Not knowing what to do, I watched the jug as it bounced around erratically.

Pimento overshot his approach and turned off the engine as the boat bumped the bottle and it bounced its way down the side into his waiting hands. As the bottle bounced closer, he reached down to pull in his fish. I sat frozen in the bow and watched as he grabbed the jug with both hands and lifted it out of the water. The fish was every bit as big as predicted and not about to give up without a fight. Pimento was standing in the boat when the fish gave a mighty tug and pulled the bottle from his hands. While everyone watched, he fell backward out of the boat and into the water. A boat close by moved to help as Pimento turned away from his boat and swam after the still-moving bottle. Laughter echoed across the water as boats stopped to watch the fight develop.

"Look at that fool swimming after his jug," Jim said. "I'll bet that the fish is damn near as big as he is. Someone over there pull up and give him a hand."

I moved to the back of the boat and attempted to start the motor. Pimento reached the jug and pulled it to his chest in a bear hug, but it continued to move. Now, the fish was dragging the jug *and* Pimento as he sputtered water and said, "I think I've latched onto Moby Dick. Somebody pull up and give me a hand." I moved to the back of the boat and pulled the motor's starter cord, but it flooded and refused to run.

Jim said, "I'm comin'. Hold on until my partner can take the bottle." Keith, Jim's fishing partner, moved to the middle of the boat and leaned over the side as they approached Pimento and his jug. Jim stopped his motor, and the boat settled in the water. Keith reached out and grabbed a handful of Pimento's shirt and pulled him to the boat. He looked at Pimento and said, "Try to turn toward me so I can get my hands around the jug." Pimento tried to turn using his feet, but the constant jerking by the fish made it impossible.

Keith reached out as far as he could and shouted, "Try to lift the jug up far enough for me to take it." The first attempt failed as the wet bottle slipped from Keith's hands and Pimento pulled it back to his chest.

The fish stopped pulling, and Pimento looked into the murky water but could not see to the end of his line. He looked up at Keith and said, "I hope he's getting tired and not just slacking off to get a better hold for the next round. I'm just about worn out."

The jug was passed to Keith as Jim slipped on gloves and stepped forward to help pull the big fish aboard. With two men pulling on the line, the forty-pound catfish was lifted out of the water and flopped over the side into the bottom of the boat. The big fish was over four feet long, with a large mouth, sharp teeth, and needle-sharp three-inch fins on each side of its head. It was hard to handle and could be dangerous.

Pimento remained in the water holding on to the side of the boat with both hands. It was clear that the fight was not over. The fish was thrashing about inside the boat and appeared to be attacking the two men who had pulled it out of the water.

Jim yelled, "Look out! Don't let him bite you. Those teeth are sharp and can do some damage."

This was clearly a fish that demanded respect. As the big fish wiggled its way down the boat Keith jumped into the water and Jim retreated to the back of the boat and was standing on the rear seat. A second boat came alongside, and a man with a 357- Magnum pistol shot the fish. That killed the fish but also put a sizable hole in the bottom of the boat. The boat started to sink as Keith and Pimento attempted to climb back into it. Both were on the same side, and their weight tipped the boat to the point of it taking on even more water.

The men in surrounding boats saw nothing but humor in this and sat back to enjoy the show. Though they had mildly bruised egos, both men finally climbed aboard. One used his shirt to plug the hole, and both began to bail to keep the boat from sinking. The bailing continued until there was less than two inches of water remaining in the boat. Some water crept in around the poorly patched hole but not enough to be a problem. It was time to stop, sit back, and enjoy a cold beer.

The fish weighed in at thirty-eight pounds and was the biggest catch of the day. Several other boats had fish, but none as large as this. As the sun began to set, they collected their jugs and returned to the dock to prepare for the evening. A day of fishing was always followed with a catfish and hush puppy dinner cooked over an open fire. The stone fire pit near the boat dock had been built for just such events. Two unpainted wooden picnic tables stood near the pit beside a stack of oak firewood. One man started a fire in the pit, while several others brought supplies to be stacked on the tables. Several large iron skillets sat on one table, prepared and ready for three men to finish cleaning the day's catch. Hush puppies were being mixed in a large bowl to be cooked over the fire in another large skillet. Cold beer from an ice cooler was passed around as men gathered at the fire to laugh and talk about the events of the day. Exaggeration and bragging were allowed as the stories began.

Pimento grinned and said, "If any of you boys want some help with how to jug fish, come around my barbershop and I'll give you a few tips."

Several men snorted; one laughed and said, "The man catches one big fish, and we have to listen to him spout off all night long!"

The fire popped and crackled, lighting the area as Pimento continued. "It takes talent, boys. Keep trying, and you'll get the hang of it."

One of the men cleaning fish said, "Are you gonna teach us how to swim, Pimento? That's the way *you* jug fish."

Men around the fire laughed. One said, "And while you're at it, teach us how to keep a boat from sinking after you've shot a hole in it!"

More laughter, and Pimento, with a glint in his eye and a slight smile, was not about to let this pass. "I've set the standard for you guys. I'll bet this is the biggest fish caught this summer."

Keith looked across the fire and said, "If there is anything bigger than that out there, it's gonna take a team effort to bring it in. Today's fight was as tough as it gets."

Sammy laughed and said, "You call that a fight? I saw you do a swan dive off the bow of your boat. Keep that up, and we're gonna have to mount a diving board off your front seat."

Uncontrolled laughter echoed around the camp as Keith responded in a loud voice, "When that big sucker started after me, I needed a gun, but I didn't even have a paddle. It was time to hit the water!"

Pimento chuckled and said, "I was swimming toward my boat when Keith did his swan dive. I thought I had lost my fish."

"No chance of that happening," Don answered. "With the fishing done, Keith had decided to go for a swim."

Everyone hooted and laughed as they stood around the fire watching skillets of catfish and hush puppies cooking over the flames.

Bill said, "With everything that was going on, nobody saw Mort follow a jug under a low-hanging tree branch and get knocked out of his boat into the water."

Mort said, "I was watching the bottle and didn't see the branch. The good news was that I had my kill switch hooked on my belt and the motor died after I fell out. I swam to the boat and climbed back in."

There was laughter all around as one man said, "Did we go fishing today or swimming?"

More laughter as the cook said, "I think a couple of people here thought we were swimming. Which was it, Pimento?"

Pimento said, "I'll let my fish do the talking."

The night was quiet, with only the sound of an owl in a distant tree. The fire crackled and sparks flew as a log was thrown on the hot burning embers. Skillets of sizzling food were carried to the tables, and paper plates were passed around as men helped themselves to dinner. As everyone settled down to eat, one man said, "It just doesn't get any better than this!"

Chapter Twelve
A Day of Fishing

Fish bite early in the morning. Bill knew that and planned to be in position as daylight broke.

Up before dawn, he made a pot of coffee, placed it on the stove, and returned to his bedroom to dress. The coffee would be done by the time he returned to the kitchen.

The room was cool, and he pulled on jeans, white cotton socks, a flannel shirt, and a jean jacket to keep warm. He could smell the strong coffee aroma as he pulled on the knee-high rubber fishing boots he had purchased at the hardware store on Friday. They were a tight fit but would stretch with wear.

Bill was over six feet tall, with a mop of blond hair and bright blue eyes. He was square-jawed, with a wide mouth and uneven teeth that were common for people in the area. Dentistry had not reached the rural areas of Arkansas, and it showed.

As a young man just out of high school, he went to work for Valley Meat Packing Company. He was suited to the work and during his first year was assigned a route truck for delivering meat to rural grocery stores on a daily basis. The stores insisted that their orders be delivered before opening, and Bill started each day loading his truck at 4 a.m.

During deliveries, he talked to the managers about product that Valley had in its warehouse. Orders increased, and Bill soon had the most successful route in the company. Because of his ability to sell, the company promoted him to sales representative and one year later placed him in charge of all salespeople as district head salesman. He had been with the company ten years and was respected in his job.

I first met Bill when he was building his house, a small, one-bedroom clapboard structure with a kitchen, living room, and porch, located near the main road about a mile from our farm. We became friends, and I visited on weekends to help while he finished the roof and then brushed on a coat of white paint. A metal wood-burning stove attached to a flue in the living room provided the only heat, when needed. His sparse furnishings were those of a confirmed bachelor. A torn but comfortable overstuffed chair faced the stove in the living room, with a straight-back wood chair the only other item in the room. An unmade bed rested against the back wall of the bedroom with a scarred and chipped end table at its side. A round metal table sat in one corner of the kitchen, surrounded by three well-worn chairs with vinyl seats.

Excited about fishing, I was awake well before daylight. This was the first time Bill had invited me, and I was not about to keep him waiting. The morning air was cool; I dressed quickly, tied my shoes, and hurried into the kitchen to add wood to the stove. Flames reached into the flue as I closed the stove door and rubbed my hands together, warming them close to the fire. The stove vibrated gently while I enjoyed the heat and waited for my jacket on the back of the chair to warm. Unable to delay longer, I picked up my coat and slipped through the door, walked across the porch and down the steps, and headed to the barn.

As I passed the doghouse, Sandy stuck his head out beside the feed sack that hung over his door. Warm and comfortable, he had decided not to move. I continued walking and stroked his head as I passed. I could hear his thick tail thumping against the wall of the doghouse as I went on my way. It was his way of thanking me for the attention.

I moved from stall to stall distributing grain, checked the water trough, broke apart a thin layer of ice, and began adding water as Bill's truck turned into our drive. I waved, making sure he saw me when he stepped out of the truck. He waved back as I started up the path to the house.

My cane pole rested against the porch beside a cigar box containing several bobbers, hooks, weights, and a bottle of 6-12 to fight off insects. Mosquitoes were not bad, but chiggers could get under your skin and make you itch for at least three days. A light coat of 6-12 around your ankles stopped that, and if you rubbed some on your face the mosquitoes left you alone.

Bill stood beside the pickup bed as I approached and said, "Good morning."

He answered, "Morning. Throw your gear in back, and let's get going."

He started the engine, and as we pulled away, he said, "We are going to fish the river today. I've got us a boat reserved at Wally's Landing, and my motor's in the back. We can go up the river and drift back. Have you ever fished for bass?"

"No, sir. I fish for crappie at a creek not far from our house."

"Well, bass are bigger and will give you a harder fight. We can fish around the sandbars; they seem to hang out around there, so it should be a good day."

Bill was the best fisherman in our area. As he talked about what to do, I listened to every word. When we arrived at Wally's, I jumped out and began carrying our gear to the boat dock while he talked to Wally and made arrangements for our boat.

With most of our gear at the dock, I returned for the outboard motor. Bill was standing beside the truck and said, "Have you ever used a rod and reel?"

"No, sir," I answered. "I just have a cane pole."

"I have an extra one in the truck. Would you like to use it?"

My heart skipped a beat. A real fishing rod and reel! I finally recovered and said, "I would, but I don't know how to use a reel."

Bill answered, "It's easy. I'll show you how." He reached for both rods and a paddle in the back of the truck. I picked up the motor, and we started toward the dock. Our flat-bottom fishing boat was tied at the end of a one-hundred-foot dock that reached out to the cove. We walked to the end; Bill stepped into the boat, and I handed him the motor and returned to the shore to collect our equipment and a small cooler filled with ice, beer, and pop. The sandwiches had been placed on top of the ice to keep them cool.

I returned to the boat as Bill finished mounting the motor and gave the starter rope a quick pull. The motor purred to life and ran at a quiet idle. I passed him our supplies as he sat on a seat at the back of the boat beside the motor.

When everything was loaded, I jumped in, untied our line, and pushed away from the dock. The water in the cove was flat and mirrored the trees that lined the banks on both sides of the dock. Bill left the motor at idle and shifted to reverse, backing the boat to the center of the cove. I sat in the front seat and removed my shirt to enjoy the warm, sunny day.

As we idled down the cove, Bill said, "We will reach the river in just a few minutes and head upstream for about a mile. I have caught a lot of bass in a cove up there. Let's see if we can find some today."

I nodded and continued to look for the river. We expected a current, but our motor was strong enough to push us upstream to the cove Bill had selected. As we entered the swollen river, a strong current pushed the boat in the wrong direction. Bill opened the throttle wide and turned into the current, stopping our drift. We began the slow move upstream. The trip would take longer than expected, and I slipped off my shoes and settled back to enjoy the day.

A half hour later, Bill made a sweeping turn into a deep cove that was lined with trees on both sides. The boat slowed as we passed a large oak that had fallen into the water. This was a wooded area that had been flooded years ago when the river changed its course. We threaded our way through trees that were dead but still standing, surrounded by water. Dead limbs floated in the water, forcing us to go slow. The motor putted at an idle while I hung over the bow and moved dead wood aside so that we could keep going. The trees began to thin, and we came to an open pool of mirror-smooth black water. Trees around the pool reflected off the ripples made by our boat. Bill steered across the pool to a high bank and said, "This is the place. We should catch some bass and a few perch here."

I nodded and reached for my rod. A mockingbird singing in a nearby tree broke the quiet. We baited our hooks, dropped them into the water, and sat back to watch our lines. I fished at the bow, and Bill cast his line in the opposite direction.

Bill caught the first fish, a four-pound bass. A few minutes later he hooked up again with another bass that weighed about three pounds. I continued to fish and had one bite, but could not set the hook and it got away.

By midday, I had caught two perch and Bill had two more nice bass. We were having a good day. Dark clouds began to drift overhead, and the moist air smelled of oncoming rain.

Bill said, "It looks like there is a storm coming up. We should quit in a few minutes and work our way downstream toward the dock."

I was getting bites and Bill was not in a hurry, so we continued to fish. A half hour later it began to rain and then turned into a downpour. The boat started to fill with water, and Bill said, "It looks like this is going to be a bad one. We had better skedaddle."

I untied the bow as he started the motor. Heavy rain continued as we worked our way back through the tree graveyard. I could see whitecaps on the river, and the current seemed to be faster than before.

As we started the turn into the main channel, whitecaps hit the side of the boat, flipping it upside down. I tried to stay with the boat, but it was floating upside down and impossible to hold on to.

I heard Bill shout, "Dubbie, are you okay?"

"Yes," I sputtered, spitting out water while we continued to drift downstream beside the boat. Waves continued to wash over my head, making it difficult to breathe. I began to choke as waves hit my face and filled my mouth with water. I was treading water and knew that I would not make it just drifting beside the boat.

I could not see Bill on the other side of the boat, but heard him yell, "I don't think we should stay with the boat. Can you make it to shore?"

I spat out a mouthful of water and said, "I think so. I'm a good swimmer." I drifted to the back of the boat and between waves asked, "Are you okay?"

He answered, "My boots are pulling me down. I've got one of them off and think I can get the other if I go under." He took a deep breath and disappeared under the water. The dark, murky water made it impossible for him to see his leg. Pulling his right knee up to his chest, he placed one hand on each side of the boot, hooked his thumbs inside the top, and pushed down hard. Water had filled the boot and made it even tighter. It would not move. *Damn new boots,* Bill thought as he reached down to grab the heel and toe and pull again. The water swirled, turning him over and over as he attempted to free himself from the weight on his right leg. Several desperate pulls moved the heel, but it was still stuck and he was running out of air. His lungs ached; he had to get to the surface. Releasing the boot, he looked for the surface and realized that he had become disorientated in the dark water and did not know which way was up. Thinking he knew, he began to swim toward the bottom of the river, growing weaker with each stroke.

I continued to drift down the river beside the boat. Bill did not come up. I called his name again and again with no answer. It was impossible to stay with the boat because the waves were too high and the boat kept slipping away.

I swam for shore while whitecaps continued to break over my head. I swallowed water and began to cough. The current pulled me downstream as I swam, making the distance to shore much longer. My arms and legs grew tired, and my lungs burned from exhaustion. I began to think I was not going to make it, but the fear of drowning kept me going. I tried floating on my back, but the waves made it impossible.

The current slowed as I neared shore, but the drift was taking me toward a large tree that was down in the water. With no way to escape, I drifted into the tree, grabbed a limb, and tried to pull myself up. The current was pulling me down; I could barely get my shoulders above the water. I hung on, but it was impossible to rest. The current was too strong, and I had to move.

One limb stuck out farther than the others and was attached directly to the trunk. I lunged in that direction, caught the limb, and started moving hand over hand toward the trunk. I reached the trunk, but the current had almost pulled me under. Still holding the limb, I pressed my body against it, and the undertow lessened. I rested there until I could pull myself up and out of the water. I tried to catch my breath as the water swirled around my waist, testing my strength. Pressing against the limb made holding on easier, and I began to feel stronger. Pulling with all my strength, I threw my right leg over the limb and rolled up onto the trunk and out of the water. I was safe but too weak to move, and lay there trying to catch my breath. I was shaking from the cold and exhaustion, but I knew I had to reach dry land. It was time to move. The rain was still falling but was no longer a downpour. Unable to stand, I slid down the trunk on my stomach and reached the muddy bank, rested, and then wobbled to my feet and started to walk, but I kept falling. The undergrowth was thick, with no road or trails in sight. I was lost and knew that men lost in the woods almost always walked in a large circle. I needed a road or better yet, a farmhouse and did my best to walk in a straight line.

It seemed like hours had passed when the woods opened up to a field with a barn in the distance. Crossing the field, I staggered to the barn and passed out just inside the front door.

Rain continued to fall as Dallas Jones slipped into his yellow slicker and walked down the path to the barn for his evening chores. He entered the barn at a run and almost tripped over the unconscious body beside the door. The rain-drenched boy was alive with a weak pulse. He took the boy's left arm and pulled him to a sitting position. Then he lowered his left shoulder, grabbed the boy's belt with both hands, and lifted him over his head and across his shoulder. Moving toward the house, he called to his wife for help. As he reached the steps, she opened the screen door so he could enter and said, "Oh, my. Is he alive?"

"Yes, but just barely. He was passed out just inside the barn."

"Take him to the back bedroom," she said. "I'll get those wet clothes off and put some blankets over him so he can get warm."

Dallas said, "I'm going to call the sheriff, report this, and ask for medical help."

The telephone was on a party line shared with two other families. Dallas lifted the earpiece from its hook to hear a conversation in progress. Listening to others' conversations was entertainment in the farming community and was tolerated in all but very personal situations. When privacy was needed, the parties that were talking would ask everyone else to hang up the phone.

Dallas interrupted the call and said, "Folks, I have just found an unconscious boy down at my barn, and I have to get hold of the doc and the sheriff. Hang up and let me have the line." Dallas heard two clicks as they departed; then he pressed and released the hook for the earpiece and spun the crank to roust the operator.

"Hello," she answered.

Dallas said, "This is an emergency. Connect me to the sheriff."

Two rings later the sheriff answered and Dallas told his story.

"Hello, Sheriff. I just found a boy passed out inside the door to my barn. He's still alive. I brought him to the house, and my wife stripped off his wet clothes and put him in bed to warm up. He's still not awake. We need the doc as fast as he can get here."

The sheriff said, "Wally's Landing called less than an hour ago to report a missing boat with two fishermen aboard. Have you seen anyone else?"

"There was no one else around. Just the boy, and he was passed out."

"I'll call the doc and send him to your place as fast as he can make it, and then call Wally's to see if the missing boat has turned up. Either way, I am coming to your house."

Dallas thanked him for his help and hung up the phone.

I was in a daze and half-awake as the doc leaned over me to check my heartbeat and pulse. It was impossible to talk and after several attempts, I stopped trying, closed my eyes, and passed out again.

The sheriff arrived, and while the doc continued his examination, he asked, "How is he, Doc? Is he going to be okay?"

The doc looked up and said, "His pulse is very weak. I need to get him to the hospital. Give me a hand, and let's put him in your car." The two men carried me through the house and laid me on the backseat of the car, wrapped in a blanket for warmth.

As the sheriff closed the car door, the doc said, "I need to stay with him. I'll ride with you to the hospital and pick my car up later."

The ruts in the road shook me awake. As my eyes fluttered, the doc asked, "Can you hear me?"

Unable to answer, I tried to nod my head. Doc understood and continued, "We have you in the back of the sheriff's car and are on the way to the hospital. Should be there in just a few minutes."

We were met at the hospital door by two formidable nurses who lifted me to a gurney and wheeled it into the emergency room as I tried to talk. The sheriff was there and leaned over me as I managed a whisper. I asked about Bill and was told that he had not been found. The sheriff asked if I could tell him what had happened.

My chest tightened, and the lump in my throat made it impossible to talk. The sheriff touched a glass of water to my lips and said, "It's okay. You don't have to talk now; it can wait."

After two sips of water, I cleared my throat and started to talk in a hoarse whisper. "It was a nice day. The storm seemed to come out of nowhere. We were caught in heavy rain, and Bill decided to leave. I grabbed a cup and started bailing out the boat. We were fine until we entered the river. The waves were big, and one flipped us over." I stopped to choke back tears. My throat hurt, and I could only whisper.

"We got back to the boat, but it was upside down and moving so fast I couldn't hold on." My throat tightened, and I gasped for breath. "Bill decided to leave the boat and swim for shore. He had on rubber fishing boots and needed to get them off. They were dragging him down. He got one off and said that he was going under to pull off the other one. He went under and didn't come up." My throat ached, and I closed my eyes, choking back tears. "I didn't see him again. The current was fast. Maybe he is okay farther down the river."

The sheriff told me that he had not been found but they were still looking. Uncle Joe and Aunt Ona Belle entered the room. She had been crying. I closed my eyes and with a low sob began to cry. My aunt leaned over the bed and hugged me close as tears continued to run down my face.

Uncle Joe waited and then asked, "Are you all right?"

I whispered, "I'm okay, but they haven't found Bill."

I was released from the hospital the following day in weak, but good condition. Bill's body was found ten miles downstream two days later. One rubber boot was stuck half-off his right foot.

Chapter Thirteen
The Bully

Because the elementary school was over ten miles away, farm kids were taken to and from there in a large yellow school bus owned and operated by a local farmer. Mr. Todd was a giant of a man, six foot six, 350 pounds, with mitt-sized hands, and a pumpkin head that looked even larger under his broad-brimmed straw hat. He rarely spoke, except to say "good morning" as we boarded the bus. I always tried to sit in the middle or front of the bus to avoid the rough kids who sat in back. When the noise got out of hand, Mr. Todd would stop the bus, stand, and walk to the back. He was so tall he could not stand straight inside the bus, and his intimidating size brought immediate silence.

As the bus moved from farm to farm each morning, he sounded the horn to announce his position for kids in the area. He owned a milk cow farm and believed in tight schedules. Our pickup area was at the mailboxes alongside the main road. Hearing the horn meant that the bus was several minutes away, so get ready; it won't wait for late arrivals.

Kids of all ages rode the same bus. Each day, we gathered at our stop to wait for the ride to school. This presented an opportunity for the older, and larger, kids to dominate younger students while we waited. One boy, two years my senior, had selected me for his daily target. Billy Joe was a head taller than me and the strongest kid at the bus stop. He enjoyed taking advantage of his size by shoving and hitting younger boys waiting for the bus. As the newest addition to the stop, I was his favorite target. As weeks passed, the problem worsened. After school one day, we loaded on the bus and I tried to stay away from him, but the only seat available was on the aisle directly across from where he sat. As the bus started, he lashed out with his fist, hitting me behind my left ear. My vision blurred with flashes of light. I grabbed the seat in front of me to keep from falling. I looked over as he grinned, enjoying his work. I shook my head and sat quietly in my seat waiting for the bus to arrive at my stop.

When Mr. Todd stopped the bus and opened the door, kids began to unload. I looked out the window and could see Sandy, his tail wagging as he waited for me to get off the bus. I wanted to avoid trouble and intended to be the last person to get off. When the bus was empty, I walked forward and down the steps to the gravel road. Billy Joe was leaning against the bus beside the door so that he could not be seen out the window. He grinned as I stepped down from the bus, and I knew that he was after me. I turned away and screamed, "Leave me alone!" I attempted to run but was tackled and knocked to the ground. He sat on my stomach and pinned my arms to the ground with his knees. With his right hand clenched into a fist, he struck a painful blow to my chin. Using both fists, the blows kept coming; I could not move but turned my head each time trying to avoid the blow. He continued until he finally became bored and stopped. Standing, he looked at me with a grin and said, "You do everything I tell you, or this will happen again."

I rolled over, sat up, and wiped the blood from my nose on my shirtsleeve as he turned and walked away.

My books were on the ground, and loose papers were blowing across the road. My vision was blurred, but I managed to chase down the papers and return them to my notebook and stack everything in a pile so I could pick it up. I returned home with a black eye, bloody nose, and bruises on the upper half of my body, and I decided to go straight to the barn. As I passed the house, I dropped my books on the steps and continued on. I planned to wash my face at the water trough, but Uncle Joe was oiling the hay mower that was parked just inside the gate and looked up as I walked into the barnyard. I wiped my bloody nose on my sleeve as he asked, "Are you having a problem at school?"

"Yes, sir, at the bus stop," I answered.

"Is it just one boy, or more?"

"Just one, but he's older and stronger than me."

"School bullies are cowards that like to pick on smaller kids that can't fight back. He will keep it up until you fix it."

"I don't have a chance of whipping him in a fight," I said. "He's bigger and has beaten me up several times."

"You need to ambush him and beat the hell out of him. Bullies are the way they are because no one fights back. If you fight back, he will stop."

I walked to the water trough, scooped up two hands full of water, and rubbed my face. It felt cool and reduced the pounding in my head. I looked at my uncle and said, "How am I gonna do that?"

"He's bigger than you," he answered. "The only way you can win is to strike the first blow. Knock him down, and you are halfway there."

"How am I gonna knock someone down that is bigger and stronger than me?" I asked.

"He's an older boy, and he's picking on you because he knows he can win," my uncle said. "Forget fighting fair. You need to get yourself an equalizer."

"What's an equalizer?" I asked.

"A club about the size of a baseball bat," he answered. "And then you have to hit him before he sees it coming. Knock him down, and keep hitting him until he begs you to stop."

With Sandy and Star beside me, I entered the woods at the back of the farm and began looking for a suitable club. It had to fit my hand but be solid enough to do some damage. Sandy sniffed the ground for squirrels while Star lapped water from a small stream. A low-hanging branch on an oak tree was perfect for the task. I measured a three-foot length and cut it with a saw I had brought from the barn. It was as solid as a baseball bat but small enough to fit my hand.

Each afternoon, Billy Joe walked a path through the woods to return to his home. It was a shortcut that he always took. Knowing this, I hid the club behind a bush well into the wooded area. I planned to hide there and hit him before he had a chance to use his size and strength on me. I had to strike the first blow and then keep hitting.

The next day, I played hooky and worked around the barn for most of the day. The bus stopped in front of our mailboxes at three thirty, and Billy Joe would be on board.

I intended to be early and walked by the mailboxes and into the woods fifteen minutes before the bus was due at our stop. I walked down the path, found the club, and took up my post behind a bush to wait for Billy Joe.

The brakes on the bus screeched as the bus stopped and Mr. Todd opened the door.

I could hear a pounding in my ears as two boys got off, followed by Billy Joe. My breathing was faster; I swallowed hard but was determined to get this done. I could see Billy Joe walking down the path with his schoolbooks tucked under his right arm. He was alone, which was exactly what I wanted. My palms were wet with sweat as I nervously worked my fingers around the club and waited for my chance to strike. Sweat dripped in my eyes and I needed to pee, but it would have to wait.

As he passed, I swung the club with all my strength. It struck at the back of his knee. He screamed and fell to the ground. Breathing hard, I stood above him with the club raised for the next blow. Tears of anger ran down my face. He grabbed his knee, rolled over, and saw me standing above him with the club raised over my head. He screamed, "You!" His teeth were clenched, and he tried to stand. I swung the club as hard as I could and struck his shoulder at the base of his neck. He fell to the ground screaming as I raised my club for another strike. He tried to roll away from me, but I stepped forward and hit his back as he made another try at standing. He fell back to the ground; I was clearly in control as I raised my club and screamed, "Are you ever going to pick on me again?"

He screamed, "I'm gonna kick your ass!" Another blow, this time on his stomach.

He screamed in pain as I raised my club once more and said, "Are you ever going to pick on me again?" He tried to roll away as I struck again, hitting him squarely across the back. He cried out in pain and tried to crawl away without standing.

I was breathing hard but raised the club once more, clenched my jaw, and yelled, "Are you ever going to pick on me again?"

He looked up at me with my club raised to strike and said in a high-pitched scream, "Don't hit me again, don't hit me again! I won't ever pick on you again!"

I swung again hitting his chest and said, "Are you sure?"

Tears ran down his face and his mouth was open as he held his hands up to avoid another blow. He moaned and said, "I'm sure, I'm sure!"

Breathing hard, I shouted, "Liar!" I hit him again, this time on his leg just below the hip. "Do you promise? Don't lie to me. If you do, I will beat you with this club all night."

He rolled to his knees, placed his hands on the ground, and tried to stand.

I raised the club high over my head and with both hands, brought it down hard on his back. He screamed, fell to the ground, and lay there with his mouth open trying to breathe and talk. "I promise, I promise," he said. "I'll never pick on you again, I swear!"

He tried to stand while I looked at him through glazed eyes and said, "If you ever pick on me again, the beating will be a lot worse than this."

He wobbled to his feet and with a moan started running down the path toward his house.

I was shaking so hard that I just stood and watched. After several deep breaths, I started to calm down and with weak knees began walking to our barn.

Still holding the club, I entered the gate to the barnyard. It was feeding time, and Uncle Joe was inside the barn. Looking at the club, he asked, "Have you used that club yet?"

"Yes, sir, I have," I said. "Just a few minutes ago."

He knew that from my tattered look and said, "You probably won't need it again, so leave it here at the barn.

I made a point of being at the bus stop early the next morning. Several kids were there waiting when Billy Joe came along. He walked slowly with a limp; there was a large bruise on his right cheek. I braced myself for a problem, but he stopped at the far side of the mailboxes and waited quietly for the bus to arrive.

My uncle Joe was right. I needed an equalizer, and it worked. I smiled to myself knowing that I had done the right thing by standing up for myself.

Chapter Fourteen
Blackberry-Picking Time

Summer was nearing an end, and there were crops to harvest and fruit to pick. The blackberry patch at the rear of our farm was loaded with beautiful berries ripe for picking. Aunt Ona Belle was an excellent cook, and cobbler pies were her specialty. Blackberry and peach topped the list, and I loved both. Several peach trees produced all we needed, but blackberries only grow wild and had to be picked when in season. The time had come; the family prepared for a day in the blackberry patch.

Protection from thorns and the hot summer sun and insects required overalls, high-top shoes, a long-sleeve shirt, a straw hat, and 6/12 insect repellent to ward away small bugs and chiggers that live inside a large blackberry patch. Those and an occasional snake.

Fully dressed, with untied shoes, I jumped from the porch and walked to the rear of the house. "I'm ready to go whenever you are!" I shouted.

Aunt Ona Belle announced, "I'm almost ready. Just give me a minute."

Gathering our pails, Uncle Joe started his walk to the back of the farm. The sun was bright; it was going to be a warm day. As we reached the patch, a crow called from his lookout post in a nearby tree to warn those in the patch of approaching danger. Several crows flew away suddenly, their feeding interrupted by our approach. High above the patch, a hawk glided in sweeping circles in search of an unsuspecting field mouse. The blackberries were ripe, and everyone looked forward to a day of picking. I tasted several while moving deeper into the patch.

I heard the buzz of a rattlesnake and looked down; he was less than three feet from my right shoe. I did not move. The coiled snake flicked his tongue, buzzed his rattle, and looked at me through beady eyes. Any movement by me would bring a strike, so remaining frozen was the only option. Time passed slowly, but the rattling finally stopped and the snake slithered away. Taking a deep breath, I backed away from that area of the patch. Well clear of the snake, I called, "There's a rattler over here!"

Aunt Ona Belle answered, "Are you all right?"

"I'm fine," I answered. "He rattled and I froze. When I didn't move, he finally left. I'll watch for him while I pick."

The blackberries were sweet and juicy. I was enjoying the morning and ate almost as many as I picked, but slowed as the sun reached noon. As I filled the bucket, I thought of the great blackberry cobbler that my aunt would cook. The thought of a warm bowl of cobbler in a buttery crust with juicy ripe blackberries covered with a large scoop of ice cream inspired me to pick faster. My hands were scratched and bleeding from thorns, but the bucket was about full. We returned to the house with several pails of beautiful, ripe berries. Some were for canning but there would be at least one blackberry cobbler this weekend. We placed the pails on the kitchen table as Aunt Ona Belle announced, "I'll make us a cobbler this Saturday."

I knew that a dish of blackberry cobbler topped with ice cream was about as close to heaven as I could get. One taste of Aunt Ona Belle's cobbler, and you were hooked. When she pulled her deep-dish cobbler out of the oven, I was always close by.

With no bus to catch on Saturday, I moved slowly through my chores at the barn. Uncle Joe stood beside the hay-mowing machine oiling the blades with a long-stem can made for that purpose. He looked over at me and said, "It looks like Cricket decided to roll in the dirt yesterday. She needs a good brushing."

Cricket stood in front of the barn swishing her tail. Her matted coat reminded me of a young girl who had been making mud pies. I said, "I'll take care of it." I led the big horse into her stall and raised the retaining bar. She turned and extended her long neck over the bar to watch me as I moved to the feed room for a brush and metal curry comb. With one in each hand, I slipped under the bar and talked to her as I brushed her neck. "You had yourself a good roll in the barnyard, girl." She stood quietly for the next thirty minutes while I brushed her coat and combed her mane and tail.

The sun was up, and the day had started to warm. I needed to chop the grass at the base of our tomato plants before it grew tall and became a problem. Using a long-handled hoe, I walked the rows for the next hour chopping grass around the plants. It was a boring job but had to be done if we wanted a good crop of tomatoes.

I worked in the center of the patch as my uncle arrived and began inspecting the plants. Bending down beside a plant, he said, "We are going to have a good crop this year."

Looking up, I answered, "There are some real big ones at the far end that are about ready to be picked."

"Yep," he said. "It looks like that scarecrow we put up down there is keeping the birds out."

I laughed and said, "We have some smart crows flying around here, but I think they have been working the cornfield and leaving our tomatoes alone."

"Crows will always go for corn first," he said. "Let's just hope they don't do too much damage."

"I go to the corn patch every day, and a crow hidden in a tree beside the field sounds the alarm and a bunch of them fly up out of the patch," I said. "They are smart birds. They always post a lookout."

Midday approached as I put the hoe away and started for the house. As I crossed the porch, I could smell the cobbler cooling on the kitchen table.

The screen door creaked as I pulled it open and stepped into the kitchen. Aunt Ona Belle was standing in front of the stove stirring a pot with a long-handled spoon. She looked up, smiled as I entered the room, and said, "The cobbler is cooling and about ready. Would you like a dish?"

My mouth watered as I looked at the cobbler cooling on the kitchen table. The lightly browned crust was loaded with butter, and the dish was filled with juicy blackberries cooked to perfection.

"Yes, ma'am," I said, but I knew to wait until she asked me to sit at the table. I watched as she opened a cabinet, retrieved a bowl, and walked to the table with a spoon in her right hand. Reaching for the cobbler, she said, "Sit down while I fix you a dish."

"Yes, ma'am," I said, pulling a chair away from the table. Taking my seat, I waited for her to place the dish in front of me. Eating the cobbler was the highlight of my day.

Several weeks passed as summer ended, and there were cooler days with an occasional frost at night. It was time to prepare for winter as crops were gathered, hay was baled, and wood was stacked near the house to burn in our potbelly stove when needed.

It was a busy time, but an occasional horseback ride always relieved the pressures of the day. Jack was an older black mule smaller than Mike and gentle in nature. Too old to pull a wagon or plow, he was retired and remained on the farm as a pet.

I had made friends with all our livestock but had a special relationship with Jack. He had a maturity that younger mules seemed to lack. I could swing on Jack's tail, hang on his neck, and climb on his back, and he didn't mind. In fact, he seemed to enjoy the attention.

This was a mule that was easy to ride. Jack approached life at a walk, which was suitable for an eleven-year-old boy. As Jack approached the water trough, I brought out his bridle and slipped the bit into his mouth. Folding his ears forward so that the leather strap slipped into place on top of his head, I gently moved the harness over his big ears. The final strap went around his neck and was secured with a buckle.

Holding the reins, I moved to the water trough. Jack followed, and I tied him to a post beside the trough so that he could get a drink. That done, I walked inside the barn and entered the feed room in search of two brushes that were designed for use on horses. They were on a shelf next to the feed bin. As I reached for them, a mouse ran across the shelf, jumped to a bale of hay, and disappeared. Where was a cat when you needed one?!

I returned to Jack and spent the next ten minutes giving him a thorough brushing that made his coat shine. I could feel his shoulder muscles relax as I ran the brush down his body. I was tall for my age but still had to tiptoe to see while I brushed his back.

We were ready to go. That is, if I could find something to stand on and get Jack in position so that I could jump on his back. I always rode Jack bareback, and this could take some time because he was not always cooperative with this part of the project. Getting him in place alongside what I planned to stand on took some effort. Then I had to get on my stand while Jack waited for me to climb aboard. If Jack stood still, everything was fine. If he moved two feet to the right, I could not jump aboard. There were times when it took four or even five attempts before I was in place on his back, but once I was there, we were on our way. I led him beside the hay wagon and climbed up on the tire to mount. As I made my jump, Jack moved and I landed halfway on his back but slipped off and fell to the ground on my feet. The second attempt was even worse; I fell to the ground like a sack of potatoes. I walked the big mule in a circle ending back at the front tire on the wagon.

He stood switching his tail as I climbed on the wagon wheel and prepared to mount. I slipped on his back, patted his neck, and said, "Good boy." Pulling on the left rein, I tapped his stomach with my heels and said, "Giddy up." Jack began to move, and I directed him across the barnyard to the back gate. His best and only speed was a slow walk. It was impossible to coax him into a trot, and I knew better than to try. Old Jack was quietly in charge and had rejected all my efforts to make him trot. Yelling "giddy up" had no effect at all, and my legs were too short to reach around his stomach to coax him with my heels.

We reached the gate, and my next challenge was to get it open without getting off. A rope looped over the fence post held the gate in place. I nudged Jack alongside the gate so that I could lift the rope off the post and push the gate open. Jack knew what to do, and I opened the gate on the first try. We moved through and circled so that I could close and secure the gate with us in the pasture. Jack was not close enough. I leaned over to reach the gate, lost my balance, and began to fall. I lunged for the gate and grabbed the top rail. Good-bye, Jack; hello, gate. Jack stood patiently by as I jumped down and gathered his reins, and then shut and secured the gate. This was turning out to be work, and I needed some cooperation. I stroked Jack's neck and said, "I could use a little help here, old man. When I get you in position, I want you to stand still while I get on your back."

He looked at me like he understood. Either that, or the game was on. I led him in a circle that ended at the gate. Jack snorted but stood quietly swishing his tail while I climbed up the boards on the gate and prepared to do my flying mount. Old Jack was wise beyond his years and did not intend to make this too easy.

I turned toward Jack and made my leap as he sidestepped. I was halfway on his back but was slowly slipping off. The gate was too far away, thanks to Jack's sidestep, and I tried to stay on his back by clamping my legs. I continued to slide, but my fall had now turned into a nosedive. I hit the ground headfirst and lay there spitting out a mouthful of dirt. I stood, spitting and shouted, "Dammit, Jack! You stand still."

I led the big mule in a circle and stopped him beside the gate. He was close this time, and I was positive as I climbed the gate, ready to leap on his back. "Hi, ho, Silver," I said as I leaped from the gate—and Jack moved. This time, I failed to get my leg over his back and began my next trip to Mother Earth. Landing flat, I managed to keep my mouth out of the dirt, which was some progress. Standing, I brushed myself off, looked at Jack, and said, "Damn you, Jack. Enough is enough. I'm gettin' on this time."

My only hope was that Jack was getting tired of the game. Another circle and back in position. I decided that a quiet, humble approach might work and talked to Jack as I rubbed his nose and scratched his ears. I had learned that mules are stubborn and usually have a sense of humor. Mike had taught me that as he pinned me to the wall of his stall just about every time I gave him his food.

I rubbed Jack's neck, gave him a pat, and said, "Okay, Jack. Easy, fellow. Stand still this time, and I'll give you extra food when we get back."

I climbed the gate one more time and rubbed Jack's back while I held on to the top board to get my balance. Jack didn't move this time, and I landed squarely on his back.

Blackberry patch, here we come! Cobbler on the table tonight! My mouth watered at the thought. The pasture outside the barnyard was an alfalfa field that would make enough hay to feed the animals through the winter. The alfalfa was a foot tall, green, and beautiful. Jack dipped his head for a mouthful; I let him enjoy a couple of bites and then pulled him up with the reins.

We moved across the patch and into the woods past the Everett's farm, which was located next to our property. Their farm was larger than ours, with a brick house and two-story barn with enough stalls for all of their livestock. Three horses were in a pasture behind the barn with their heads down eating grass. As we moved beside the pasture, I stayed in the woods to avoid fences and gates. One gate was enough challenge for the day, and I knew the way through the woods to the blackberry patch.

The woods thinned, and I could see the patch up ahead. The berries were big and had changed from red to black, which meant they were ripe and still at their peak.

I slipped off Jack and tied him to a nearby tree. He stood patiently swishing his tail while watching me move inside the patch. A crow cawed, clearly irritated that I was in his territory. It was an alert to several crows eating berries. Three of the big birds flew out of the patch toward a wooded area. I entered the patch and picked several berries for a taste. They were sweet and delicious. I picked a few more, selecting the large ones that were at their peak of ripeness.

Beautiful, ripe berries surrounded me. I had found the mother lode and was not prepared for such an opportunity. I had not thought to bring a bucket. The berries were perfect for making a cobbler, and I intended to pick enough to accomplish that goal.

To protect myself from the sun and heat, I wore a tan hard-shell safari hat. It was great for riding and useful when you wanted to pretend you were on an African safari searching for the king of the beasts, a lion. Removing it from my head, I realized that it would hold all the blackberries my aunt would need for a cobbler.

I cradled the hat upside down against my stomach and began picking. The hat began to fill, and I ate a few along the way. Berries were so plentiful that I filled the hat to overflowing. It was time to return home with my bounty.

Untying Jack, I looked for a stump I could stand on to climb on his back. With no stump in sight, I began walking toward the woods, being careful not to spill my stash of blackberries. There should be something there I could stand on to mount Jack. I spotted a large log lying flat on the ground. Perfect!

Leading Jack alongside the log, I placed the reins over his neck and climbed on the log for the mounting. So far, so good. I was being careful and had not spilled any of my blackberries.

Time to mount. As I jumped toward Jack, he moved slightly away. I missed and fell to the ground, landing on my feet. Blackberries flew out of my hat, hitting me in the face and throughout most of my upper body. The purple juice from the berries left stains on my face, shirt, and pants. I still had blackberries in my hat and was not about to give up on a project that was this important. I started over, led Jack around, and repositioned him next to the log. All I had to do was fix the reins on his neck, climb the log, and make the short leap to Jack's back.

Mules seem to have a sense of humor that is lacking in other animals. As I jumped, Jack moved slightly away and I missed once again. More blackberries spilled from my hat, hitting my face and shirt.

Half of my berries had been lost during my attempts to mount, but I still planned to return home with the remainder. After two more attempts, Jack, apparently bored with his game, stood still and allowed me to mount.

As Jack and I arrived at the porch, I called, "Aunt Ona Belle, I brought you some blackberries for a cobbler." I sat astride Jack, cradling the hat with the remaining blackberries by my side.

The screen door creaked as she walked through from the kitchen to the back porch. If I had not been sitting on a mule, she would have thought I had been in a car wreck. Looking me over, she reacted. "What happened to you?"

"The blackberry patch is loaded with berries, and I picked some for you. I spilled some, but it looks like I have enough for a cobbler."

Aunt Ona Belle said, "It looks to me like you got more on you than in the hat." As she looked up and down my blackberry-stained clothes and body, she began to laugh. "Give me your hat, and take Jack to the barn. When you come back to the house, take your clothes off outside. Leave them on the porch steps, and I'll put them in the washtub."

I handed her my hat and walked Jack toward the barnyard gate. Once he was inside his stall, I removed the bridle and patted his neck. He had earned a treat, so I gave him a scoop of corn. As he munched away, I returned to the house for a cold-water bath in a washtub.

Placing my clothes on the steps, I hurried into the back room for the unavoidable tub bath. Aunt Ona Belle had filled the metal tub half-full and was pouring in boiling water from her stovetop teakettle. I was thankful for that. A cold-water bath could be a real shocker. The water was lukewarm, and I stepped in as she handed me a cloth and said, "Be sure to soap your face, because it's stained and you look like you have been in an accident."

"Yes, ma'am," I answered, hurrying through the wash. That done, I dressed quickly and returned to the barn for the evening feeding.

I saw Uncle Joe's car pull in our drive as I was brushing Jack's coat. Supper would be ready in about an hour, and I wondered if my aunt would make us a cobbler with the blackberries I had picked. I filled the water trough as the supper bell rang. I hurried up the path to the house and entered the kitchen as Uncle Joe said, "Hi. Is everything okay at the barn?"

"Yes, sir," I answered. "I just finished feeding the livestock."

Uncle Joe pulled his chair back from the table and said, "Good. Let's eat."

We took our seats and bowed our heads while he said the prayer.

I reached for an ear of corn as Uncle Joe looked at me with a glint in his eye and said, "What's that on the side of your head?"

"What?" I asked. "Where?"

"Just below your right ear," he answered. "It's a dark spot. Are you getting sick?"

"No, sir," I said. "I'm not sick. I'm fine."

My aunt and uncle howled in uncontrolled laughter, and I realized that the joke was about me.

Uncle Joe finally stopped laughing and said, "I heard that you went blackberry picking today. Could that be a blackberry stain on the side of your head?" He snorted and laughed again.

"Yes, sir," I answered. "I rode Jack down to the blackberry patch and used my hat to pick some and bring them home. I fell off Jack when I tried to get on him and spilled blackberries all over me."

Uncle Joe roared with laughter and between gasps said, "Did you get 'em all over the mule too?"

Aunt Ona Belle chuckled as she rose from her chair and moved to the kitchen stove. Opening the oven door with a cloth, she removed a small blackberry cobbler and placed it on the corner of the table.

She smiled and said, "You saved enough for a small cobbler, and there is a piece for each of us."

I licked my lips and smiled as she passed the dish to me. I took a bite and said, "It was worth it. I would do it again."

Uncle Joe chuckled and said, "You might want to take some time first and learn how to get on a mule!"

Chapter Fifteen
The Hunt for Supper

Midday sun on the five-acre field of corn reflected off the broad green leaves, causing Uncle Joe to squint as he walked the patch inspecting his crop. He moved from row to row, making occasional stops to peel back the leaves on an ear to inspect the kernels for maturity. The stalks were over seven feet tall, and the corn was ready for harvest.

As he finished his inspection, Uncle Joe could see his neighbor's barn through the trees that separated their fields. Sam was thirty-five years old, about five feet six inches tall, and had a ruddy complexion that blended with his red hair and deep blue eyes. His face was wrinkled from years of working in the fields and looked sunburned even during the winter months. It was a warm day, and he was working in his barnyard in jeans but without a shirt.

Uncle Joe walked to the edge of his field, bent at the waist, and slipped his right leg between the top two strands of barbed wire as he pushed down on the bottom strand to keep from tearing his coveralls. Still holding the wire, he brought his left leg through and stood erect in Sam's pasture.

Sam had his back turned and was fueling his tractor. Uncle Joe walked to him and said, "Mornin', Sam."

Sam looked around, set the fuel can down, and said, "Mornin', Joe." He pulled a red handkerchief from his back pocket and wiped his face.

"I was inspecting my crop," Uncle Joe said, "and saw you working over here, and I've come to ask a favor."

"What can I do for you?" Sam asked.

While they talked, I stepped out of our chicken pen and moved closer so I could listen to them.

Uncle Joe looked at the tractor as he answered, "If I remember correctly, you used to have a single-shot 22 rifle that you used to scare off crows several years ago. Do you still have it?"

"Yep," he answered, "but I haven't used it since I stopped planting corn in my back field. The crows have left me alone and are picking on your corn." He chuckled.

"You've got that right." Uncle Joe grinned. "I would like to borrow the gun for a few weeks, but not to scare crows. I want to teach Dubbie how to shoot."

"No problem. Let me finish fueling my tractor, and I'll get it for you," Sam said, and he picked up his can to finish the job.

I was twelve years old and had watched my uncle use his shotgun to hunt quail. He was a good shot and never shot more birds than we needed for dinner. Each time the gun was fired, it kicked against his shoulder, and I had no interest in giving it a try. I was happy following along to retrieve each bird as it fell to the ground.

It was a sunny day, but fall was approaching and my denim jacket felt comfortable. I sat on the dirt floor of the barn trying to nail together two stilts that would make me ten feet tall. That is, if I could stay on them without falling over.

Uncle Joe opened the door to the feed room, stepped inside, and returned with a 22 rifle in his right hand. I looked up as he said, "You can work on the stilts later. Let's take a walk to the back of our property."

I walked alongside but was not sure where we were going until he said, "There is a knoll back here that we can use for a backstop for shooting. I picked up a box of shells and am going to teach you how to shoot."

I took a deep breath, swallowed hard, and said, "Yes, sir." My heart raced as I took another deep breath and thought about shooting a gun.

We crossed the barnyard and followed a path that would take us through the woods to the back of the property. As we reached the knoll, Uncle Joe searched for a piece of wood the thickness of a coffee can that we could use for target practice. We walked to a brush pile close by and began digging through branches in search of what was needed. I found a piece of log and held it up for Uncle Joe. "Will this do?" I asked, hoping he would like it.

"It should be big enough. Let's use it," Uncle Joe said as he turned it in his hands and started toward the knoll. While we walked, he talked to me about how to handle a gun safely.

"A gun is not a toy. Never point it at anything unless you intend to shoot it. Make sure your gun is unloaded until you are ready to shoot. Never put a loaded rifle in the trunk of a car. Remove the shell from the chamber, and leave the bolt open. That tells everybody the gun is empty." He continued, "And don't ever lean a rifle against a wall, a tree, or anything else where it could fall over and go off. Be sure it's empty and lay it down where it will be out of the way and no danger to people around you."

My uncle knew how to safely handle a rifle, and I listened closely. He was teaching me to be safe; hunting would start as soon as I could be trusted to handle the gun. I watched as he placed a shell in the chamber and locked the bolt.

He raised the rifle toward the target, clicked off the safety, and said, "The front sight on the barrel has to line up with the sight at the back. Look down the barrel, line the sights up on the target, and squeeze the trigger. Be gentle. If you pull the trigger too hard, you are sure to miss the target."

He squeezed off his shot, and the wood log jumped as the bullet struck its target. Looking at me, he said, "Are you ready to give it a try?" He handed me the gun.

I swallowed hard and blinked to clear my eyes. I looked the gun over and opened the chamber to let the empty shell fall to the ground. Uncle Joe handed me a bullet that I inserted into the chamber, with the barrel pointed toward the ground. After it slipped into place, I closed and locked the bolt and was ready to go.

I raised the rifle to my shoulder and pointed to the target while Uncle Joe gave me pointers on how to aim. Holding the rifle steady was harder than I had expected. With a gentle squeeze of the trigger, the gun fired. A small puff of smoke a foot below my target verified the miss. The smell of gunpowder filled my nose and caused my eyes to water. I lowered the gun as Uncle Joe looked at the target and said, "Not bad for your first shot. Let's try a few more."

I practiced for the next hour, with Uncle Joe teaching me how to stand, hold a gun, and aim. With his help, I improved and was consistently hitting the log at the end of the day. He stood beside me and watched as I continued to load and fire until the shell box was empty.

Sunlight had started to dim in the thick forest, and dew had started to rise. As I opened the bolt to remove the shell casing, Uncle Joe said, "The sun is going down. We need to get back and feed the livestock."

"Yes, sir," I said and laid the gun over my right shoulder; then I started down the path to the barn.

Uncle Joe followed and said, "Is your bolt open?"

"Yes, sir," I answered and continued walking. My heart was pounding, and I was short of breath and excited about learning to hit a target over fifty yards away. Uncle Joe was a good teacher, and I wanted him to be comfortable with how I handled the gun.

The animals stood close by the barn waiting for their feed. Cricket watched us approach and snorted. I moved in her direction. She was hungry but deserved a pat on her head and a gentle scratch on both ears. She lowered her head, enjoying the attention.

Uncle Joe opened the feed room, and I stepped inside to lay my gun on a bale of hay. Mike and Cricket had walked into their stalls and were waiting for their grain. I fed Cricket first, refilled my bucket, and entered Mike's stall to dump the grain in his trough. As I walked beside Mike, he leaned against me, pinning me against the wall.

The game was on, and he would hold me there for as long as he wanted. "Come on, Mike! Move over!" I said. Mike snorted but did not move. I pushed against his stomach and said, "Get over, Mike!" No luck, but I knew he would eventually let me go because I had his food in my bucket. I tried again. "Get over, Mike, if you want your grain!" Maybe the mule knew English, because he moved, and I stepped to the trough and filled it with his grain.

Uncle Joe was filling the water trough as I stepped out of Mike's stall. He looked up and said, "There is going to be a light snow tonight. That will make it easy to track rabbits. I've seen several at the back of our woods, and the hunting should be good there. Why don't you give it a try tomorrow after you finish the feeding? I have another box of shells for you at the house."

"Thanks, I will," I answered as I stepped inside the feed room to retrieve my gun. I intended to polish the stock and give the barrel and chamber a light coat of oil to be ready for tomorrow.

Aunt Ona Belle rang the dinner bell as we reached the barnyard gate on our way to the house. Both dogs moved through the gate, followed by Uncle Joe. I stepped through, and then closed and secured the latch.

I hardly tasted dinner as I thought about how to hunt rabbits. As we ate, my uncle asked, "Do you know what a rabbit's tracks look like?"

"I think so." I had seen some but was not sure.

Uncle Joe laid a piece of paper beside his plate and with a pencil, began to draw tracks like a rabbit would make. He drew several and asked, "Do you know which direction he is going?" He continued, "It's easy to track a rabbit in the snow, but you have to know which way he's going." He explained the tracks so that I would understand.

After dinner, I moved to my bunk on the porch to prepare for the next morning. The sun had set, the evening had started to cool, and small flakes of snow began to fall. The light dangling from a tree near the steps provided enough light for me to work.

Using a soft cloth dampened with oil, I laid the gun across my lap and began to polish. Starting with the tip of the barrel, I applied a thin coat of oil on the entire gun. I applied furniture wax to a clean cloth and polished the wood stock. The entire process took about a half hour. After a final inspection, I placed it under my bed to be ready for tomorrow morning.

A gust of wind blew snow from the steps to the edge of the porch. It was going to be a cool night. I unfolded another wool blanket, tucked it under the foot of the mattress, and began to undress. I removed my coveralls and shirt, placed them on the chair next to my bed, and slipped under the covers. The bed was cool but warmed quickly after I pulled the covers tight around my neck. I could see the snow falling on the steps as I pulled the blankets around my ears for warmth. The night was quiet, with only the call of the whip-poor-wills as I drifted off to sleep.

Excited about the coming day, I was awake before daylight. The porch was cold, but I was warm and comfortable under the covers on my bed. I could hear Uncle Joe stoke our potbelly stove and knew the kitchen would be warm in just a few minutes. Delay was the answer, and I decided to stay under my covers for a little longer.

Uncle Joe opened the kitchen door, pushed open the screen door, and said, "Get up, Dubbie. The kitchen is warm, and I have a pot of coffee on."

It was time to set a new speed record for getting dressed. I rolled out of the bed, slipped into my flannel shirt, pulled on my coveralls, and scampered into the kitchen. The fire was warm, and I settled into a chair just inside the door. My shoes and socks were sitting close by the stove and were warm as toast. I slipped them on as Uncle Joe placed two coffee mugs on the table and reached for the tin pot on top of the stove. It had been perking, and he used a towel to avoid burning his hand. The coffee sizzled as it ran down the spout into our cups. He handed me a cup, and I spooned in two scoops of sugar and some cream and began to stir. The cup warmed my hands as I took a small sip. It was hot but felt good.

As daylight approached, I slipped on my jacket, opened the door, stepped through, and took a deep breath of the cool morning air. The steps were covered with a light dusting of snow. I reached under the bed for my rifle, placed the shells in my jacket pocket, and headed for the barn. As I passed the doghouse, Sandy and Star greeted me with tails wagging. I continued to walk but gave both a pat, and Star licked my hand. They would be with me on my first rabbit hunt.

The sun's rays broke through the trees as I finished my chores and locked the feed room. The snow crunched under my shoes as I crossed the barnyard, with Star and Sandy close behind. As we entered the woods, I began looking for rabbit tracks while the dogs went separate directions with their noses sniffing the ground. The thin blanket of snow seemed to quiet the forest. I stopped and looked around, and there was no noise or movement to be heard or seen. The trees filtered the sunlight but the snow had reached the ground, making the forest beautiful.

Since there were no tracks in the snow, I decided to walk to the creek that cut across our property. At the water's edge, I discovered rabbit tracks that led into a briar patch. Without moving, I searched the patch with my eyes but with no results. The rabbit had to be in the patch. I searched again, this time paying close attention to detail.

The rabbit sat, without moving, beside a scrub bush less than twenty yards from where I stood. Its gray coat provided good camouflage, and it was almost impossible to see. Without moving, I slowly raised the rifle to my shoulder. My breathing increased and my hands shook as

I attempted to take aim. This was harder than I expected. My hands shook as I looked down the barrel. The rabbit had not moved. I aimed and gently squeezed the trigger. Nothing happened. Oops, the safety was still on.

I clicked the safety off and raised the gun to my shoulder for a second attempt. The gun fired, and dirt kicked up two feet behind my target. The rabbit still had not moved.

My rifle, a single-shot gun, was empty and needed to be reloaded. I fumbled in my pocket for a shell, found one, and opened the chamber to eject the empty shell. The rabbit still had not moved. If I hurried, I had another chance.

The shell slipped from my fingers and fell to the ground. I looked down, but no shell. It had fallen in the snow and could not be seen. Okay, back in my pocket for another shell, found one, slipped it into the chamber, and closed the bolt.

The rabbit sat quietly, unconcerned about my confused activity only a few yards away. I stopped moving and stared at the animal, wondering if it was mocking me. It seemed to know that I didn't know how to shoot and was going to prove it by letting me try again.

Taking a deep breath, I raised the gun, took aim, and fired. The shot was closer but missed once again. The rabbit took a casual hop forward and stopped, seeming to make a point. If this was a contest, the rabbit was the winner. I laughed out loud and said to myself, "Okay, I can't shoot. Have a nice day, Mr. Rabbit!"

I bent down to recover the shell I had dropped. As I moved, the rabbit, taking his time, moved farther into the brush and disappeared. I stood quietly but could hear Sandy barking in the distance. The high pitch of his barks told me he was chasing a rabbit. *Give it up, Sandy,* I thought. *You never catch rabbits; they're too quick for you.*

The barking stopped, and Sandy trotted through the woods. He was panting, and his tongue was hanging from the side of his mouth. He looked happy with his chase but wanted my approval, and I gently stroked his head. He licked my hand as I said, "You don't have to catch a rabbit to have fun. Let's go home."

At the supper table that night, I told my story. Uncle Joe laughed so hard that he choked on some of his food. Aunt Ona Belle sipped her tea, chuckled, and said, "You have just had a hunting trip that you will always remember."

Later that evening, I cleaned the gun, placed it under my bed, and decided that I needed to practice more before my next hunting trip.

Chapter Sixteen
The State Fair

The sun had set and it was dark as I crossed the barnyard, stepped through the gate, and started up the path to the house. The evening had cooled, and the moon lighted my way to the house.

Supper was my favorite meal, and tonight was special with Aunt Ona Belle's signature meat loaf, complemented with corn on the cob, mashed potatoes, cornbread, and tea.

I opened the door to the kitchen, carrying two bowls to feed the dogs. Aunt Ona Belle smiled as I used a cup to dip food from the sack into their dishes, and she said, "It looks like fall is on the way. Is it cooling down outside?"

"It's going to be cool tonight—perfect for sleeping," I said.

Uncle Joe opened the door to our potbelly stove, added a piece of wood, and said, "Our first frost is at least three weeks away. Our next two weeks are going to be really busy. We have to get our crops in before the frost to keep from losing them."

He slammed the door shut as I nodded and said, "I can take some days off from school if you need me during the week."

He rubbed his hands together and then turned his palms to the stove, enjoying the heat. "Let's see how much we get done this weekend, and if we fall behind I may need you next week."

I walked outside and placed the bowls near the steps, and the dogs began to gulp their food. My aunt and uncle were at the table waiting for me to take my seat. I pulled back my chair, sat, and bowed my head for the blessing.

While plates were passed around, Uncle Joe said, "The State Fair opens in two weeks."

I grinned and said. "What day are we going?"

The State Fair was the biggest event of the year, and every farmer in the area attended. Some entered livestock and produce in contests that would take place during the five days that the fair would be open to the public. It was a competitive time and a fun week at the end of summer.

Uncle Joe ignored my question and asked, "Have you looked over our tomato crop in the last few days? It's the best I have seen in years." He knew that one of my favorite things was a ripe tomato sandwich with mayonnaise on fresh white bread, and he suspected that I had been watching the crop develop.

I said, "Yes, sir. The vines at the far end of row three have some of the biggest I have ever seen. Several of the big ones have splits from growing too fast, but we do have one that is perfect and it's a big one."

Uncle Joe chuckled and said, "Why don't we pick our best and enter it in the tomato contest the day the fair opens? It's worth a try; that big one could be a winner."

We had never entered a contest at the fair, and it sounded exciting. I watched the vines closely for the next two weeks. One tomato was perfect in looks, and we guessed that it would weigh in at well over two pounds. The day before the fair, Uncle Joe looked it over and said, "That's our baby! We'll pick it tomorrow right before we leave for the fair."

As I climbed under the covers on my bunk that night, my thoughts were on the contest that would start the next day. Farms large and small from all over the state would be participating. Did we have a chance? A half moon hung just above the trees, casting a dim glow on the yard and porch beside my bed. I pulled the blankets around my head. I was expecting a cool night and had added an extra blanket in case it would be needed. The evening was quiet, with only the whip-poor-wills calling in the distance. I began to drift off to sleep as two owls hooted and made strange-sounding calls back and forth in distant trees. Owls have a strange language. It's not really a hoot, although they start with a hoot and then begin making strange noises that I can't describe. When one does it, a second one always answers. It's a language that only they understand. I fell asleep and dreamed about holding my prize tomato in front of the judges and accepting the blue ribbon while the audience applauded.

The next morning, I was too excited to eat breakfast. Who cares! There was always plenty of food at the fair. The box I had prepared for moving the tomato was padded with soft mulch for protection from bumps as we moved from the field to the fairgrounds. Uncle Joe drove with Aunt Ona Belle in front, and I sat in back with the box on the seat touching my leg.

We parked as close as we could to the poultry barn. No directions needed there! The hens and roosters have a smell all their own. The three-hundred-foot building was forty feet wide and twelve feet high, with an arched roof supported by wood beams. Windows just below the eaves lined the length of the building on both sides and were open for ventilation. Rows of waist-high cages filled the inside, with aisles between the rows. Each cage had room for one or more birds, with a glass water feeder attached to the front beside the door.

The back wall of the building opened into an attached wing one hundred feet long with a low ceiling. The sign above the door announced, "PRODUCE." Ten-foot-long tables had been positioned along both walls. A three-foot-high stage along the back wall had steps attached to the sides for easy access. That was where the winners were announced and the awards were presented.

Each of the tables had a sign that announced the type of produce to be judged. One person sat in a folding chair behind each table to sign in contestants and label their entry. The tomato table was halfway down on the right side. I sat my box down gently and announced to the lady behind the table, "I would like to enter this tomato in the contest."

She stood and looked down into the box containing my prize. "My," she said, "that's a beauty. Fill out this form while I tag your box." I did as she asked and was given a receipt for my entry.

The judges would announce their decision at 4:00 p.m. the next day. I had some free time and knew that hog judging went on all day. The animals are judged in an arena surrounded by bleachers for use by interested observers. The owners and their hogs are in the arena for about twenty minutes so that the judges have enough time to closely inspect each animal and take notes. When the judges are finished, they signal the owners to move out of the arena so that the next set of contestants can enter.

It is common for six or eight hogs of a breed to be in the arena at the same time. Hogs are more intelligent than most dogs and independent in nature. Each hog is required to have a handler before being allowed inside the arena. The handlers know that their hog must be separated from the other animals in the pen as it is judged. To accomplish this, each owner carries a three-foot-square board and attempts to stay in front of the hog so it can't see other hogs in the arena. The handler's goal is to keep his hog quiet and still so that it can be judged.

The hogs, being well-fed, active animals, want no part of "still and quiet" and actively move about the arena. Each handler tries to stay in front of his hog and keep him separate from other hogs. From my view in the stands, it looked like the hogs were in control as the handlers jumped around, trying to stay in position. This was more fun than a Laurel & Hardy movie.

Carrying a double-dip ice cream cone, I took a seat in the bleachers beside Mr. Revere as he waited for the action. He looked at me and said, "The next round of judging will start in just a few minutes. I have a hog entered in this round, and James Charles is the handler."

"Great," I answered. "I hope he wins!"

Mr. Revere nodded and said, "We have a good animal this year. I think we have a chance at a ribbon."

While we waited, I licked the drips on my cone and watched the arena for the next contest. The gate opened and six hogs entered the arena, followed by their owners, who were carrying boards. As the hogs moved about the arena, each owner positioned himself in front of his animal, holding up a board so that the hog was separated from the others.

James Charles entered the pen alongside his hog, with a board tucked under his right arm. I waved, and James looked in my direction with an unhappy frown on his face. He turned and looked down at his hog, ignoring me and Mr. Revere.

I looked at Mr. Revere and said, "He looks upset. I don't think he likes showing a hog."

Mr. Revere snorted and said, "You are right about that. I had to talk him into it and told him that if we win a ribbon, it's his to keep." The judges entered the arena, and the fun was about to start. This was too good for me to just sit quietly and watch.

James Charles positioned himself in front of his pig and raised his board as I yelled, "Go get him, James! Stay in front of him!" James frowned and gave me a look that could kill. This was so much fun that I yelled again, "He's movin' to the left. Get after him!"

James moved in an attempt to stay in front of the pig, but I was having too much fun to stop. "Keep your board up! You're looking good!" James was so mad his face was red and the veins stood out on his neck. I was laughing so hard that tears ran down my face and I was having trouble catching my breath. I took a deep breath and yelled, "Watch him, watch him; he's moving to the right. Keep your board up!"

As the judging continued, I yelled at James again and again while he worked the pig with occasional mean glances at me. I could not stop laughing, while James looked meaner every minute.

When the pigs moved out of the arena, I jumped down from my seat and started to the fairway as James Charles charged through the arena gate and came after me at a dead run. Trouble was on the way, and I took off at a run, trying to lose him in the crowd. As he closed in on me, I made a right turn between the bearded lady's tent and the hamburger stand and entered an open field. James Charles tackled me from behind, yelling, "I'm gonna beat the hell out of you for what you did back there!" We rolled in the grass as he punched me in the stomach, but I could not stop laughing. We exchanged blows but finally stopped, as this was too funny for a serious fight. I sat up in the grass and pushed James away so that I could stand. He stood beside me, and I could not resist making one more comment: "You looked really good out there today, Hog Man."

That did it! He jumped at me, and I took off running. The chase was on, but he was fastest and knocked me to the ground at midfield. We exchanged blows until I yelled, "I give! I give! I won't call you Hog Man again."

He sat up, glaring at me, and asked, "Do you promise? Cross your heart and promise."

I crossed my heart with my right hand and said, "I cross my heart and promise."

While we walked back across the field, I looked at James and said, "I have entered a tomato in the contest, and the judging will take place tomorrow around four thirty. We have to go home this afternoon to feed the livestock but will come here tomorrow for the awards. Our tomato weighs almost three pounds and has a perfect color with no splits. We have a chance at a blue ribbon. Are you going to be here tomorrow?"

"Dad told me that the hog judges will announce their decision tomorrow after dinner, and we're coming back for that. He thinks our hog could be a winner."

"When you finish, come on over to the poultry barn. The produce section is in the back of the poultry barn, and that's where they will make the awards. You can't miss it; just follow the smell." I grinned and then laughed at my joke.

James wrinkled his nose and said, "I'll be there rooting for you!"

There are no secrets on a farm that has a party line telephone. News, good and bad, travels about the community at a speed that would make a newspaper green with envy. The farms around us knew that we had a tomato entered in the contest at the State Fair, and plans were made to be there when the ribbons were awarded.

I spent the morning working around the barn with Uncle Joe. He was working in the feed room as I stuck my head inside and asked, "What time are we going to leave for the fair?"

He looked at me with a smile and said, "If we leave by two o'clock, we'll be there before the judges make their awards. They are probably working at it right now and will be ready to announce their decision at four thirty."

I walked to the water trough, splashed water on my face, and said, "If it's all right with you, I'm going to the house to change my clothes."

Winning a blue ribbon at the fair would be talked about around fireplaces and potbelly stoves for the remainder of the year. Uncle Joe knew I was excited and said, "You go ahead and clean up. I'll be along in a few minutes."

The trip to the state fairground took about one hour. I sat stiffly in the backseat while my uncle drove the car and we listened to Aunt Ona Belle talk about the fair. Her patchwork blanket had won second place, and she was excited. "There were over fifty blankets entered in the contest," she said and continued, "I didn't think I had a chance and almost fell off the chair when they called my name for second place."

I stared out the window, not listening, and daydreamed about winning with my big tomato.

We arrived at the produce barn early, but the judges were already at work inspecting entries in the first five categories. Tomatoes would be judged after that. We took our seats on folding metal chairs directly in front of the stage. The seats behind us began to fill with friends giving us moral support. I turned and looked back as several smiled and waved to let me know that they wanted me to win. I nodded and turned toward the stage with a funny feeling in the pit of my stomach.

The judges took their seats behind a table as the chief judge approached the microphone at center stage and announced the winners of the first five categories. As the winners crossed the stage, they were greeted with polite applause.

It was four thirty and time to judge the tomato entries. I sat on the edge of my chair as the chief judge announced the third-place winner. There was no mention of our entry. Then came the second-place winner, a farm we did not know. I sat back with a sinking feeling and thought that we had not made it into the top three. After a brief pause, the judge held up our beautiful red tomato and made his announcement. "First place goes to the Peaceful Valley Farm."

We had won the blue ribbon. My friends stood and broke into wild applause. I was too shocked to move and sat staring at the tomato and ribbon in the judge's hands.

Uncle Joe put his arm around my shoulder and said, "It's your tomato. You won. Go up there and get your ribbon."

I leaped up the stairs and stood before the judge as he handed me the blue ribbon with congratulations. The audience continued to applaud, and several shouted, "Speech, speech." I was too stunned to say anything, so I just shook my head and smiled. Several men patted me on the back as I walked to my chair, and Aunt Ona Belle gave me a hug while Uncle Joe patted my shoulder and smiled.

The awards ended, and several people gathered around for a look at our tomato. One farmer said, "That tomato is almost as big as a cantaloupe, and it has perfect color. There was nothing even close to it in the contest."

I smiled and said, "Thanks."

Someone in the crowd said, "What are you going to do with it, Dubbie?"

I looked down at the tomato in my right hand and answered, "I don't know. Eat it, I guess." The crowd around me roared with laughter.

I held the tomato in my lap for the trip home and then carried it inside the house to be placed on our dinner table.

Aunt Ona Belle looked at me and said, "It's a shame it won't keep and it will go soft in about a week. It's fully ripe now and won't last very long."

Uncle Joe stood beside the table and said, "I'll bet a center slice will make one fine tomato and mayonnaise sandwich. What do you think, Dubbie?"

Aunt Ona Belle crossed the kitchen, opened the bread box, and handed me two thick slices of soft fresh bread and said, "It's your tomato, Dubbie. Make yourself a sandwich."

Using a long kitchen knife, I made a center cut of the tomato and then sliced a thick piece and laid it on the bread I had placed on my plate. The slice was so big it completely covered the bread, hanging over on all sides.

Aunt Ona Belle was right. It made one great sandwich!

Chapter Seventeen
The Widow Williams

The bus slowly screeched to a stop in front of our mailboxes as the driver opened the door for us to load. Kids were climbing aboard. Sandy stood by the door wagging his tail. It was his way of saying good-bye. I gave him a pat on the head and started up the steps to my seat. The big setter turned and trotted toward the house but would be there when the bus brought us back at the end of the day.

Mr. Todd closed the door and placed the bus in gear, and we were on our way. The fields on both sides of the road would soon be replaced by tall oak trees that reduced sunlight and provided shade for most of the day.

I sat on the right side of the bus and looked out at the creek as we crossed a small bridge built by local farmers last year. We started up a slight incline and approached a knoll on my side of the bus. Thick brush and scrub trees covered the hill, with only a small path winding from the road and disappearing into the undergrowth. The shack on top of the hill was surrounded by trees and could not be seen from the road, but I always looked for it as we passed by on our way to school.

The small shanty was occupied by a woman who had never been seen. She was known as the Widow Williams. We believed she was a witch and had a witch's powers. As Halloween approached, tales about "the witch on the hill" were told by older students while we listened quietly with our mouths hanging open. I wanted to see the witch but was afraid that she would wave her wand and turn me into a frog. One of the older boys said that had been done, and I was not about to take a chance and climb the hill for a look.

I had visions of her stirring a witch's brew in a large pot over an open fire with a black cat at her side. Inside the safety of the bus, I watched the hill each day, expecting to see her in a black robe and pointed hat with a wooden-handled broom in her hand. The bus trundled down the road beside the hill while I stared at the trees in search of the witch.

Sam, the older boy sitting beside me, said, "Have you ever seen the witch?"

I turned to Sam, stuck out my chin, and said, "No, but I am not afraid of her."

The bus bounced over ruts in the road as I turned away and looked out the window, thinking about how a witch would look.

Sam grinned as he leaned toward me and said in a whisper, "She only comes out once a month, at night when the moon is full."

I chewed on my lip and continued to look out the window as we passed the hill.

He leaned to me and with his lips beside my ear, spoke barely above a whisper, "She's always out on Halloween." He paused, and then continued, "I've heard she flies on a broom that night."

"Have you ever seen her?" I asked. "What does she look like?"

"I saw her in the sky on Halloween last year." He chuckled. "I'll bet she'll be out again this year. You'd better be careful if you go out on Halloween."

I pushed him away from me and shouted, "I'm not afraid of that old witch!"

Sam could see the doubt in my eyes as I spoke. The bus was almost at the school, but this was too much fun to stop now. He licked his lips and said with a smirk, "She cooks over an open fire almost every night. Her and that big black cat. Why don't you sneak up there after dark one night and see if you can get a look at her?"

"Maybe I will," I answered. *But not by myself,* I thought, *and not without a plan that included several of my friends.*

Sam could see that he had scared me and decided to see if he could make me pee my pants. I stood to get off the bus, but he blocked my way, leaned down to look into my eyes, and said, "I'd be careful if I were you. I heard that she turns boys your age into frogs by waving her magic wand. If she sees you around her place, you are going to wind up croaking and eating bugs just to stay alive."

138

The bus stopped, and Sam started down the aisle with me close behind. I stepped off the bus thinking that trying to see the witch might not be worth the risk. I rushed to the boy's restroom and approached the urinal to satisfy my immediate need. Standing at parade rest, I decided to stop sitting beside Sam on our bus rides. I didn't think my kidneys would hold up to many more talks about the Widow Williams. I was scared and needed to know more about just how bad the witch could be.

My uncle Joe would know about witches. I decided to talk to him after school at the barn without my aunt. I took my time feeding the livestock, expecting him to come to the barn while I was still there. I carried a bucket of feed to Cricket's stall as he stepped out of the outhouse, turned, and walked toward the barnyard gate. I fed Cricket, patted her neck, and returned the bucket to the feed bin. As I closed the door, Uncle Joe reached the trough and started to add fresh water.

Looking up, he said, "Are you about done?"

"Yes, sir," I answered and made ripples in the water with my hand. While he shut off the water, I asked, "Uncle Joe, have you ever known a witch?"

He looked up, surprised by my question, thought for a moment, and with a gleam in his eye said, "Well, I have known a few, but they weren't the broom-ridin' kind." He snorted.

"In fact," he continued, "several women in the next county are ugly enough to be witches. I heard that when they held a beauty contest over there, nobody won. The best girl there placed third; they kept second and first open. At least that's what I was told." He roared with laughter at his joke.

He continued to laugh as I said, "Halloween is two weeks away. Have you ever seen a Halloween witch? One that comes out on Halloween?"

Uncle Joe could see that I was serious but thought this was too good to shut down, and he said, "Why are you asking? Have you seen any witches around here lately?" He gave a low chuckle while continuing to fill the water trough

"No, sir, I haven't." I kicked a clod of dirt beside the trough, looked down, and continued, "I was just wondering."

I swirled my hand in the water and then asked, "What about the Widow Williams? Could she be a witch?"

Uncle Joe looked at me, laughed, and said, "She's not a witch. She is a hermit. Doesn't like people. Lives alone in that shack her husband left her when he died."

He opened the feed room door, stepped inside, and said, "It's starting to cool off at night, and with fall coming, our animals' coats will get shaggy unless we keep them brushed." He handed me a brush and said, "You brush down Cricket, and I will do Mike. We will finish up with Jack before we go to the house for supper."

I slipped under the retaining bar to Cricket's stall and stepped inside. I stopped to enjoy the rich aroma inside the stall and listened to Cricket crunch the dried corn in her feed bin. "Easy, Cricket," I said, just to let her know I was beside her inside the stall. I had learned that she could deliver a painful kick when frightened and knew better than to walk to her without speaking. She continued to eat while I brushed her mane and neck and continued down her back. This was a job I enjoyed, and she would stand quietly while I brushed her coat to a smooth sheen. I took my time finishing as Uncle Joe was brushing out Jack's tail. We put our brushes away and walked toward the house, enjoying the cool evening.

I climbed into my bed that night thinking about witches. The Widow Williams could have turned into a witch after her husband died. That could be why she never comes out of her shack on top of the hill. No one has ever seen her or knows what she looks like.

I was going "trick or treatin'" on Halloween, and if she was a witch she would be out that night for sure. I decided to go to the Revere farm the next day and talk with James Charles. He was my age, in my class, and would go trick or treating with me on Halloween night.

I pulled the blankets around my neck and buried my head in the soft pillow. Warm and comfortable, I drifted off to sleep listening to the whip-poor-wills call in the quiet of the evening.

It was mid-morning when I finished my chores and mounted my bike for a ride to the Revere farm. It was an easy trip down the gravel road about a mile away. I expected to find James Charles either in the house or somewhere around the farm.

I turned off the road and pedaled down a path leading to a sprawling three-bedroom home with an L-shaped porch extending the entire length in front and on one side of the building. An oversized swing hung on chains beside the door, and there were several straight-backed wooden chairs strewn about at odd angles. All had printed cushions that were worn but looked comfortable. The clapboard house had a fresh coat of white paint that stood out in the morning sun.

I dropped my bike in front of the porch and shouted, "Hello. Is anyone home?" No answer. I walked up the steps to the screened-in porch and knocked on the door. There was no one inside the house. They had to be at the barn or in the fields; I started around the house to the barn and saw James Charles hitching a hay wagon to their John Deere tractor.

As I approached, he looked up, smiled, and said, "Hey, Dubbie."

"Hi," I said. "What'cha doing?"

"I've got to pick up some firewood that's stacked by the trees at the back of our alfalfa patch. Want to come along?" He turned, sat on the wagon bed, and continued, "If you help me load, it won't take very long. I only have to haul one load."

"Okay," I said. "I'll ride in the wagon." I stepped on the rubber tire and settled on the wagon floor, crossing my legs as he climbed to the seat of the tractor and started the engine. The wagon jerked forward; I placed one hand on the sideboard while we bounced along through the patch toward the trees at the back of the field.

The wood had been cut into pieces less than two feet long, stacked, and left to cure in the summer sun. It was dry and would burn well in their stove during the cool winter months.

I loaded the front of the trailer, James Charles the back. When our stack met, we would drive to the house and unload it into a rack beside the kitchen door. It was easy work for two twelve-year-old boys used to farm labor, and we expected to finish in about an hour.

We tossed wood into the back of the wagon, and the pile grew until James Charles said, "We've got a good-size load. Let's stop while the tractor can still pull it."

Throwing one final piece into the back of the wagon, I said okay and climbed on the pile, taking a seat. James Charles mounted the tractor and looked back to check on me before pushing the starter. The engine coughed, fired, and settled into a smooth idle. The rear wheels sprayed dirt as the tractor strained to move the loaded wagon forward.

We crossed the field and approached the rear of the barn, a red two-story structure with doors that opened on both ends for easy access by loaded hay wagons. Preparations had been made for winter; the loft was stacked high with bales of freshly cut hay. Several cows stood quietly near the barn and watched us approach.

The tractor moved around the barn and stopped at the wood rack at the rear of the house. I jumped down from my perch on the wagon and started unloading. James Charles stepped down from the tractor, and the unloading increased as we quietly competed to see who was fastest.

Our shirts were damp with sweat as I placed the last log on the pile. James Charles wiped his brow, climbed on the tractor, and said, "Climb on, and we'll go down to the barn and have a drink of water from the well."

"Good idea!" I said and climbed into the wagon for the short trip to the barn. The well had a hand pump with the outlet beside a six-foot-long water trough that was half-full. A priming dipper hung on a hook beside the pump handle. I dipped it in the trough and poured water in the top of the pump as James Charles worked the handle. Several pumps later water began to flow, spilling into the trough. I rinsed the dipper, filled it with water from the pump, and took a long drink. The cool water was pure and had a great taste. We swapped positions so James Charles could have his turn.

When his dipper was full, I stopped pumping, sat on the edge of the trough, stretched, and crossed my legs. A slight breeze blew across the yard and felt good against my damp shirt. It was time to talk.

I said, "Are we going trick or treatin' on Halloween?"

"You bet!" he said. "I've got a couple of ideas about some tricks we may be able to pull off. Jimmy and J.C. are going with us. That should be enough people to do what I have in mind."

I splashed water in his direction and laughed as it fell short. He stepped back and yelled, "Hey, watch it!"

James Charles had gotten us into trouble before with some of his harebrained ideas, and the sound of his voice made me wary. I watched him closely as I asked, "What do you have in mind?"

With a sly grin, he answered, "If I tell you, do you promise not to tell anyone until we do the trick on Halloween?"

I knew from the tone of his voice that this was not going to be good. I paused and rinsed my hands in the water trough before saying, "I know how to keep a secret. You can trust me. I promise." I wiped my wet hands on my pants.

"Cross your heart?" he challenged.

I put my right hand over my heart and said, "I cross my heart."

"Do you know the church that's about a mile from here?"

"Yes," I said. I wondered what a church had to do with Halloween night.

He looked at me with a glint in his eye and said, "Well, it's got a steeple. It has steps inside that make it easy to reach when someone has to ring the bell. The room at the top is just about big enough for a cow. I want to swipe a cow from the farm next to the church and put it up in the steeple."

A cow in the church? I was stunned and said, "Are you crazy?" I stood, waved my arms, and shouted, "We can't put a damn cow in a church steeple! That's the craziest thing I have ever heard." I laughed so hard that I had to sit back down on the edge of the water trough.

"With four of us, it should be easy," he said. "You take the front, pull the cow up on a rope, and the rest of us will get behind her and make her move. When we get her up there, you can tie her off and we will leave her there for the night."

This had the makings of real trouble. First, swipe a cow, and then get it into the church and up the steeple without being seen. There was a real risk here, but if we could pull it off, it would be the best Halloween trick ever done in these parts. It was scary but could be worth a try. If we couldn't get the cow up the steps, we could just leave it in the church and run for the hills.

"I'm about as crazy as you are, but this could be an awesome trick. If we don't get caught, it will be the best trick ever pulled around here." I laughed, punched his shoulder, and asked, "Do you really think we can do it?"

"You bet I do," he answered. "But it's going to take some planning, and everyone has to do their part."

"Do Jimmy and J.C. know about your plan?" I asked. They had to join us, or the trick was off. Two people couldn't put even a small cow up in the belfry.

"No," he answered, and after a pause he said, "We need to get together next Saturday to go over it and get ready for Halloween."

As we walked to the house, I thought of the Widow Williams and her shack on the hill. She could be a problem on Halloween.

I said, "Witches come out on Halloween. I've heard that the Widow Williams is a witch and can fly on that night."

James Charles looked at me, shook his head, and laughed. "Witches won't come near a church. We'll be okay there."

I looked worried and said, "If she's out riding on a broom that night, we could get into trouble before we even get to the church. She has a magic wand and can turn boys into frogs."

James Charles leaned an elbow on the wood piled beside the back door and said, "I don't think she's a witch."

"Have you ever been up to her shack on the hill and taken a look?" I demanded.

"No, but I'm not afraid to." He clenched his jaw, pursed his lips, and said, "I've just never had a need to go up there."

I thought about that for a minute and said, "She has a big black cat and cooks over an open fire behind her shack every night. Why don't we sneak up there after dark one night and see what she's doin'? We could circle around the back of her place and hide in the woods."

James Charles sat on one end of the woodpile, crossed his feet, and asked, "Why do you want to go up there?"

"Because I've heard that she can turn you into a frog, that's why!" I yelled. "If it's true, I don't want to be anywhere near the old witch on Halloween night!"

James Charles sat quietly on the woodpile looking out at the barn while I stood close by with my hands stuffed in the rear pockets of my pants. I wanted to check out the Widow Williams but was not about to do it alone.

"Look," I said. "If the four of us go together and stay hidden in the woods, we should be okay." He stared at me with his mouth open but did not move. I could see that he didn't want to visit the witch, and I shouted, "What's the matter? You afraid?"

He clenched his jaw but did not answer. I decided to push it. "I double dog dare you to go with me!"

I was looking and sounding stronger than I felt. I really did not want to get near the witch, but I was even more afraid of what could happen on Halloween and was trying to appear fearless.

James Charles frowned and looked at me with a hard stare. Standing from the woodpile, he said, his voice harsh, "I'm not afraid. Can you get Jimmy and J.C to go with us?"

"I'll talk to them at school on Monday," I answered.

It was dark as we mounted our bikes and started down the road, but a bright moon lighted the way. Our bikes trundled across the bridge as we continued the short trip to the hill below the Widow Williams's shack. Scrub oak trees occupied the hill, surrounded by weeds and briars that made walking difficult. We left our bikes in the brush beside the road and formed a circle to talk about our next move.

Jimmy spoke first. "If we aren't careful, we will make a lot of noise going up the hill. I think we should go single file with the leader making a path for everyone else."

I nodded and answered in a low voice, "Try to avoid the bushes. The leaves are dry and will make a lot of noise when you brush up against them. No talking from this point on. I will lead, so follow me." I started up the hill. The hillside was steep and strewn with moss-covered boulders surrounded by half-dead scrub bushes.

My breath came faster as I wound my way near the top of the hill. I stopped and squinted through the trees, trying to locate the Widow's house. The small, unpainted wooden house looked black in the moonlight. The wall nearest me had one small window. There was a light on inside the room, but it appeared to be empty. A fire in a stone pit behind the house crackled beneath a black metal pot, dangling from a rod supported by posts mounted on each side of the blaze.

I dropped to the ground as the door to the shack opened and the Widow Williams stepped out with a small pail and walked to the fire, followed by a black cat. She dumped the contents of the pail into the hissing pot and stirred with a long-handled spoon. That had to be a witch's brew used to turn boys into frogs. Could she have known that we were coming and be making up a fresh pot of her brew just for us? She moved about the fire in a full-length gown that was a dark color but impossible to see in the moonlight. I had expected a pointed hat and a broom, but they were nowhere to be seen.

I took a deep breath, blinked my eyes, and puffed out air but remained frozen watching her every move. J.C., directly behind me, crawled forward, rustling the dried leaves on the bush over my head. The cat arched his back, yowled, and hissed as it looked in our direction.

As she looked toward the noise, the Widow Williams screeched, "Who's out there?! Is anybody out there?" I gasped for air and crawled backward, bumping into James Charles as he turned to run. I was closest to the Widow and would be the one she would turn into a frog. The answer was to run, and in a panic, I started down the hill at a fast gallop. The noise that four boys made charging down the hill resembled a cattle stampede.

As we ran, we could hear the Widow Williams screaming, "You git out of here! Git off my property!"

My legs were burning and the scratches on my arms were bleeding as I found my bike and made a running start down the road. I pedaled home in record time and was thankful that the Widow Williams had not turned me into a frog.

The next two weeks passed fast as we made preparations for the big event. Jimmy checked the farm beside the church and reported that the cows stayed in the pasture at night. It would be easy to rope one and lead it to the church.

We had to know if the church remained open at night. I was closest and volunteered to make a late-night visit on my bike. This had to be done after Uncle Joe and Aunt Ona Belle were sound asleep.

I slipped under my covers wide awake and waited. An owl hooted in a nearby tree, and the whip-poor-wills were calling down by the creek. Sandy was curled up at the foot of my bed, asleep. It was a clear night; the stars were bright, and a half moon lit the yard beside my porch. I started to doze and shook my head to stay awake.

The door leading from the porch to the back bedroom was open, and I could hear Uncle Joe's light snore. He was asleep. I slipped out of my bed, dressed, and carried my shoes across the porch to the steps. Sandy followed, expecting some attention, and I gave him a quiet pat.

It was almost midnight when I pedaled my bike out of the yard and down the gravel road. Moonlight made it easy to follow. The only sound was the crunch of gravel as I pumped the pedals to get to the church.

The road made a sweeping turn through the trees, and I could see a silhouette of the church at the back of a well-mowed lawn. A dirt road led across the lawn to the church and continued to the preacher's house in the woods behind the church parking lot. There were no lights in either the house or the church.

I stopped my bike at the steps in front of the church, let it fall to the ground, and walked up the steps to the front door. Sandy stood close by quietly watching me move. The handle to the large door turned easily, and I eased it open. No noise; all was well so far.

I stepped inside and waited for my eyes to adjust. I could see steps just inside the entrance that would take me up to the belfry. They looked wide enough for a cow, but what about the bell tower? Was it big enough for a cow? I had to know. Worried about noise, I slipped my shoes off and started up the steps.

A dog outside the church began to bark. It wasn't Sandy; I knew the sound of his bark. I mumbled, "Please keep quiet, Sandy. I don't need a dogfight now." I waited on the steps until the dog finally quieted down.

I moved farther up the steps as a light came on in back of the pulpit. The dog had rousted the preacher, who decided to check out the church. I backed up the belfry out of sight but had left my shoes on the bottom step. If he saw them, I was caught!

The preacher walked in my direction down the center aisle, moving slowly as he checked the pews on both sides. I held my breath and waited. Nearing the last pew, he noticed that the entrance door was slightly cracked, so he walked forward and pulled it closed. My shoes sat unnoticed on the first step leading to the steeple. Satisfied with his inspection, the reverend returned to the pulpit, turned out the light, and left the building.

I took a deep breath and exhaled. I was safe; it was time to check the belfry to see if it was big enough for a cow. I moved up the steps to a room that was smaller than I had expected. It was square, four feet wide, with a beam just above my head that divided the room in half. A bell and clapper were attached to the center of the beam. A six-foot rope dangled from the clapper, touching the floor below. Louvered shutters decorated the walls so that sound would not be restricted. I stepped to the front wall, looked through the shutters, and could see the lawn below. A light breeze blew through the openings and cooled the room.

To pull off our trick, we needed the right-size cow. A milk cow would not work, but a heifer probably would because it's smaller. That would be my report to the guys at our meeting the next day. I crept down the stairs, stepped into my shoes, and left the building for the short bike ride home. Uncle Joe and Aunt Ona Belle were sound asleep in their bedroom, so I undressed and slipped under the blankets on my bed.

I was the first to arrive at the Revere farm. James Charles was in front of the barn motioning for me to bypass the house and come straight there.

"Hi," I said, stepping off my bike and leaning it against the wall.

"Hi," he answered. "Did you go to the church and check out the belfry?"

"Yep, and I almost got caught because a barking dog woke up the preacher. When he turned on the lights to see if anyone was there, I was halfway up the steps with no way out. I hid at the top of the steps, and he didn't see me."

Jimmy and J.C. arrived as I was finishing my story. James Charles was in charge of our plan and began asking questions.

"Jimmy," he said, "did you check out the farm beside the church?"

"That's the Carlson farm. He leaves his cows in the pasture at night, and it will be easy to get a rope on one and lead it to the church."

"Did you hear what happened to old man Carlson's bull on Halloween last year?" J.C. asked. "My brother and a couple of his friends painted the back of his prize bull red. Old man Carlson was really mad, but no one ever found out who did it. I didn't know my brother did it until he told me a couple of weeks ago."

"We can't do this before midnight," James Charles said. "We have to be sure the Carlson house is dark before we try to get the cow."

I nodded and said, "The belfry is small. A big cow won't make it through the door. We have to pick out a heifer, one that is not too fat."

"Since you have seen the belfry, we will let you pick out the cow," James Charles said, pointing at me.

Jimmy smiled, looked at me, and said, "You pick out the cow, and I'll rope it and lead it to the church."

I said, "You have a deal. It looks like we have it together. Now all we have to do is pull it off." My concerned look was shared by Jimmy and J.C. Both frowned but sat quietly with nothing to say.

James Charles saw our doubtful looks and tried to cheer us up by saying, "This is gonna be a lot of fun, and it's not gonna be that hard. We should be able to do the whole thing in fifteen minutes and be out of there. We'll do it after midnight and let the reverend bring the cow down in the morning. By then everyone will know about the best trick that has ever been pulled in this county."

I smiled and nodded while J.C. and Jimmy joined in with nervous laughter.

Chapter Eighteen
Halloween Tricks

The day had finally arrived. Aunt Ona Belle worked throughout the day making a supper that we would enjoy before the start of the evening. The smells from the kitchen wafted across the porch, making my mouth water. A chicken was roasting in the oven beside cornbread. Mashed potatoes and green beans were cooking on the stove. Several pumpkin pies had been prepared for dessert with whipped cream made from the morning delivery by Hess's Dairy Farm. She had made a big plate of red candied apples and oatmeal cookies to be passed out as bribes to keep the pranksters from playing tricks.

I was working with Uncle Joe at the table next to the house carving two pumpkins for the front porch. We planned to place candles inside each so their evil smiles could be seen from the road.

As we carved, Uncle Joe said, "Some mighty good smells are coming out of the kitchen. Your aunt is fixin' a real feast for supper tonight."

I nodded and said, "It's making my mouth water. I'm ready for it."

I looked down at my pumpkin's frowning face and said, "My pumpkin looks meaner than yours!" I laughed as I picked it up and started to the porch.

Uncle Joe followed with his pumpkin and said, "I carve a friendly pumpkin." He placed it on the porch beside a post.

I looked over at his smiling pumpkin with round, friendly eyes and said, "That pumpkin wouldn't scare anybody."

"It isn't meant to scare, but to welcome kids looking for a treat. It works for me."

We stepped inside for candles as my aunt placed a large bowl of steaming mashed potatoes on the table. She looked up, smiled, and said, "Wash up. Supper is ready."

Uncle Joe looked around the room, taking inventory, and said, "You've been busy in here today, girl." With a wink, he walked to the sink to wash. I waited close by for my turn.

She looked around and said, "It's kind of fun having a boy in the house on Halloween."

Uncle Joe stepped aside so I could wash my hands, tousled my hair, and with a crooked smile said, "Yep, it sure is."

I was so excited about the evening that I hardly tasted the food. That is, with the exception of a large piece of pumpkin pie covered with whipped cream. My aunt's pie crust was every bit as good as the filling, and I left nothing on my plate.

Uncle Joe watched me finish and teased, "Are you planning on going somewhere tonight?"

"Yes, sir," I said. "Several of us are going to meet at James Charles's house."

He looked out the window as the shadows moved across the yard and said with a chuckle, "Well, it's just about dark, so you'd better get going. You boys stay out of trouble tonight."

"Yes, sir," I said as I slipped out of my chair and moved to the porch.

I put on my darkest coveralls, a blue print flannel shirt, white cotton socks, and high-top shoes, and began to blacken my face with charcoal. I had a mask in my jacket that would cover my face and would put it on later. Equipped with a bar of soap for marking car windows, I clomped across the porch and down the steps to my bike. The sun had set, and I was on my way to the Revere farm to meet my friends.

I was the last to arrive; they were playing pitch in the front yard. I laid my bike on the ground and joined the circle. As the moon began to rise over the trees, we stopped playing to talk.

James Charles said, "We have to wait until midnight before going to the church. Let's trick or treat some of the farms and get some candy."

Four stops at farmhouses produced enough candy and cookies for the evening. As we left the last house, I said, "I brought some soap so we can write on car windows."

Jimmy sat on his bike with his hands on the handlebars and said, "I've got some balloons we can fill with water and throw at passing cars."

J.C. joined in. "Let's go down by the bridge, fill the balloons, and wait for cars to come along. We can hide our bikes in the woods."

I said, "Let's go!" We mounted our bikes and pedaled down the dirt path to the main road.

Jimmy had four balloons, one for each of us. I filled mine with creek water and knotted it tight to make sure the water stayed inside until it hit the car. I planned to aim for the driver's windshield and wanted a big splash. We crouched down in the ditch beside the bridge and waited for a car to pass. It was a good place to hide and close enough to the road for throwing accuracy.

James Charles went first. As the car went by, he threw too soon and the balloon landed on the hood. We laughed as the car kept going.

J.C was next. His car was traveling fast, and the balloon hit the rear door. We booed the shot, and I said, "You will never make the shot-put team with that arm!"

My turn was next. The road was quiet as we waited for a car to come along. Finally, a slow-moving pickup truck came around the curve. It was Mark on his way home after a night of drinking while sitting around the stove at the country store. With my feet apart and firmly planted, I leaned forward and watched the truck approach. I expected to have a perfect shot and brought the loaded balloon up to my shoulder, holding it tight in a shot-put stance. The truck reached my side as I heaved the balloon with all my might. Mark had his window down, and the balloon went inside and broke as it struck his head. The truck wobbled to a stop, and we knew it was time to leave.

The driver jumped out of the truck yelling, "I'm going to break somebody's head!"

We were laughing so hard it was difficult to run. But run we did. Down by the creek and into the thickest part of the woods. Safely out of range of the driver, we came together, still laughing about the best shot of the night.

It was almost midnight as Jimmy led the way to the cows in the pasture beside the church. Twenty or more cows stood quietly, half-asleep. As we approached, none moved or bellowed. The night was quiet as we stood beside the gate thinking about our selection.

I whispered, "A full-grown milk cow will get stuck before she gets to the top. We need a heifer that's not that fat."

We stood close together, reviewed the herd, and whispered our opinions about what to do. James Charles pointed to one and said, "How about that one? It's not fat and doesn't look very old. What do you think?"

It looked good to me, and I said, "Jimmy, you've got the rope. See if you can get a loop on it, and let's go."

Jimmy opened the gate and stepped inside with a loop ready to slip over the cow's head. One milk cow moved slowly to the back of the herd. The others stood quietly without moving as Jimmy approached our prize selection. He planned to walk up to the heifer and slip the loop over its head. This guy was no Buffalo Bill, but if it worked, fine. We opened the gate as he led the animal through and walked quietly to the church. The cow, having no idea about what was in store for it, followed along. J.C. closed the gate as I took the rope and coaxed the animal toward the steps to the building. So far, things were going well.

James Charles moved around me and opened the church door. The cow followed Jimmy up the steps and into the room, stopping behind the last pew.

We were at the base of the belfry stairs. The cow stood quietly while I whispered my plan to get her up the stairs. "One of you stay on each side of her until we get her on the staircase. Take your belts off, and if she balks, I'll pull and you whip her so that she will move. Got it?"

They agreed, so I led the animal to the bottom step. She shook her head and refused to move. James Charles got behind her, placed his shoulder on her butt, and pushed. It worked, and we moved up several steps, but she balked again. I pulled, but she reared her head and pulled back without moving. This was not going to be easy. I looked over the cow's back and said in a loud whisper, "We're stuck. Hit her with your belts while I pull."

I heard leather slapping the cow's rump and jerked hard on the rope. She moved a few more feet and then stopped and thrashed her head from side to side in a panic. The rope was tight around her neck, and I stepped closer and said, "Easy girl, easy." I stroked her head and began to scratch her ears. It worked, and she settled down as I released some of the pressure on the rope.

Several minutes passed, and I whispered, "She's calmed down. Let's try to move her again." I started to pull as somebody down there hit her with a belt, and she lurched forward. I backed into the belfry, but it was really tight. The cow was between me and the door, and I had no room to get by her. I decided to loop the rope that dangled from the bell clapper around the cow's neck so that she would stay in the belfry. That done, I squatted and crawled between the cow's legs back to the stairs. Everyone was waiting for me at the bottom of the steps.

James Charles said, "Did you tie her up so she will stay there?"

"Yes," I said, giving Jimmy his rope. "I used the rope dangling from the clapper. Her rear end was too broad to go through the door. She's wedged in there and can't move."

We walked outside, and James Charles said, "My pa is going to tan my hide if I don't get home pretty soon. See you later."

We jumped on our bikes and scattered like leaves in the wind.

Dawn was breaking, and the cow was still stuck in the belfry. Irritated at being confined, she thrashed her head from side to side. With each movement, the bell rang as if announcing the call to church.

The pastor was asleep but awoke to the irregular noise made by the bell. Throwing the blanket back, he sat on the side of the bed in his quiet room and listened. Minutes passed, and then the bell rang again. Thinking it had to be the church bell, he dressed and walked from his house to the church as the uneven ringing continued. Entering the rear of the church, he walked to the belfry and started up the steps. Halfway up, he could see the tail of the cow that was stuck inside the tiny space.

Stunned, he sat down on the steps shaking his head and mumbled, "A cow in my belfry? What am I gonna do?" He held his face in his hands and groaned. The bell continued its sporadic ringing.

Returning to his house and collecting his thoughts, he knew he needed help. He decided to call members of the parish board and ask them to help him get the cow out of the belfry.

His first call was to the board president, who fumbled for the phone and answered from a sound sleep. "Hello." He was clearly unhappy at being rousted out of bed before daylight. He nervously smacked his lips and cleared his throat while he waited for the caller to speak.

"Bill, this is the reverend," the pastor said. "I apologize for waking you up, but there's a cow stuck in our belfry and I need your help."

"What?" Now fully awake, he shook his head in disbelief.

"A cow. There's a cow that someone put in our belfry, and I don't know how to get it out. I need your help."

"Reverend, it's too early in the morning for a joke. How could a cow get up in the belfry? Are you serious?"

"I'm serious. It's stuck with its rear end sticking out toward the steps. It's too tight up there for it to turn around. I guess we are gonna have to bring it down the steps backward. Can you get some men to help with this?

Bill collapsed with laughter. "That's the damnedest thing I have ever heard!" Still laughing, he said, "I'll round up several guys, and we should be there in about an hour."

The reverend said, "Thanks, Bill. I'll wait here for you."

Hanging up the phone, he returned to the belfry for a closer look at the problem. The cow was firmly stuck in its position. A turn was impossible. He could not enter the room, because the cow's rear end was firmly stuck in the door frame. As he stood on the belfry steps looking up at the cow's rear end, the bell gonged and the cow relieved herself! She urinated and then deposited a sizable cow patty directly in front of the pastor.

"Dear Lord," he mumbled, stepping back to avoid a direct hit. "A cow has just shit on my church." The cow shook her head, and the bell gave a loud clang.

Bill made his calls for help knowing that farms shared their telephone lines with at least two other farms in their area. Listening to telephone conversations was a great pastime and could be fun. As Bill made his calls trying to explain that a cow was stuck in the church belfry, the party lines became alive with activity.

Cars began to arrive at the church—some with men to help, others just to enjoy the show. A crowd began to gather in front of the church, all watching the belfry for a glimpse of the cow. An occasional clang always brought laughter and applause.

Several men inside the church gathered below the steps of the steeple to talk about what to do.

Bill said, "The first thing we have to do is get that damn cow untied from the bell. Every time she shakes her head the bell rings, and the people out front are laughing their heads off."

"Yep," Melvin said. "But the way the cow is wedged in the door, no one can get in there."

"We need someone small enough to crawl under the cow to her head. Does anyone here want to give it a try?"

"My son is out front," Homer said. "He's small enough to be able to crawl under the cow." Walking toward the door, he said, "I'll get him in here."

The fearsome foursome had just arrived by bicycle to admire last night's work. I watched what was happening with my mouth hanging open. Over fifty people had gathered in front of the building. James Charles sat on his bike resting his arms on the handlebars while I talked. "Do they put thirteen-year-old boys in jail for doing something like this? If they do, we probably would not get out until we are eighteen"

James Charles was visibly shaken as he said, "Probably juvenile detention, but that's just as bad." Our trick had gotten out of hand, and after a quiet talk, we swore each other to silence forever and ever. We would never admit that we had done it.

We watched at a distance as the front door to the church opened and a man called, "Tim, come here. We need you inside."

A small boy walked up the steps to the door and followed his father inside.

I heard a siren wail as I climbed off my bike and let it fall to the ground. The sheriff's car rounded the curve with red lights flashing and slowed as it reached the church drive. He had been called to deal with the problem. The police car stopped behind the crowd, and the sheriff opened his door and stepped out.

Someone yelled, "You're just in time, Sheriff. We need you to get a cow out of the belfry."

The crowd hooted and laughed as the sheriff frowned and began his solemn walk to the church door.

Sam Carlson and his wife, Marie, owned the farm beside the church. Sam was blunt and outspoken with a booming voice, all characteristics that did not endear him to people in the community. At six foot four and 260 pounds with a full head of white hair and piercing blue eyes over a handlebar mustache, Sam was a favorite target for pranks by kids living nearby. It was never said to his face, but his nickname in the community was "Wimpy" because he always wore cowboy boots and a broad-brim western hat that made him look like a cartoon character from the local newspaper.

He looked out his window at the crowd gathering in the churchyard and said to his wife, "Something is going on over there, and I would like to know what it is."

Marie answered, "Why don't you walk over and take a look?"

Sam ran his hand through his hair and reached for his jacket. "I think I will," he said. He crossed the room while buttoning his coat and opened the door to the porch.

The sheriff had just arrived as he stepped through his barbed-wire fence and walked toward the crowd, asking, "What's going on?"

Mrs. Revere answered, "Someone put a cow in the belfry, and it's stuck up there."

Sam followed the sheriff inside the church, looked up at the cow's rear end, and could tell it was one of his.

"That's my cow up there. Sheriff, you have got to do something about the pranks that are happening around here. Enough is enough. Every year, Halloween tricks get worse. Last year, someone painted the back of my prize bull red. It ain't grown all the way out yet. Now, one of my best cows is stuck in the church belfry."

The sheriff nodded, continued to look at the confusion, and said, "I'll ask around and see if anybody knows who did it." He hesitated and then said, "I know you are upset, Sam, but I have to say that this is the funniest thing that has happened around here in years!" He chuckled, and then frowned as he looked up at the backside of the cow.

Sam chuckled and said, "It may be funny, but I still want my cow back."

He looked down at his shoes and grunted as he stuffed his hands into the back pockets of his jeans.

Melvin turned and sat on the bottom step to begin coiling his rope. Looking up and grinning at Sam, he said, "We've been trying to get her out for over an hour. You should've taught her to back up, Sam."

The men on the stairs laughed as Sam said, "That's one of my best heifers. Take it easy getting her out."

The door opened, and a skinny eight-year-old boy walked over to his father. He took his son by the hand and said, "Timmy, do you think you can crawl under that cow up there and see if it's tied to something? We think that's why we can't get her to back up."

The boy looked up the stairs and then at his father and said, "I don't know, Dad. What if the cow steps on me?"

His dad placed his arm around Timmy's shoulders; then he bent down to look into his face and said, "The cow is not going to move. It's stuck in the doorway. All you have to do is crawl around her legs and into the belfry. Then, if there is a rope on her neck, take it off."

Timmy looked scared and clearly did not want to do as he was told. Trying to think of a way out, he said, "I'll get my clothes dirty if I have to crawl under the cow, and Mom will be really upset."

Homer looked down at his son and said, "Don't worry about your clothes. The cow dumped on the steps, and the floor between her legs is clean. Step around the mess on the steps, and you'll be fine."

Timmy stood frozen with his mouth half-open while he tried to think of anything else that would get him out of this mess. Homer reached out and took his son by the hand to lead him up the steps. Standing one step below the cow, they looked up at her rear end, and Homer said, "You can slip through beside her left leg, and once you get inside, you should be able to stand up beside her head."

Unable to avoid this any longer, Timmy dropped down behind the cow and began to crawl under her stomach. There was room to stand when he reached the cow's head. The heifer saw the boy, shook her head, and bellowed. The rope around her neck jerked the clapper, ringing the bell.

Timmy stood beside the cow and looked through the louvers at the crowd that had gathered below, and he reached for the rope attached to the bell clapper.

He rang the bell several times while his dad stood behind the cow's rear yelling, "Forget the bell! Get the rope off the cow!"

Timmy tried to slip the rope over its head, but it was too short and needed to be untied. He picked at the knot, but it would not come loose. It had tightened with each shake of the cow's head. He tried again and again, but it would not work loose. He decided to crawl out leaving the rope around the cow's neck. He climbed down the steps, looked at his dad, and said, "The rope is too short to slip over the cow's head. I tried to untie it, but the knot is too tight. I couldn't get it loose."

His dad turned and shouted to the men below, "Has anybody got a screwdriver in their truck? The knot holding the rope is too tight. Timmy needs to work it loose."

A ten-inch screwdriver was passed up the stairs, and Timmy's father showed him what needed to be done. "Work the blade through the center of the knot, and wiggle it so that it loosens up. You should be able to get it out that way."

The sheriff watched and then stepped back from the crowd on the stairs, crossed his arms, frowned, and tried to look serious.

Timmy climbed the stairs and dropped to the floor for a return trip to the cow's head. He stood and worked the screwdriver blade through the knot. After a brief struggle, it came loose and the rope dangled beside the cow's neck.

The ringing stopped as he shouted, "I got it, Dad!" He dropped beneath the cow and crawled to the steps.

Homer placed an arm around his son's shoulder and said, "I knew you could do it."

During the next hour, several men tried to get the cow to back down the stairs, with no success. They concluded that cows don't know how to back up. Sam tried to help but only irritated the two men working at the rear of the cow who were attempting to get it to back out of the belfry. Finally, Melvin said, "Back off, Sam, and let us work this out. Three people at the ass end of this cow are one too many."

The men inside the church snickered as Sam clomped down the stairs grumbling, "You be careful and don't hurt my cow. Take it easy."

The party line was alive and well. As the ladies talked, one suggested a picnic on the church lawn and said, "There's no tellin' how long that cow is gonna be stuck up there. We might as well have a picnic and enjoy the day." The idea was born, and baskets were filled with sandwiches, cookies, and jugs of iced tea. As the women arrived at the church, blankets were spread on the lawn while the crowd continued to watch the belfry.

I saw Mrs. Revere, nudged James Charles, and said, "Let's go get one of your mom's sandwiches."

Mrs. Revere, an ample lady with a light complexion, bright smile, and big brown eyes, always kept her dark hair in a bun. She dressed in jeans and a long-sleeve cotton shirt that she thought hid her oversized breasts. As we approached, she was sitting on her blanket removing cellophane-wrapped sandwiches from a basket and stacking them on the blanket.

"Hi, Mrs. Revere," I said.

She looked up and said, "Hi, Dubbie. Is the cow still stuck in the church?"

"I think so," I said, trying not to laugh. "I haven't seen a cow come out of the church. We've been out here watching, but I don't know much about it," I lied.

James Charles said, "I heard it bellow a few minutes ago, so I think it's still there."

Mrs. Revere shook her head in disbelief and said, "I can't imagine who would do such a thing, but it *is* funny."

We turned away looking at each other and smirked.

She watched us starting to walk away and said, "Would you like a sandwich? Ham and cheese on fresh bread."

"Yes, ma'am," we answered as she handed us two cellophane packages.

As we were walking back to our bikes, I looked at James Charles and said, "Everyone had better keep their mouths shut about this. One leak, and we are gonna wind up in jail."

He nodded and said, "They will, they will. But I'm going to talk to Jimmy and J.C. just to be sure."

Work inside the church continued with no cooperation from the cow. Someone said, "We need to get a rope around her neck so we can pull her back. Let's send the boy back in to put a loop over her neck. We should be able to get her to back up by pulling on the rope."

"That might work," several men said, nodding. Melvin made a loop in his rope and gave it to the kid, and he began to crawl under the cow. Reaching the cow's head, he stood and looked through the louvers at the crowd gathered below.

This was just too good. He grabbed the rope dangling from the clapper and gave the bell a ring. The crowd below howled in delight.

The continuous ringing of the bell irritated the cow, and she shook her head and bellowed, knocking Timmy against the louvered wall.

Homer heard the racket and called up to his son, "Everything okay up there?"

"Yeah, Dad," Timmy said. "I'm trying to stay away from the cow's swinging head, but it's pretty tight up here."

The bellowing and ringing echoed inside the church while the men below the belfry steps huddled to talk about what to do next. The sheriff stood back from the steps with his arms folded across his chest and watched with a humorous grin on his face. *I wouldn't miss this for a million dollars,* he thought.

The crowd outside was making more noise than fans at a football game. Several men inside the church yelled at the boy to stop ringing the bell, but he could not hear and kept at it while the crowd outside howled at every strike.

The boy's father leaned over the rump of the cow and screamed, "Stop ringing the damned bell, and put the rope on the cow."

After one more strike of the bell, he slipped the loop over the cow's head and made his exit. The men on the stairs pulled on the rope, but there was no movement by the cow. Several tugs later, Melvin said, "This isn't going to work. We are gonna have to think of something else."

Someone said, "Hell, let's tie her back legs together, put a rope on them, and drag her down the stairs. That ought to work. Send the boy back in to take the rope off her head, and we can use it to tie her legs and slide her down the stairs."

Homer bent down beside his son and said, "Tim, can you crawl under the cow one more time?"

Timmy looked up at his dad, stuffed his hands in his jeans pockets, and turned toward the steps. It was Timmy to the rescue as he smiled at his dad and said, "Sure, Dad."

Crawling under the cow was getting easier and starting to be fun. As he stood beside the cow's head, the clapper rope dangled beside his left shoulder. He stuck his hand through the louver and waved. The crowd below watched as someone said, "Look. Someone is in the tower with the cow." Everyone silently watched the tower as Timmy's hand flapped up and down in a continuous wave.

The crowd in front of the church erupted with applause and laughter. Someone said, "Now they've got a cow and a boy stuck in the tower."

Forget the rope around the cow's neck. Timmy was onstage, and the crowd was his audience. The cow shook her head, knocking Timmy against the louvered wall and then gave a long and very loud bellow.

Tim moved away from the wall while the cow continued to shake her head and bellow. He tried to slip the rope over her head, but she shook her head, knocking him off balance.

His dad stood on the steps behind the cow and screamed at his son, "Leave the bell alone! Take the rope off, and crawl out of there!"

Timmy stayed away from the cow's swinging head but rubbed her neck and said, "Easy, girl, easy. We are going to get you out of here."

The cow stopped shaking her head, and Tim slipped off the rope and dropped to his knees for the crawl to safety. The cow brought her left rear leg forward and kicked at him while he crawled for the door. Once outside the room, he stood laughing and gave the rope to his dad.

With Timmy out of the way, two men mounted the stairs to tie the cow's legs together. One produced a short rope while the other eased the cow's hind legs together. When that was done, they attached a long rope so that the cow could be eased down the stairs. The men on each side of the animal lifted while two men below pulled her rear legs out straight. As the cow dropped on her stomach, the men eased her down the stairs to the floor of the church. When her legs were untied, she wobbled to her feet unharmed. Only the cleanup of the stairs remained.

Sam inspected his cow and said, "Thanks. She's okay." He took the rope and led her through the door and down the steps to the lawn. The crowd applauded, and several commented on a job well done. With the pressure off, Sam smiled and said, "You have to understand, folks, this here is a religious cow. I'm bringing her back next Sunday to be baptized." Everyone laughed as he led the cow across the churchyard, opened the gate, and turned her loose in the pasture. He watched as she slowly walked toward the herd, and he could see that she was unharmed.

I returned to my bike for the ride back to our farm. It was time to feed the livestock. I leaned the bike against the porch and started down the path to the barn. Sandy sniffed the ground and followed along. There had to be a rabbit in the area.

I walked through the gate as my uncle's car turned into our drive. He would come to the barn after a brief stop at the house.

I continued to feed the animals as he came through the gate and checked the water trough. As I closed the feed room door, he said, "I heard there was a cow stuck in the belfry at the church. Everyone's laughing their heads off about it. It's the funniest Halloween trick to be pulled around here in years. Do you know anything about it?"

"I was over there today. They got her down, and she's okay."

"Do they have any idea who did it?" he asked.

"It was probably some high school boys, but nobody knows who," I lied.

He looked at me with a twinkle in his eye and said, "We may never find out. Anyone would be crazy to admit to doing a trick like that."

As we walked to the house, I nodded and said, "You are right about that."

Chapter Nineteen
Christmas on the Farm

The harvest was over, with hay and corn safely stored in the barn. Fall was in the air, with cool days and light frost on the ground at night. The ice on our grass crunched under my feet as I walked across the yard and down the path to the barn. Cricket saw me coming and snorted out a puff of air that changed to a small cloud and then evaporated.

I opened the barnyard gate and stepped inside as she walked toward me expecting some attention. I gently rubbed her nose, stroked her muscular neck, and walked toward the barn as she turned to follow. I loved all our animals, but Cricket, with her big brown eyes and dark mane, was my favorite. The big Clydesdale was as gentle as she was strong, with muscular shoulders and powerful legs that could pull a wagon loaded with oak firewood and then gently nudge my arm while I unhooked her harness at the end of the day.

Thanksgiving was approaching; days were cool with a light frost on the ground at night. With the harvest complete, we fed the livestock before dark and retreated to the house as the sun set and the temperature dropped below freezing. After an early supper, we always gathered around the potbelly stove to warm ourselves and listen to the radio. The Sears catalog that rested on top of the wood box beside the stove was torn and dog-eared from constant use. Pages were missing from the linen and silverware sections and had been used to start the morning fire, while other sections were intact for reading beside the fire.

My aunt moved about the kitchen washing and putting away dishes while I sat by the stove with the catalog on my lap, opened to the gun section. As I concentrated, she said, "Do you see anything there that you like?"

"Yes," I answered but did not want to mention my favorite. She laid her dish towel on the counter, walked to my side, and placed her hand on my shoulder. Looking down at the guns on the page, she said, "Which one do you like?" I pointed to the Stevens semiautomatic 22 rifle with a steel-blue barrel, handmade blond wooden stock, and military shoulder strap and said, "It's the best one Sears has. It's beautiful."

She paused and quietly said, "We don't have the money to afford that."

I looked up at her and said, "I was just looking. They have a single-shot that is a lot cheaper. If I save my money, I might be able to buy it someday."

She returned to the kitchen counter, picked up the towel, and said, "Maybe in the spring, if things get better."

Christmas was two weeks away, and our teachers kept us busy decorating the classrooms. Two of my friends found mistletoe growing in a tree, brought small branches to school, and gave them to their buddies. We had heard that if you held a piece over a girl's head, she would give you a kiss. We were willing to give it a try. It didn't work. Some girls screamed and others laughed, but all ran away. I was not sure I wanted a kiss and was relieved that the idea didn't work. So much for mistletoe.

I thought back to my last Christmas at home with Mom and Dad. We had a small tree about three feet high in the living room. I did not know where Dad got it, but it was so beat up I thought it had been dragged behind a truck. Limbs were missing, and those that were still attached drooped and had bare spots. Mom made popcorn, and we strung it on thread and draped it around the tree in an attempt to deal with its sad condition. Dad came home with a set of colored lights that almost never worked. When one went out, the entire set stopped working and we had to swap bulbs until the burned-out one was found and replaced. It was too much work, and after a while we decided to leave the lights off.

Several presents decorated the floor around the tree, and one was addressed to me. The box was about two feet high and almost as wide with red paper that stopped me from peeking inside. Could it be a baseball glove? Maybe spike shoes; some of the kids had them, and they were really neat.

Christmas day arrived, and I ripped off the paper to find that I had been given a chemistry set. It was a wooden box that sat on its end and opened to display the wonders of chemistry. Bottles filled three shelves on one side, while all sorts of glass tubes and things filled the other. I had no idea about what to do with any of this but mumbled thanks and left it sitting open beside the tree. Later that day, I learned that if you burned sulfur, it really stunk up the house and Mom made me take everything outside. So much for chemistry. Scratch that one off my Christmas list.

I had just finished the morning feeding and looked at the house to see Uncle Joe come down the steps and walk toward the barn. Expecting a project for the day, I closed the feed room door and waited. With a twinkle in his eye, he said, "Let's hitch up the team and see if we can find a Christmas tree!"

"Great! I'll harness Mike," I said. Uncle Joe favored Cricket and would harness her and meet me at the wagon. Mike turned to face me as I stepped into his stall. The mule knew we were about to go somewhere and was not always excited about our trips. I took my time, scratched his ears, lifted the bridle, and slipped the bit into his mouth. He stood quietly while I rigged his harness and then followed me to the wagon. Uncle Joe hooked the team to the wagon while I returned to the feed room for a saw.

It was a cool, partly sunny day with a light snow on the ground. Using the wagon wheel for a step, I climbed up and sat beside my uncle as he slapped the reins and told the team to move.

Enjoying the day, we wandered about in the woods looking for a tree suited to our small living room. I pointed to one that Uncle Joe turned down because of its size and said, "It has to be less than five feet. Let's go down by the creek." He slapped the reins on the animal's rumps, and they jerked to a start. Sandy and Star trotted beside the wagon as we moved deeper into the forest.

The trees on the back lot were the tallest ones on our property. There was only dim sunlight reaching us as we wove our way between the trees in search of a suitable small pine for our home. Mike and Cricket stopped moving and began nervously stamping their feet. Cricket gave a deep whinny while shaking her head in a panic. A bobcat was crouched on a fallen log thirty feet in front of the team. Sandy stood frozen beside the wagon and growled as he looked at the big cat. He lowered his head, and the hair on the back of his neck stood up.

Star stood frozen beside Sandy and attempted a bark that sounded more like a groan than a bark. Her hind legs quivered as she poised to make a retreat if the bobcat moved.

Uncle Joe looked at me and whispered, "Look straight ahead. Don't move! That bobcat in front of us doesn't look happy."

Where was a gun when you needed one? I sat frozen as the bobcat bared its teeth and hissed in preparation for an attack. Uncle Joe, in one swift movement, jumped to the ground and ran directly at the bobcat waving his arms and screaming, "Get out of here!" Sandy barked and charged at the cat, jumping in front of Uncle Joe as he continued screaming. Star ran under the wagon to hide, and I watched from my seat with my mouth hanging open.

The bobcat turned and ran deeper into the woods. It was no longer a threat, and my uncle returned to the wagon and picked up the reins to continue our search. I looked at him and said, "You scared me half to death." I was breathing hard and beginning to sweat as I wiped my hands on my pants.

He smiled and said, "It was the bobcat I was trying to scare. It's better to be aggressive with an animal like that, because it confuses the critter and it usually runs."

"What happens if it doesn't run?" I asked.

"Then your bluff didn't work, and you are in big trouble. Back off and call the dogs, because you are gonna need help!"

The wagon bounced along in the woods while I thought about how to fight a full-grown bobcat. Sandy had attacked in front of Uncle Joe but stopped short of making contact. He would help me by diverting the animal's attention. Star, our sweet little cocker, was not a fighter and would be no help. I decided that if screaming and waving my arms didn't work, then running like hell would be the fallback plan.

We found a small cedar that was growing underneath a stand of mature trees. This was a tree that would never reach sunlight, so cutting it for Christmas would not affect the forest, and it was the perfect size for our living room.

We returned to the barn to build a stand and nail it to the base of the tree. Holding each end, we carried it to the house and placed it in the corner of the living room beside the front door. Aunt Ona Belle was happy with that and had made popcorn to string on thread for decoration. She draped the string around the tree, and then stepped back and said, "It's a start, but we need more decorations. Dubbie, there's a pine tree at the back of our lot that has lots of cones. Take a bucket and gather some of the smaller ones, and we can hang them on the tree with thread."

"Yes, ma'am," I answered, slipping on my coat and starting for the door. I crossed the yard followed by the dogs as the sun began its descent behind the trees. Long shadows stretched across the field when I entered the forest in search of a pine tree that produced cones. Sandy ran in front of me in a zigzag pattern with his nose sniffing the ground in search of a rabbit. As darkness approached, the forest was quiet and I looked around enjoying the solitude. The stately pine at the back of our property was surrounded by cones that had fallen on the needles that coated the ground beneath its limbs. I gathered half a bucket of those that I thought would look good on our tree and started for the house.

After supper, we gathered around our potbelly stove to tie thread to the cones so that they could be hung on the tree. Our popcorn-decorated tree was a nice addition to the house.

Saturday is the busiest day of the week during spring and summer. Crops needed planting and attention that was interrupted on school days. Saturday became the "catch-up" day until school was out for the summer months. After the fall harvest, Saturday becomes an easy day, with little work and lots of free time.

I tucked my borrowed single-shot rifle under my arm for the trip to James Charles's house. We had built a rifle range at the back of his property, and the competition was fierce.

My knock on the kitchen door was met by Mrs. Revere. "Hi, Dubbie. Are you here for James?"

"Yes, ma'am. Is he here?" I asked. I heard movement in the kitchen, and James Charles came to the door with a rifle tucked under his right arm. Opening the door, he stepped out, looked at me, and said, "Hi. I've got a sack of empty cans down at the barn. We can use those for targets. Let's go."

Our walk to the range was a good time to talk about Christmas. The Reveres had a tall tree in the corner of their living room and had decorated the house in a festive way. Presents were stacked under the tree, waiting to be opened. Mrs. Revere always cooked a turkey with all the trimmings, which made a fun Christmas Day even more enjoyable.

James Charles looked at me and said, "I can hardly wait! It's going to be so much fun. How about you? Are you expecting anything special this Christmas?"

"Nah," I answered. "My gifts are always clothing—shirts and jeans—but they're things I need for school. I wanted a 22 rifle, but we can't afford it. Uncle Joe borrowed this one from our neighbor, and I can use it as long as I want."

Christmas morning arrived with freezing temperatures. I was warm and comfortable in my bed as dawn broke and not interested in placing my feet on the cold porch floor. I knew what to expect for Christmas. Coveralls, shirts, and socks were needed and high on the list.

The kitchen door opened, and Uncle Joe pushed open the screen and said, "Dubbie! Get up! It's Christmas!" I looked over my blankets to see his smiling face peeking through the screen. "Coffee is brewing," he said. "Come in by the stove, and I will pour you a cup."

"I'm coming," I answered as I threw back the covers and reached for my coveralls and shirt. I scampered through the door to my chair and warmed my hands beside the stove. My shoes and socks sat near the stove and were warm as toast. I pulled them on and reached for the coffee at the corner of the kitchen table.

We stood quietly around the stove enjoying the warmth until Aunt Ona Belle said, "Let's see what Santa Claus has brought. It's time to open our gifts." We each opened two gifts, all of which were clothing needed to get through the winter. I knew it was all we could afford and was thankful just to have a place to live. I thanked them as Uncle Joe turned and left the room. Minutes later, he returned with a long, flat package and laid it across my lap. Caught by surprise, I was too stunned to move.

"Don't just sit there," he said. "It's your present, so open it."

I untied the bow and carefully slipped the paper off one end of the carton. With the carton flat on my lap, the side opened easily. I looked down at a new Stevens 22 semiautomatic rifle, exactly like the one in the Sears catalog. I blinked to keep from crying and took a deep breath but was too choked up to talk. Aunt Ona Belle was smiling as Uncle Joe said, "Well, what do you think?"

I tried to swallow the lump in my throat without success and managed a weak answer, "It's the most beautiful gun I have ever seen."

Uncle Joe said, "It's yours. We wanted you to have it."

I sat smiling with the gun across my lap as I ran my fingers over the cool barrel and stroked the smooth blond stock. It was a beauty, and it was hard to believe it was mine.

Later that morning, we had breakfast, but I was too excited to eat. My uncle, enjoying the moment, said with a gleam in his eye, "Why don't we do a little target practice after breakfast? Get two or three cans, and we'll set them up on the log we used the other day."

Swallowing a mouthful of food, I said, "I'll get some cans out of the trash. My gun and jacket are on my bed. I'm ready to go." I stood, pushed back my chair, and walked around the table to the porch door. Hearing Uncle Joe's low chuckle, I turned as Aunt Ona Belle stood to clear the kitchen table. I walked back, gave her a big hug, and thanked her for my gun. Uncle Joe was standing and gave me a bear hug, and then said, "We love you and wanted you to have it!" Blinking back tears, I thanked him, turned, and started to the door.

Aunt Ona Belle looked at her husband and said, "It's a sunny day and not very cold. Have fun teaching Dubbie how to shoot his new gun. I am going to stay here and cook us up a good Christmas dinner."

Uncle Joe had two boxes of shells, a supply that was more than adequate. During the next three hours, I learned several ways to shoot, hold the gun, and steady my aim using a limb or log for support. The prone position on the ground was the most challenging, but with his help, those became my most reliable shots. The gun fired as good as it looked. I was having a fantastic Christmas!

The afternoon had slipped away and the sun was setting over the trees when Uncle Joe said, "It's time to stop. We have to feed the animals."

I opened the chamber to my new rifle, the empty shell casing ejected, and the gun remained locked in the open position. It could not accidentally fire, and I threw it over my shoulder and followed him to the barn. Feeding took a half hour but was over just as Aunt Ona Belle rang the bell for supper. Uncle Joe started for the house as I filled the water trough and locked the feed room door.

Sandy followed me down the path beside the outhouse and into the yard. I bounded up the steps, crossed the porch, and stored the gun under my bed.

The smells from a great supper wafted across the porch and made my mouth water. I opened the screen door and stepped into a room warmed by an afternoon of cooking on a woodstove. The table was set with a golden brown turkey, bowls of corn, peas, mashed potatoes, and a plate piled high with steaming cornbread, fresh from the oven.

We took our seats and bowed our heads, and Uncle Joe said a brief blessing. As we raised our heads, I said, "Bow your heads again. I would like to say a blessing." They bowed their heads, and I closed my eyes and said, "Father, thank you for this day. Thank you for sending me here to live with Aunt Ona Belle and Uncle Joe. I love them very much. Amen."

As we raised our heads, my aunt wiped away tears. Uncle Joe remained silent with his head down while rearranging his plate and tea glass. I sipped my tea while waiting for him to start the meal.

The meal was excellent, followed by a dish of warm apple pie topped with ice cream. I helped clear the table and dried the dishes as Aunt Ona Belle washed. Uncle Joe sat by the stove tinkering with the radio in search of a station. It was a day I would always remember.

With the dishes done, I slipped out to the porch to get my gun and bring it inside. It was clean, but I wanted to break it apart and rub it down with gun oil on a soft cloth. Uncle Joe watched as I rubbed the barrel and said, "It will last you the rest of your life if you take care of it."

I looked up and answered, "I know it will. I'll clean it after every use and always keep it oiled so it won't rust."

"Good boy," he answered, placing another stick of wood in our potbelly stove.

I sat back in my chair with the gun across my lap and thought that this was the best Christmas ever and I would always remember this day.

Chapter Twenty
The Watermelon Patch

Winsome Manard was respected as a farmer and liked by everyone in the area. His muscular six-foot frame and long, thin legs gave the appearance of a larger man. Gray-streaked brown hair, piercing blue eyes, and a broad nose over a wide mouth produced a friendly smile that inspired people to smile back as he talked.

He purchased a farm and small acreage on his thirtieth birthday and added surrounding plots over the next fifteen years to develop one of the largest farms in the area. He and his wife, Susie, produced corn, tomatoes, strawberries, pumpkins, and watermelons for markets in the Little Rock area.

Win knew that high school kids believed that swiping a watermelon from a patch was sport. Watermelons growing in a field beside a road were overly tempting to teenagers looking for excitement on a Saturday night. He knew this and decided to plant his melons in a field at the back of his property. He hoped that they would go unnoticed as the crop grew to maturity.

His well-thought-out plan proved to be the ultimate challenge to teenagers in search of Saturday night fun. A melon swiped from the Manard patch was a badge of honor to be bragged about the following week at school.

Win had been a victim of these Saturday night raids over the years and felt that it was his duty to catch anyone roaming his field after dark. He inspected his melons every Friday as they grew to full ripeness. Walking the patch, he thumped some of the larger melons. The thunk,

thunk, thunk told him they would be ready to market the next week. Tuesday would be his day to truck them into town for sale to grocers stocking their shelves for weekend shoppers. It was a job he looked forward to and enjoyed.

Farmers have a communications network that would make Ma Bell pale with envy. Their nerve center in our area was the potbelly stove at the country store. Any trip to town required a mandatory stop at the store. The black six-foot-high cast-iron wood- stove resting against the back wall of the store was surrounded by chairs, stools, and wood crates used by visitors to get comfortable as they joined the day's conversation. Talk about crops, complaints about the weather, gossip, and tall tales about recent events were all covered if you had time to stay and participate.

Win walked to the back of the store and took a seat on a crate beside the rocking chair. Several men sitting around the stove nodded hello as he said, "Are any of you raising watermelons this year?" He waited for an answer.

One farmer answered, "I'm raising one acre, and they are looking good. I plan to sell 'em at the weekend farmer's market when they are ready."

Win nodded and said, "I've got five acres, and they are the best I have had in years. They are about ready. I plan to pick on Monday and drive them to market on Tuesday."

Win looked at me and said, "Dubbie, do you want to help me load melons on Monday?" I nodded yes and continued to sit on a crate beside the stove.

. Win was easy to work for and paid in cash at the end of each day.

Greg sat on a stool beside the stove, stretched as he crossed his legs, and said, "Have you had any raids by schoolkids this year? You damn near need a guard to protect a big crop like that."

Win nodded and said, "I'm worried about this weekend. I may spend the night in the patch with my shotgun."

Roy moved back and forth in his rocking chair smoking his pipe and said, "Why don't you load your shells with rock salt? It stings but won't kill anybody, and it sure sends a signal for everyone to stay out of your patch."

Win thought quietly and said, "That sounds like a good idea. I'll take some salt back with me and load some shells before Saturday."

Leon leaned back in his chair looking at Win and said, "Did you hear about what happened to Billy Evans last week when he was dusting cotton at the Stratford farm?"

Mark sat on a wooden crate beside the stove whittling on a piece of wood and asked, "No, what happened?"

"I always thought he flew that plane too low. He used to brag about having leaves from cotton plants on his wheels when he returned to the airport. Well, he couldn't pull up enough to miss the power lines at the end of one of his runs, hit the lines, and crashed."

Roy rocked forward in his chair and asked, "Damn, did he live through it?"

"Yep, but just barely. The plane didn't burn, but he was busted up in the crash. He's still in the hospital, but they say he is going to be all right."

Roy nodded and said as he looked around the room, "That's good. He gets a little crazy sometimes but is a good boy. I hope he gets well."

Mark nodded in agreement and said, "Last summer, he landed his plane on the road beside the 76 station, got out, bought a Coca-Cola, jumped back in his plane, and took off. I don't know many people that would do that."

Several men laughed as Win said, "You could not pay me enough money to get in a plane and dust cotton. You have got to be a little crazy to like that kind of work."

Roy nodded and added, "Crazy or just plain dumb."

Laughing, Win stood and said to the clerk, "I'll take a small bag of rock salt, the smallest you have." The clerk placed the bag on the counter and said, "That will be fifty cents." Win dug in his pocket, produced two quarters, paid the man, and started to his truck.

I followed along and spoke as he opened the door to his truck.

"Mr. Manard, Monday is no problem for me." I said, " Could you use some help today?"

"I sure could," he answered. "In fact, I could use some help with the afternoon feeding. Throw your bike in the back of the truck, and come with me."

Win lowered the truck's tailgate and helped me lift my bike inside. He slammed the tailgate as I opened the passenger door and stepped inside to my seat. I looked forward to the work, but throwing hay around with a pitchfork needed some preparation. Hay down the back of your shirt always caused an itch, and it was wise to chew gum so you kept your mouth closed. The adults chewed tobacco, but I was not old enough to participate. With no gum and an open-neck shirt, I knew I would need a bath that night. The feeding went fine until a bull chased me and I jumped into the back of the wagon, while Mr. Manard roared with laughter.

"You are pretty fast on your feet, kid," Mr. Manard said, smiling.

"Nothing gets you going better than a bull running at you with his head down," I answered. "I just have never had any luck trying to make friends with a bull! Running like hell is the answer."

Mr. Manard shook his head and laughed as we loaded the last rack with hay. I took a seat at the back of the wagon with my feet dangling over the side as he started the tractor and drove to the barn. When he stepped down from the tractor seat I thanked him for the work and mounted my bike for the ride to our house.

The next morning Several cows lingered at the rear of the barn for their ration of hay as dawn glowed above the treetops beside their pasture. Win opened the front and back barn doors and hitched the tractor to the wagon, which was loaded with enough hay to feed the herd. The cows followed along as he stopped at each rack to load it with hay. The racks were full and the wagon was empty as he slipped into the seat on the tractor for the short ride to the barn. Lights were on at the house, coffee was on, and Susie would be cooking breakfast.

The sun's rays beamed through the kitchen window, lighting the table as he walked across the porch to the door. Glancing through the window, he could see Susie opening the oven door to inspect her biscuits. Her worn jeans and long-sleeve flannel shirt were covered with a white apron printed with red flowers. Expecting a busy day, she had pinned her shoulder-length blond hair in a tight bun.

He stepped through the door into the kitchen. She looked up from the stove and said, "Good morning. Coffee is still hot." She reached for the pot, poured a cup, added cream, and placed it on the table.

Win pulled back his chair, slipped into the seat in front of his cup, picked up his spoon, and stirred to cool the brew. Lifting a spoonful to his lips, he slurped and said, "It's going to be a beautiful day—not a cloud in the sky."

The eight-foot-long rectangular table was the nerve center of their farm. Worn from years of use and surrounded by six wooden chairs, it was the centerpiece of the room. Three wood-frame windows provided light and could be opened for ventilation when needed. A hutch against the back wall had glass doors and display shelves stacked with china that had been collected during their marriage.

Susie turned to the stove, opened the oven door to check her biscuits once more, and said, "They are almost done. Do you want sausage with your eggs, or bacon?" The smell of biscuits drifted across the room as she talked.

"Just eggs," he said. "I have a lot to do today, and a big breakfast will just slow me down."

"Are you going to need me to help?" she asked. "I want to wax the living room floor but will put it off if you need me outside."

"I have several things to do but expect to finish by noon. I can do my jobs alone, so you do your floor and we can take the afternoon off."

Eggs sizzled in an iron skillet as they talked. She placed two on Win's plate and one on hers, along with buttered biscuits still warm from the oven. Carrying the plates to the table and taking her seat, she asked, "How do the watermelons look? Are they about ready for market?"

"Yes, I plan to pick them Monday and take them to town the next day. The crop looks good, and I am worried about some midnight runs by kids this weekend. I am going to load that little 410 shotgun with rock salt and hide in the field Saturday night. Rock salt is not that dangerous, and the noise from the gun will probably make them pee their pants."

Susie frowned, but she knew her husband had his mind made up and no amount of pleading could get him to change. She worried that someone might get hurt and said, "Why don't you just shoot the gun over their heads so that the salt will fall on them? That should make them think they are being shot at and scare them away."

Win raised his left hand to his lips, rubbed his chin, and said, "That might work. I don't want to hurt anybody; I just want my watermelons left alone."

He pushed his chair back from the table, took a final sip of coffee, and stood. Susie turned from the stove, walked to the table, gave him a brief kiss, and said, "Just be careful and don't hurt anyone. It's not worth it for a watermelon."

"I know," he said. "It's more than just one watermelon. I don't want my patch supplying melons to every kid in the area. I want it stopped."

He turned, crossed the kitchen, opened the door, and stepped onto the porch.

He walked to the truck and reached through the open window for the bag holding the salt. It was more than was needed but was the smallest amount that could be purchased. With the bag in his right hand, he walked inside the barn, opened the tack room, and set the bag on a wooden chair resting against the wall just inside the door. The left wall of the room had wood pegs that held bridles and harness that had been collected over the years. A round wood post along the back wall held two well-oiled saddles. A dusty shelf above the saddles was stacked with parts used for repairs and the box of shells Win needed to prepare for his guard duty at the melon patch.

Opening the carton, he removed three shells—the amount the pump shotgun would hold—sat in the doorway, and reached in his pants pocket for his knife. The front of the shells opened easily, and he dumped the BB-size shot into a trash basket beside the door and filled each shell with pellets of salt. He loaded one shell into the gun, jacked it into the chamber, and slipped the other two into the reserve. He stood and leaned the weapon against the wall, and shut and locked the door so that he could begin the day's chores.

The sun was setting behind the trees as I fed the livestock. I was allowed to stay out late on Saturday night and planned to ride my bike to see James Charles after supper. Jimmy and J.C. would be there, and it would be a fun evening.

My aunt rang the bell as I finished feeding Cricket, and I returned the pail to the feed room, closed the door, and started toward the house. Sandy and Star appeared beside me as I walked up the path. They were expecting their meal, so I would feed them first and then have supper.

I crossed the porch, opened the screen door, and stepped inside to the kitchen. My aunt said, "I made us a meat loaf and have some corn on the cob. Are you hungry?"

"Yes, ma'am, but I need to feed the dogs before we sit down. Sandy is looking through the screen door watching my every move. Look at the drool hanging out the side of his mouth. That's one hungry dog," I said, laughing.

Aunt Ona Belle turned to look at the dog, smiled, and said, "I think you'd better feed him before he tries to break through the screen."

The dogs wagged their tails and followed as I crossed the porch carrying two dishes of food. The sun had set, but a wire from the house was attached to a tree with a lightbulb dangling from a socket. I set the dishes near the tree, reached up, and pulled the chain to light the backyard. The dogs noisily attacked their food as I returned to the house.

Uncle Joe was seated at the table spooning sugar into his tea. As I walked to my chair, he added lemon, stirred, and said, "Are you going down to James Charles's house tonight?"

"Yes, sir," I said. "Jimmy and J.C. are going to meet me there, and we will probably go for a bike ride to the creek."

Aunt Ona Belle handed the plate of meat loaf to Uncle Joe, who forked a slice, placed it on his plate, and passed the dish to me. I took a slice and set the dish in the center of the table beside a platter piled high with steaming ears of corn. I slipped an ear onto my plate, using my thumb and one finger because they were so hot.

"Our corn is looking good," Uncle Joe said. "It's almost three feet high, but we need to chop the grass before it takes over the corn and messes up our crop. I want to start early, so don't stay out too late."

Buttering the ear of corn with my knife, I said, "Yes, sir. I'll get a good night's sleep and be ready."

Win finished dinner and settled into his easy chair to read the paper. The sun had set, but he intended to wait until nine o'clock before taking up his post in the watermelon patch. Susie walked into the room. He looked up and said, "How about making me a thermos of coffee to take to the field? It's going to be a little cool out there, and a cup of coffee would be nice."

She nodded and returned to the kitchen to begin her search for the thermos. The rattle of pots increased as she went from cabinet to cabinet, moving pots around with no results. Win thought, *She's tearing the kitchen apart. I had better help.* He folded his paper, stood, and stepped into the kitchen. Susie had her back to him and was standing on a chair with her head inside a cabinet above the stove. He gave her a playful pat on the fanny and said, "How's it going?"

Surprised, she jerked, bumped her head against the top of the cabinet, and said, "Winnnnnnn, I'm looking for your thermos. We haven't used it in years, and I can't remember where I put it."

"Have you looked in the pantry?" he asked. "It might be in there."

She stepped down from the chair and crossed the room to the pantry door.

Win returned the chair to the table as she entered the pantry to resume her search. Shelves stacked with canned goods and sealed mason jars filled the three pantry walls. Susie spotted the top of the thermos behind her canned peaches on a shoulder-high shelf and shuffled the peaches around so that she could retrieve her prize. With the thermos in hand, she called to Win, "I found it."

"Great," Win answered, and he returned to the living room to finish reading his paper.

I was the last one to arrive at the Revere farm. The guys were at the barn waiting for me. I parked my bike beside theirs, entered the gate, and walked to the barn. Jimmy had a straw dangling from his mouth and was bouncing a beat-up tennis ball against the wall of the barn. J.C. sat on the tractor seat, and James Charles sat on the edge of the water trough making ripples with his right hand.

J.C. looked down from his perch on the tractor and said, "What are we going to do tonight?"

"We could ride our bikes down to the creek and look for night crawlers," I answered. "We are going to need some for fishing tomorrow."

"You want to do something that is really fun?" James Charles said. "The Manard farm has a watermelon patch at the back of their property. We could slip down there later tonight and swipe one. It's so far from the house they can't see us down there."

Jimmy pulled the straw from his mouth and said, "I have never swiped a watermelon. You could get in trouble doing that."

"Nah," James Charles answered. "High school kids do it all the time."

"They drive cars, and all we have are bikes," I said. "How are we going to carry a watermelon and ride a bike?"

"I have a basket on my bike," Jimmy said. "If we get one that will fit in the basket, I can carry it."

Win slipped into his jacket, picked up the thermos, crossed the porch, and bounded down the steps toward the barn. It was a cloudless night with stars twinkling and a thumbnail moon that provided enough light as he walked. Opening the barn door to retrieve his gun, he thought, *This isn't my best idea, but I am into it and can't call it off now.*

With the shotgun over his right shoulder and the thermos in his left hand, he crossed the barnyard toward the back lot. As his eyes adjusted to the darkness, the moon provided enough light to navigate across the field to the trees at the front edge of the melon patch. An oak tree at one corner of the patch stood watch over the field. Win decided that was the place to be. He seated himself at the base of the tree, leaned against the trunk, and laid his shotgun on the ground beside his right leg.

The moonlight on the melon patch made the field look beautiful. Win took a deep breath and puffed out steam as he relaxed against the tree. The quiet was broken by the call of a nearby owl. An hour passed, and his chin collapsed on his chest as he dozed off.

James Charles stopped his bike beside the road at the edge of the Manard farm. As the other bikes skidded to a stop, he said, "The melon patch is at the back of their property beside a stand of trees. If we stay in the woods, we can reach the patch without being seen."

We hid our bikes in the tall grass beside the road and stepped into the edge of the woods. I stopped walking, kept my voice low, and said, "We don't need all four of us to get one watermelon. When we get to the patch, one of us should get the melon while the other three wait at the edge of the trees."

"That's a good idea," Jimmy said. "Who wants to go get the melon?"

J.C. answered, "Let's draw sticks, three long and one short. The short one goes in for the melon while the rest of us wait."

I broke four toothpick-size sticks off a bush, and made three the same length and one short. Shuffling them in my hands behind my back, I said, "I'll hold them up in my right hand with them sticking up the same length."

Jimmy looked at me and said, "What about you? You'll know which one is short."

"Okay," I answered. "I'll take the last stick. If it's the short one, then I go get the melon."

We pulled the sticks, and I opened my hand with the last stick and we compared lengths. Jimmy had the short stick; we crept through the trees toward the patch. J.C. motioned us close and whispered, "No more talking from this point in case someone is watching the field. Voices carry on a night like this."

We nodded agreement and took our positions in line behind James Charles. Stopping at the edge of the field, he pointed at Jimmy and motioned him into the patch. We remained crouched in the undergrowth at the edge of the trees.

Jimmy crouched low, entered the patch, and began searching for the right-size melon. We waited and several minutes passed, but it seemed like hours. Jimmy moved about in a crouch but stood out against the glow of the moon. Finally, holding a melon football style, he turned and ran toward the woods.

The rustling of leaves rousted Win from his slumber. Half-awake, he saw Jimmy pass less than twenty yards away as he ran from the field. Caught by surprise, he picked up his gun, raised it to his shoulder, and shot at the person running toward the woods. The exploding gun broke the quiet with a boom equal to a Civil War cannon.

Most of the rock salt hit Jimmy's buttocks, with some lodged in his back. He screamed, continued to run holding the watermelon, and disappeared into the undergrowth beneath the trees.

The shotgun blast was our motivation to leave the area. The short trip back to our bikes was taken at a dead run. Jimmy arrived, laid the melon on the ground, and said, "I've been shot! Someone was in the patch, and they shot me! My back is burning like crazy. Someone look at it and tell me how bad I'm hurt." With both hands on his behind, he danced around the grass as he talked.

I stepped behind him and raised his shirt. I could see several spots oozing blood and said, "Hold still. There are several small holes, and some blood is coming out. They are not big and don't look deep. I don't know much about rock salt, but I'll bet that's what it is. Your pants have holes in them. How does your butt feel?"

"It hurts!" Jimmy moaned, pulling down his pants so I could check the damage.

"It looks like most of the shot hit your ass," I said. "Your pants are torn up and the spots are bleeding, but not bad."

"Not bad? What do you mean, *not bad*!?" Jimmy said, continuing his dance with a pained look on his face. "I've been shot, and my ass is burning like it's on fire. *It's bad!*"

James Charles said, "Let's go back to my barn. I have some iodine in the tack room, and that should help."

Jimmy picked up his bike, swung a leg over the seat, and remained standing. "Can you sit on the seat?" I asked as I placed the watermelon in his basket.

"No," he said. "I'll pedal standing up."

James Charles jumped on his bike and said, "Let's get out of here before someone shows up and takes another shot at us."

No cars passed as we pedaled to the Revere farm. James Charles opened the tack room door, stepped inside, and turned on the light. We followed and closed the door to keep from being seen.

"We can see better with the light," I said, looking at Jimmy. "Take your clothes off so we can look you over."

I watched as he took off his shirt and pants. He was pale, sweating, and disoriented. I stepped behind him and could see that some of the salt had barely penetrated the skin.

The bleeding had stopped. I said, "Does anyone have a pocketknife? I can get some of the salt out with a knife." James Charles produced a knife, and I dug the salt out of the holes while Jimmy groaned in protest. J.C. smeared iodine on an open hole I had cleaned, and Jimmy screamed in pain. I dropped the knife, placed my hand over his mouth, and said, "You have to be quiet, or we are going to wake the family." Jimmy nodded, and I removed my hand, picked up the knife, and continued digging salt out of the punctures.

Iodine on the wounds burned at first but then seemed to relieve Jimmy's pain. He dressed while we cut the watermelon and enjoyed a slice before leaving for home. Jimmy joined us but was in too much pain to enjoy our prize. Giving up after two bites, he dumped his watermelon in the trash and said, "I am hurting too much to eat. I am going to go home, slip into bed, and try to get some sleep"

I looked at his torn shirt and said, "You need to get rid of your clothes, or your mom will know you have been shot."

"Don't worry" he answered, "I'll hide them under my bed and throw them out when no one is around. My problem is my back. I can't work outside with my shirt off for a couple of weeks, until the spots have time to heal."

I watched as he mounted his bike and said, "Take it easy. Let's get together tomorrow," as he turned and pedaled across the barnyard.

Chapter Twenty-One
The Target

Win had not intended to shoot anyone. The shot was an automatic reflex while he was half-awake. The gun fired, the boy screamed, and it sounded like a direct hit. His breath came in gulps, and his heart raced. He walked to the edge of the woods. There was no blood; the wounded person had disappeared into the woods. In the darkness, it was impossible to follow his trail.

He returned to the tree, picked up the thermos, and walked across the field to his barn in shock. His hands shook as he returned the gun to the tack room. With two pumps of the gun, he ejected the unused shells, returned them to the box, and leaned the gun against the wall beside the saddle post.

This was a real stupid idea, he thought while locking the door. *I might have killed someone over a damn watermelon.* He entered the house too shaken to go to bed. He sat in his easy chair nursing a double bourbon until dawn broke.

Win heard the bed creak as Susie sat up and reached for her robe. Standing, she threw the robe over her shoulders and walked to the kitchen to place coffee on the stove. Win entered the room, walked to the table, and slipped into his chair as she turned and said, "Hi, sweetie. Did anything happen last night?"

He frowned and said, "I shot someone last night. I didn't mean to, but I did. He kept running, and I don't know how bad he was hurt. For all I know, I could have killed the guy."

Susie was stunned. Her mouth hung open and she stood frozen, looking at Win as he talked. "What happened?" she asked.

Win said, "I was sitting on the ground leaning against a tree and fell asleep. I don't know how long I was asleep, but I woke up just as someone ran past me carrying a melon. I picked up the gun and shot at his back as he entered the woods. I know I hit him because he screamed. He kept running and disappeared into the woods. I checked the area where I shot him, and there wasn't any blood." He continued, "I came back here but was too worked up to sleep and poured myself a drink to try and think about what to do next."

"If the person you shot was hurt bad, he would go to the hospital," she said. "If you call the emergency room, they should tell you if anyone came in with a gunshot wound."

"That's a good idea," Win said as he walked to the phone on the kitchen wall. When the switchboard answered, he said, "I need to speak with the head nurse in emergency."

The line clicked, and after several rings, a voice said, "Emergency room." Win took a deep breath, let it out, and said, "Can you tell me if anyone came in during the night last night with a gunshot wound?"

The nurse hesitated but then said, "I worked the graveyard shift last night, and it was a quiet evening. No gunshot victims; it was an easy evening."

Her comment about "graveyard" reminded him to ask, "Were any deceased brought in?"

"Yes," she answered. Win gasped as she continued, "One older man died of a heart attack, but that was it."

Win thanked her, said good-bye, took a deep breath, and turned to share the news with Susie. Puffing out air, he said, "No one checked in at the hospital. I don't think I killed anybody. I must have hit him when I fired, because of the way he yelled. Either that, or I scared the hell out of him and he screamed."

He paused, scratched his head, and continued, "I don't think rock salt can cause that much damage. It's not like I was using buckshot."

Susie nodded and said, "All my life I have heard stories about people being shot with rock salt for stealing watermelons. I have never heard of anyone killed or even seriously injured. Rock salt burns but just barely penetrates the skin. It's painful but goes away in a couple of days."

Win rubbed his nose with his finger and said, "I hope you are right. After I take care of the livestock, I'm going to drive to the store to see if there any tales flying around about someone being shot last night."

As he fed the livestock, he decided to keep quiet about what had happened in the field. That is, unless someone had admitted being shot and talked about it. Sunday was always an active time at the store, and he planned to arrive before noon and take a seat around the stove.

Susie watched out the kitchen window as Win opened the door to his truck, stepped inside, and started the engine. She was concerned, knowing that Win was scared, but she doubted there was a problem. The person Win had tried to shoot might never admit to stealing a watermelon and getting shot at. After all, having a load of rock salt in your ass is not exactly a badge of honor. *Yes*, she thought, *this will blow over.*

Win parked in front of the country store, stepped out of the truck, and was greeted by several people on the porch. He waved, slipped out of his jacket, and laid it on the seat before closing the door.

The talk was about cotton as he pulled up a chair in front of the stove.

Roy slipped into the seat of the rocking chair and said, "I was down at the cotton gin yesterday, and the line to unload had over fifteen wagons in it. Most of them were from the Monroe farm. I hear their cotton crop is the best they have ever had."

Mark smiled and answered, "Yep, and they aren't the only one. Everybody that planted cotton this year is having a hell of a crop. It's about time! The last couple of years haven't been so good."

Several men nodded as Greg walked to the back of the store, looked at Win, and said, "I hear you've got a good watermelon crop this year. Is that right?"

Win inhaled a deep breath and said, "Yes, and I plan to bring half of them to market on Tuesday. The crop is so good it's going to take more than one trip, so I intend to do the rest of them the following week."

"Did you use any of that rock salt you bought in here last week?" asked the man at the counter.

"I bought the smallest bag you could get, but when you are loading 410 shotgun shells it's a lifetime supply," he answered and waited to see if anyone knew what he had done.

Leon leaned on the back legs of his chair as he rubbed his chin and said, "I've heard that if you shoot one thief, they won't bother your farm anymore. Word gets out, and they know better than to come around."

Win sat quietly thinking, *Here it comes.*

Leon frowned and continued, "Several years ago, a high school kid got shot stealing a melon on a farm down south. I understand that rock salt burns like hell but after a couple of days goes away."

Roy leaned forward in his rocking chair and with a chuckle said, "And it's not nearly as dangerous as bird shot. Rock melts out of the hole it makes and is not a problem. That is, other than hurting like hell."

Win listened quietly as the conversation moved through several subjects, but it never returned to watermelons. After an hour, he left the store feeling that his secret was intact. He returned to his truck, slipped into his jacket, and drove home.

Chapter Twenty-Two
A Hospital Visit

I crossed the porch, sat on my bunk bed, and began untying my shoes. I stopped suddenly when I realized my aunt and uncle were in the kitchen talking about my mother. Eavesdropping on conversations was my specialty, and I sat back to listen.

Aunt Ona Belle said, "We need to find Alice. We know she is in the hospital. My guess is that it is the county asylum in Little Rock. Do you think we ought to try there?"

Uncle Joe stroked his chin in thought and said, "That's a good place to start. Call them and ask if they have her as a patient."

"I'll call tomorrow," she answered. "If I can find her, I might be able to locate Wesley. He has dropped out of sight—hasn't even taken the time to call or write Dubbie. He is one sorry human being."

The sun was up and the day was starting to warm as I walked to the house, thinking about breakfast. I crossed the porch, opened the kitchen door, and stepped inside, enjoying the smell of biscuits baking in the oven. Uncle Joe was seated at the table with a cup of coffee in his hand. I used a towel to lift the metal pot off the stove and said, "Are you ready for more?" He pushed his cup across the table and said "thanks" while I filled it to the brim.

Aunt Ona Belle stacked hot biscuits on a plate and stepped to the table to place them beside a dish of scrambled eggs. I filled her cup on the kitchen counter and reached for my cup on the shelf above the sink, filled it with coffee, and set it on the table next to my plate. The chair scraped the floor as I pulled it back to take my seat and stir sugar into my steaming cup. I reached for a biscuit, cut it in half, and buttered both sides. My aunt watched, quietly sipping her coffee, while I reached for an open jar and spooned honey on and around the biscuits.

She continued to watch me and spoke quietly, "Dubbie, I think I know where your mother is." I looked up as she continued, "I believe she is in the county hospital in Little Rock."

I lost interest in my food and sat back in my chair and waited for her to continue. Our eyes locked as she said, "I'm going to call the hospital after breakfast and try to find out if she is a patient. Would you like to listen to the conversation?"

Thinking about how great it would be to see my mom, I smiled and said, "Yes, ma'am, I sure would." I finished eating, helped clear the table, and dried the dishes while Aunt Ona Belle washed.

I sat on the living room chair watching my aunt as she placed the telephone on her lap and began to dial. I leaned forward, and she held the receiver away from her ear so that I could hear the conversation.

After several rings, the line clicked and a high female voice said, "County Hospital."

After a pause, my aunt said, "I am calling to inquire about Alice Black and believe she is a patient there. Please check and tell me if that is correct."

The voice said, "One moment, please." There was a clunk as she laid the receiver on the table.

I sat frozen watching my aunt and waiting for the operator to return to the phone. My chest pounded as minutes passed that seemed like hours.

Finally, the voice said, "Yes, she's a patient of Dr. Benson's."

"Thank you," my aunt answered. "Please transfer me to Dr. Benson's office."

After several rings, a nurse answered, "Dr. Benson's office."

Aunt Ona Belle said, "I am calling about Alice Black, a patient of Dr. Benson's. Is he available to speak with me?"

"Please hold on a minute," she answered. "I will see if he is available."

Several minutes passed, the line clicked, and a deep baritone voice said, "This is Dr. Benson. Can I help you?"

"Yes," Aunt Ona Belle answered. "I am a relative of Alice Black's. Her son is living with me and would like to visit his mother. Is she allowed to have visitors?"

The doctor hesitated and then said, "Her condition is very fragile. There are times when she will not communicate and is out of touch with reality." Aunt Ona Belle heard a deep sigh as he continued, "How old is her son?"

"He is eleven but mature for his age," she answered.

The doctor hesitated and then said, "At this stage in her treatment, you can expect a visit to be hard on the boy, but it could help his mother. When she is lucid, she always talks about her son and wants to see him. I will agree to it, but want you to limit the length of the visit to no more than a half hour. Is that acceptable to you?"

The doctor sounded concerned about my mother and reluctantly agreed to let us visit. I realized that Mom was very sick as thoughts raced through my head. Would she ever get well? What would I say to her that would help? Did "out of touch with reality" mean that she might not even know me?

Aunt Ona Belle watched me and continued to talk as I sat back and took several deep breaths and blinked rapidly, fighting for control.

"Yes," she answered, "I'll keep the visit short."

"Good," Dr. Benson answered. "I will transfer you to the switchboard, and they will give you our visiting hours."

She used a pencil to write on a pad, and then looked up at me and smiled. "We know where she is, and the doctor will let us see her. The nurse said that a week from Friday is okay for a visit. What do you think?"

I tried to speak, but with the lump in my throat could only whisper, "Yes, Friday is fine."

I crossed the porch and stepped into the yard, thinking about my mom. The doctor had nothing good to say about her progress. I wanted our visit to be good but was expecting the worst. Sandy, a natural retriever, stood beside me, tail wagging, waiting for me to throw the stick I had left on the ground beside a lawn chair. I tossed it over the fence into the barnyard. Sandy was off at a run and would be there when it hit the ground, pick it up, and return to me for the next throw. He could do this without tiring for as long as I continued to throw. He dropped the stick at my feet, and I threw it as far as I could into the corn patch beside our yard. The big setter was off at a run and would remain in the patch until he found the stick and laid it at my feet.

With each throw, the stick went farther as thoughts about Mom brought a lump to my throat and tears to my eyes. I loved her very much and didn't understand why our life was so complicated. Other families did not seem to have all these problems. They lived together, loved each other, and had a happy life. Tossing the stick again, I silently wished we could live that way.

Thoughts about Mom were constantly on my mind for the next week while I waited for Friday's visit. Aunt Ona Belle knew I was upset and with occasional hugs tried to assure me that Mom was doing okay in the hospital. I tried to believe that but knew better. I had been having bad dreams every night about Mom and the hospital. In one dream, I was surrounded by ugly people with scowls on their faces while Mom ran around in circles screaming things I could not understand. I tried to reach her, but the people around me held me back. I tried to push them away, but everything happened in slow motion and nothing I did worked. The screaming did not stop until I woke up in a cold sweat.

I reacted by staying up late at night to avoid going to bed. When bed could no longer be delayed, I slipped under the covers and lay there wide awake until well after midnight, avoiding sleep and the dreaded dreams it would bring.

My aunt noticed the dark circles around my eyes and asked, "Dubbie, are you getting enough sleep?"

"Yes, ma'am," I answered.

"It doesn't look like it." She placed her hands on my head and turned my face up so she could look in my eyes. Looking down, she pursed her lips, shook her head, and said, "Sit down. I'll fix you a glass of iced tea, and let's talk."

I took my seat at the table and watched as she poured tea into a glass and added sugar and lemon. She crossed the kitchen, handed me the glass, and took her seat at the end of the table.

"I know you are upset. Do you want to talk about it?"

My aunt was a good listener, which made talking easier. We talked for the next hour about the family, and I left the table feeling better. That night, for the first time in almost a week, I slept without having the recurring dream.

Finally, Friday arrived. I was up early, finished my chores, and returned to the house to prepare for the trip to Little Rock. I took a bath, washed my hair, and went out to the porch to put on clean jeans and a shirt for the occasion. The jeans were a little short and one shoe had a sole coming off, but it was my best and I was ready to go. Uncle Joe stepped onto the porch with a bottle of rose hair oil in his hand and said, "Put some of this on your hair. It makes it easy to comb and smells good." I took the bottle, removed the cap, and shook some into the palm of my hand. The oily liquid was red but did smell a little like roses. I rubbed my hands together, ran my fingers through my hair, and said, "Thanks."

He looked me over and chuckled. "You look fine," he said, "And you smell like a rose bush!" He laughed at his joke.

I wrinkled my nose, grinned, and said, "It smells good. I'll bet that John Wayne wears it." We both laughed.

Our 1937 Plymouth was parked under a tree near the road. It was a four-door sedan, painted dark blue, with whitewall tires and chrome bumpers. Aunt Ona Belle had named it Blue Boy, and the christening had stuck. The car seemed to have a personality of its own, but with regular attention it was reliable. One of my chores was to keep it clean. I always washed it with Tide in a bucket of water. The color of the car seemed to hold up, but each time I rinsed the soap off with a garden hose, the yard around the car turned blue.

Uncle Joe held a greasy, well-used towel with both hands as he walked toward the car. I followed with a gallon bucket containing a couple of quart cans of oil and a spout. He opened the hood, pulled the dipstick, wiped it clean, and pushed it down the pipe to check the oil level. It was low, and he said, "Dubbie, add one quart. That should do it."

I opened a can while he checked the radiator water level and announced, "It's good. Finish adding the oil, and it's ready to go." I finished and tossed the empty can back into my bucket.

While my aunt backed the car down the dirt path to the road, I sat beside her and thought about the day ahead. I had not seen my mother since the men in white took her away in their van. As we started down the road, I gazed out the window at our cornfield and wondered if my mother would remember how I looked and know me when we walked into her room. Memories that I had forgotten about the bad times we had before Mom was taken away came rushing back, and my heart pounded as I gulped a deep breath and blew it out.

As the old car trudged down the gravel road, Aunt Ona Belle looked at me and saw the concern on my face. She asked, "Are you looking forward to seeing your mother?"

"Yes, I think so." I tried to avoid looking upset and watched out the window while we passed a dairy farm. Cows were grazing in the pasture, while some were standing quietly in the shade of an oak tree near the road.

"Dr. Benson told me that your mother talks about you all the time." Aunt Ona Belle continued, "I haven't seen your mother in several years and am looking forward to today."

The right side of the car bounced through several holes and settled into a rut as we rattled on while she struggled with the wheel, trying to keep the car straight. I sat quietly and looked out the window as we passed tall oak trees that filtered the sun and cast shadows across the road. I was afraid of what would happen when we reached the hospital and had doubts about making the trip.

The hospital was on a small hill surrounded by blooming magnolia trees on a manicured lawn. The road up to the building wound through the trees to a parking area just outside the main entrance. The main building was six stories high with shorter wings attached to each side.

Aunt Ona Belle braked the car to a stop directly in front of the main entrance. The building glared in the bright sunlight, and I did not want to go inside. I sat frozen in my seat. My aunt opened her door and stepped onto the tarmac. She looked through her open door at me and said, "Come on, let's go inside!"

While she waved her arm and signaled me to move, I opened the car door and stepped out. The hospital loomed over us, and I slammed the door and stood frozen beside the car. My aunt, realizing my concern, walked around the car and took my hand. She spoke, almost in a whisper, "It's going to be okay. You are going to enjoy seeing your mother. Let's walk inside." I didn't believe her but knew she was just making small talk to make me feel better. She began walking to the front entrance with me in tow. The tall double doors were propped open, and we stepped through into a twenty-foot-wide reception area with a desk at the back wall. Several unoccupied metal chairs with vinyl seats lined one wall. The windowless room was painted gray with the cold look of a military bunker. Hooded lights dangled from the fifteen-foot-high ceiling, glaring down on an off-white marble floor.

My aunt walked me toward the reception desk to talk to the nurse and make arrangements for us to see my mother. After a one-hour wait, we were escorted into a large room full of people. There was no furniture. Wooden seats attached to each of the four walls provided the only place to sit.

People were moving around. Some were making strange noises. Several screamed. Some talked but to no one—only to themselves—as they paced back and forth. I realized that this was not a hospital; it was an insane asylum. I crossed the room and sat on a bench trying to ignore all the activity. A man in an off-white gown walked the length of the room screaming, but no one seemed to notice. I leaned back trying to blend into the wall and looked down at the floor. Aunt Ona Belle took a seat beside me and looked across the room in a daze.

A door in the far wall opened, and my mother walked through. She was very thin and dressed in a worn cotton gown that hung loosely on her body. Her hair was caked and badly in need of a wash. She reminded me of a scared animal as she scanned the room in search of no one in particular. We sat along one wall, but she did not appear to notice. She remained frozen in her position just inside the door the attendant had pushed her through.

Aunt Ona Belle stood, walked toward her, and called her name, "Alice, its Ona Belle. How are you?" Mom continued to look around the room, with no response to my aunt.

Aunt Ona Belle reached out and took my mother's arm, trying to get her attention, and said, "Dubbie is here with me. Would you like to see him?"

She had not moved but continued to watch the room with her mouth hanging open.

I remained on the bench along the wall, too stunned to move. The activity in the room was almost too much to absorb. The attendant released Mom and stepped back through the door, leaving her with Aunt Ona Belle. I sat frozen looking at Mother, then at my aunt and back again, not knowing what to do.

Mom appeared to be in a trance as my aunt led her toward me, saying, "Let's go see Dubbie. He's right over here."

As they approached, Mom muttered her first words. "This is all a dream. It's not real."

Aunt Ona Belle took Mom by the shoulders and helped her to turn and sit on the bench at my side. She took her seat and continued to look straight ahead. She did not look at me. In an attempt to get her attention, I said, "Hi, Mom. It's me, Dubbie."

She did not look at me, but whispered, "This is all a dream."

I said, "It's not a dream, Mom. It's me, here for a visit." I started to sweat and felt my heart racing. I was scared but trying to keep it inside.

I looked her over as she continued her whispered chant, "This is all a dream." She repeated it over and over again. She was only five feet tall and very frail. The loose gown looked as if it would hardly stay on her body. I later learned that she weighed only fifty-five pounds. I tried repeatedly to talk to her, but she didn't answer. She did not seem to know I was at her side.

The reactions of the crazy people in the room made this appear to be unreal. I concentrated on my mother and tried to ignore the screams and rants of the people moving about, but it was impossible. A nightmare could not have been worse than this. I moved closer to Mom and placed my arm around her shoulders while she continued to gaze around the room. I wanted her to know I was there and pulled her closer and sat quietly in a warm embrace. Minutes passed as she slowly looked down and spoke in a low voice, "This is all a dream."

I hoped that she would look at me and said, "It's not a dream, Mom. It's really me. Here for a visit."

The half-hour visit passed without Mom knowing that we were there. Aunt Ona Belle sat quietly and watched while I made repeated attempts to talk with her, without success.

Finally, Aunt Ona Belle reached out to touch my shoulder and said, "Our time is up, Dubbie. We have to go." I gave my mother a hug and told her that I would come back to see her soon. She stood with slumped shoulders, her arms dangling at her sides. An attendant in a white smock took one of her arms and led her from the room while we watched.

We left the hospital and walked silently to the car. This was too much for a young boy to understand, but I tried to think it through. The lump in my throat was making it difficult to breathe. Aunt Ona Belle looked straight ahead and did not see the tears in my eyes.

Would my mother ever be well? Would she ever get out of the hospital? Would I ever see her again? Aunt Ona Belle knew I was hurting and was quiet during the drive home. I looked out the window but do not remember making the trip.

When we arrived at the farm, I sat on the porch steps and petted my dog, Sandy. His head was in my lap, and I felt a little better.

Aunt Ona Belle called out from the kitchen, "I've got a hot apple pie in here and have cut you a piece. It's on the table." She knew I was hurting and was trying to help.

I entered the kitchen as she placed a glass of milk beside the pie and said, "There's nothing like a big piece of pie to brighten a man's day."

I slipped into my seat, picked up the fork, and ate a mouthful of the warm dessert. She was right; it did make the day a little better.

The following day, Aunt Ona Belle called our family doctor to talk about our hospital visit. I listened nearby as she said, "Dubbie was very upset and didn't talk at all during the drive home."

I had no interest in the conversation, so I crossed the room, opened the screen door, and walked onto the porch, where Sandy was waiting. He licked my left hand as I sat on the steps and pulled him to my lap. Sandy loved me, and I loved him back. He was my best friend, and I needed some attention. A few minutes of quiet time with Sandy made me feel better.

The screen door creaked as Aunt Ona Belle opened it, crossed the porch, and sat on the steps beside me. We sat quietly and watched the animals move around the barnyard. She patted Sandy's back and said, "The doctor thinks we need to give your mother time to heal. He doesn't think we should visit her again until later this year. I thought I should let you know." Not knowing what to do, I nodded and said "okay" and picked up a stick for Sandy to chase.

It would be two years before I would see my mother again. Aunt Ona Belle made regular calls to the doctor and always told me what was said. Progress was slow, she said, and we talked about the hospital visit. I admitted that the room where we met Mother was a scary place. My aunt pursed her lips and said, "To tell the truth, I think about that visit almost every day. It was like a bad dream." She paused in thought, and then continued, "Sometimes I see images of it while I am in bed trying to go to sleep."

We talked when Uncle Joe was not around, and she always asked me if I was okay. I told her that I had dreamed about being locked inside the room where we met my mom and it was impossible to get out. The dream seemed to go on and on, with people yelling and screaming as I tried to hide in a corner. I remembered one thin old man with no teeth and wearing a white robe, pacing back and forth in the room while screaming. When he reached my corner of the room, he screamed in my face, but I could not understand what was said. The dream came to me again and again, always the same, seemingly endless. She listened, cocked her head in thought, and said, "You are having nightmares. I am too, and I think we need to do something about it."

It had been almost two years, but the dreams were still so vivid that she decided to talk to Uncle Joe when the time was right.

As the sun dropped behind the trees, Uncle Joe crossed the porch, opened the door, and stepped into the kitchen. I sat at the table working on a book report for school, but Aunt Ona Belle saw this was a good time and said to Uncle Joe, "Would you like some tea? I just made a pot."

He pulled a chair back from the table and said, "Sounds good. I'm done for the day."

The teakettle hissed as she poured steaming liquid into a mug and sat it in front of him. She returned the kettle to the stove, picked up her cup, and walked back to the table.

Uncle Joe stirred his tea, looked up at her, and said, "You look like you have something on your mind."

"I do," she said. "It's about Alice. I can't get her off my mind. There must be something we can do. The hospital is a nightmare." She paused to stir milk and honey into her cup. "The room where we met her was like a horror movie. Some of the people in there were scary enough to make you run for the door." I listened but continued to do my homework. She sipped tea from a spoon and continued, "It affected me, so it had to affect Dubbie."

As she refilled Uncle Joe's cup, he said, "I've heard about that hospital, and none of it was good."

"I agree," she said and continued, "There has to be some way we can help. What do you think we should do?"

Uncle Joe sat quietly in thought, sipped his tea, and said, "I don't think we can get her released from the hospital, but even if we could, we couldn't bring her here. We don't have enough room." He leaned forward, placing his elbows on the table and cupping his chin into his right palm.

Aunt Ona Belle nodded her head in agreement and said, "I'm going to call the hospital again and get the latest on her condition."

I finished my book report but remained at the table doing busywork so that I could listen to the conversation.

Uncle Joe said, "Good idea. While you are at it, see if you can find out if Wesley has been visiting her. He seems to have dropped out of sight."

Aunt Ona Belle rinsed her cup, placed it in the sink, and said, "Wesley could help if he would just quit drinking and get a job. I'll ask the hospital if they have a way to contact him."

After breakfast the next morning, Aunt Ona Belle dialed the hospital. I remained seated at the table expecting to listen to the call. Aunt Ona Belle held the phone away from her ear so that I could listen. The constant ringing was finally answered by a woman who said, "Little Rock State Hospital."

"Hello," Aunt Ona Belle said. "I am calling to ask about one of your patients, Alice Black. Please connect me with her doctor."

The voice said, "The doctor is not available. I can connect you with the head nurse, Mrs. Tidwell."

The line clicked and then rang, and a woman answered, "Hello, I'm Nurse Tidwell. Can I help you?"

Her voice was gentle, and Aunt Ona Belle warmed to her as they talked about Alice's condition. Wesley had visited Alice two times but had not been seen for several months. Aunt Ona Belle asked if they had contact information on Wesley and was told that none was available.

As the conversation ended, Aunt Ona Belle said, "Mrs. Tidwell, can I call you from time to time to see how Alice is doing?" She agreed and gave Aunt Ona Belle her direct phone number.

My aunt hung up the phone, feeling good about Mrs. Tidwell. Her concern for Alice sounded genuine. She turned to me and said, "Were you able to hear what Mrs. Tidwell said?"

"Yes, ma'am," I answered. "Thanks for holding the telephone away from your ear. I heard every word."

Mom's first year in the hospital was tightly controlled, but after the first year, Mrs. Tidwell felt that she had improved and began taking her home on weekends. Mom would stay in Mrs. Tidwell's spare bedroom and do housework as well as washing and ironing. These weekend trips were helping her to return to a normal life.

Mrs. Tidwell told Aunt Ona Belle that I was constantly in Mom's thoughts, and she felt that a weekend visit by me while Mother was at her house would be a good idea. Aunt Ona Belle agreed because a trip to the hospital would not be necessary. A visit was arranged for the following Saturday.

Mrs. Tidwell lived in a modest area of North Little Rock. Her two-bedroom clapboard house was freshly painted, and the fenced yard was neatly mowed. A large magnolia tree just inside the gate provided shade for the yard and house.

As Aunt Ona Belle parked our car beside the fence, Mrs. Tidwell opened the door and stepped onto the porch. She waved, walked down the steps to meet us at the gate, and said, "Good morning. It's a nice day for a visit." The sun was up, and the day was starting to warm.

She opened the gate as Aunt Ona Belle answered, "Good morning, Mrs. Tidwell." I stood quietly behind my aunt with my head down. I remembered our first visit and was worried about how Mom would look.

Mrs. Tidwell looked past Aunt Ona Belle to me and said, "Good morning, Dubbie. Your mother is looking forward to seeing you. Y'all come on in." As we walked toward the house, she said, "It's such a nice day, why don't we sit on the porch?" She waved a hand at the two wicker chairs sitting beside a swing that could seat three people. I slid into the closest chair, with Aunt Ona Belle beside me, as Mrs. Tidwell entered the house and called for Mom.

Mrs. Tidwell opened the screen door and stepped through, leading my mother by her right hand. Her hair was clean and swept back in a bun. The white print dress she was wearing almost reached the floor and hung loosely on her small frame. She was very thin with sunken cheeks and a hollow look in her eyes.

Not knowing what to do, I sat frozen. As they walked toward us, Mom looked dazed but smiled when Mrs. Tidwell said, "Dubbie and Ona Belle have come for a visit."

Mom continued to smile as she looked at me and said, "Hi." She knew me! I jumped up from the chair, ran to her, and threw my arms around her in a big hug. She was okay, and it warmed my heart. Holding her close, I took a deep breath and blinked back tears, thinking, *My mom is better!*

Once the ice was broken, conversation was easy. Mrs. Tidwell went inside and returned with a tray holding a pot of coffee and four thick cups. She poured steaming coffee into the mugs and handed one to me and one to my aunt. Coffee is not my favorite drink, but sugar and cream were on the tray and I added two large scoops of sugar and some cream to my cup. That made it drinkable, and I took a sip, being careful not to burn my tongue.

The next hour passed quickly. Aunt Ona Belle stood and said, "I have enjoyed our visit, but we need to get back to the farm."

Mrs.Tidwell nodded as I stood and gave Mom a hug and said, "We'll be back."

Mom took my face in her hands and said, "I need to look into those big brown eyes." She smiled and said, "You have gotten to be as tall as me. Don't worry. I'm better and will be home soon."

I looked into her eyes and knew it was going to be all right.

I walked to the car smiling and waved as we started down the road. I felt sure that Mom would get well, and that was all that mattered. I leaned back in my seat as Aunt Ona Belle said, "This was much better than our first visit. Alice has improved, and it looks like she will get well. How do you feel about it?"

"She is a lot better," I answered, "and Mrs. Tidwell is a nice lady. I really enjoyed spending time with Mom today. Maybe the nightmares I have been having will go away now."

Aunt Ona Belle continued to drive but looked over at me and said, "After today, I feel a lot better. There is an ice cream store up ahead, and I'll treat you to a cone if you're interested."

She knew my weakness for ice cream, and I answered, "That would be great. A double-dip strawberry is my favorite."

The days grew shorter as fall approached, and the trees changed from green to bright orange and red. Autumn was in the air, with crisp days and cool nights that made wearing a jacket enjoyable. I finished feeding the livestock and crossed the barnyard at a fast pace in anticipation of supper.

I crossed the porch as Aunt Ona Belle opened the kitchen door to stick her head out and say, "Supper's ready, so let's eat."

The evening meal was always the highlight of the day during the winter months. We enjoyed the warmth of our potbelly stove and talked about the day while enjoying our food.

I finished eating and moved to the couch to read the Sears catalog and dream about the things I wished we could own. Guns and farm equipment were high on the list, but when my aunt and uncle were not nearby, I would sneak a look at the women's lingerie section because the women had great butts and good-looking boobs. Times were a-changin'. Puberty was on its way!

I flipped the catalog pages and was lost in thought, and I jumped when the telephone rang. It continued in sets of three choppy rings, which was our code on the party line. I watched as Aunt Ona Belle crossed the room and picked up the receiver. "Hello," she said and waited for a response.

Her eyes flashed in anger as she began to understand the gravity of the call.

"Wesley?" she said and then shouted, "What do you want?"

She paused to listen and then said, "Dubbie has been living with us for almost two years with no help from you. Where the hell have you been all this time?"

My aunt bit her upper lip while listening to Dad talk and then said, "You are going to take Alice out of the hospital and move to Phoenix. What does the doctor say about that?" I watched my aunt's eyes as she listened to his answer. She lowered her chin to her chest and said, "What about Dubbie? Are you going to leave him here with us?"

As she listened to his response, she clenched her jaw and shook her head from side to side. Her eyes flashed, and she said, "You know you are not welcome here. We don't want you on our property. If you want to visit Dubbie, park beside the road and I'll send him out to you."

I was too young to understand the problem but knew that they were not on talking terms. When Aunt Ona Belle hung up the phone, she looked at me with a frown and said, "Your dad will be out tomorrow and wants to see you. I told him to park beside the road and wait for you to walk out to the car."

I sat on the couch and began to think about how Dad had treated Mom and me. Living alone in a house with no food was scary, but he didn't seem to care. He disappeared after Mother was taken to the hospital, and I rode my bike here because I was desperate. I did not know if I still loved my dad but knew that things were much better here than they had been living with him. I dreaded seeing him but realized that it was unavoidable.

The next day, I watched the road until Dad finally showed up.

Uncle Joe stood by the front door and said, "He's here."

Aunt Ona Belle walked from the kitchen to the front room and stared out the window with a strained look on her face. The tension in the house was so high you could cut it with a knife. I stood quietly in the center of the room with my hands in my back pockets. Aunt Ona Belle looked at me and said, "You go on."

I took a deep breath, walked out the front door, jumped down from the porch, and started toward the car with Sandy by my side. I gave him a pat and thought that it was good to have one friend.

The car looked like it had survived a wrecking derby, but miraculously it was still running. It was a 1937 two-door Plymouth so badly rusted it looked too beat-up to run. The front bumper and windshield wipers were missing. The backseat had been stacked to the roof with clothing. It was obvious he was living out of the car.

As I approached, Dad opened his door, stepped out, and leaned against the front fender alongside the hood. His six-foot frame was thin but hidden under loose-fitting jeans that needed washing and a well-worn oversized flannel shirt. His gray-streaked black hair was long and in need of cutting. His eyes had the hollow look of a man who had been on a two-week drinking binge.

The two-day growth on his face covered bloated cheeks that reached the dark areas surrounding his eyes. Glasses that needed cleaning were perched on his red nose. He looked down as I approached and avoided eye contact.

Sandy, normally easygoing and friendly, lowered his head, bared his teeth, and began a low growl. This was not a warning; the dog was upset and ready to attack. I grabbed him by his collar and shouted, "No, Sandy, no!" I wanted him to stop.

As I reached the front of the car, Dad said, "Nice dog. Is he mean?"

"No," I said. "He just doesn't like strangers."

Dad took a deep breath, blew out the air, and said, "How have you been?"

I wanted to say, *Better now that I am living here*, but decided to answer by just saying fine.

"Are Joe and Ona Belle treating you all right? How are they to live with?"

"They treat me fine and never fight," I answered. I regretted my comment and looked back at the house wishing that this was over.

Dad rolled up his shirtsleeves, taking time to think, and then said, "I guess that's better than living with me."

He looked across the road at the trees, turned, sat on the fender, and said, "I wanted to come and see you before I leave for Phoenix. I'm going to get your mother out of the hospital and move her there."

I nodded but made no other response.

He pulled a cigarette from a pack in his shirt pocket, lit it, and inhaled deeply. Blowing out smoke, he said, "Phoenix is a beautiful place. Warm all year with almost no rain. It's desert country with lots of cactus and palm trees."

I heard him talking but was too nervous to pay attention. My heart was pounding, my chest tight, and I wanted this finished and Dad gone.

Finally, he said, "Well, I have to go." He stood, opened the car door, and slipped into the seat while I watched. He started the car, looked through the open window, and said, "You be good. I'll let you know where we are when we find a place to live."

As he pulled away, I mumbled my thanks and watched the car move slowly down the road. Our brief time together was uncomfortable, and I was relieved when it was finally over. Several years would pass before I would see him again.

Uncle Joe and Aunt Ona Belle remained in the house during the entire visit. I know Dad could see them, but he made no effort to speak or even wave. They watched out the window as Dad started the car and left.

With our meeting over, I walked back to the house but was unable to tell my aunt and uncle anything that was said. My mind drew a complete blank. I could tell that they were upset by the visit. My aunt was frowning, and Uncle Joe had a grim look.

The only sound at the supper table was the clinking of knives and forks. While we ate, I remembered that Dad had talked about moving to Arizona and told them that he wanted to get Mom out of the hospital and take her to Phoenix. Uncle Joe glanced at Aunt Ona Belle while I talked. Her eyebrows went up as she listened. "He is going to try to get

Mom out of the hospital." I continued, "That's all he talked about. He said he was going to do it soon."

Uncle Joe looked across the table and said, "There's no telling what he will do. I just hope he doesn't mess up Alice's recovery."

I finished eating, carried my plate to the sink, and retreated to the porch. They were upset and I was not sure why, but I wanted to help. I could feel the tension in the house and wanted it to go away, but had no idea about what to do. They needed time to talk, and I was in the way. I walked across the porch, bounded down the steps, and, with Sandy at my heels, trotted toward the barn.

Chapter Twenty-Three
A Visit with Grandparents

The bus glided to a stop, and I stepped down while Sandy watched, wagging his tail. Giving him a pat, I started for the house. As we passed the mailbox, I said, "Go get the paper, boy!" The big dog was a natural retriever and scooped up the newspaper with his mouth as he continued his trot to our porch. It was a daily ritual always done with the wagging of his tail. He understood that I caught a school bus on weekdays and walked with me to the bus stop each morning. As I boarded the bus, he returned to the house but seemed to know that I would be back that afternoon.

Our first frost happened in October. The crops had been harvested, there was fresh-cut hay in the barn, and the pantry was stocked with newly canned fruits and vegetables. We were ready for winter but had very little money.

With the sun going down and the feeding complete, I closed and secured the door to the feed room. Sandy appeared as I started up the path and licked my hand as he wagged his tail. I stopped, gave him a pat, and scratched his ears before opening the gate to leave the barnyard. He had become my best friend and followed me everywhere.

It was dinnertime, and he waited on the porch beside my bunk as I entered the kitchen to prepare his food. Star, our little cocker, appeared and looked through the door expecting her dinner. I prepared both bowls and carried them to the yard while the dogs followed.

I returned to the kitchen, where Uncle Joe and Aunt Ona Belle were talking about bills they needed to pay. I sat quietly on a straight-back chair close to our wood-burning stove and listened to them talk. I could see the strain on my aunt's face and knew there was a problem. I also knew that I was a part of it but didn't know what to do, so I sat very still.

Uncle Joe worked hard at farming, but it did not produce enough money for a comfortable living. Summer months were easiest because crops were ripe for market and could be sold in town. Corn, tomatoes, and peas were our best crops, and we sold them to food distributors as well as at the weekend farmer's market. During the winter months, the farm produced very little income, which was the problem.

Uncle Joe looked at his wife and said, "We are going to have to have some help. That's all there is to it."

Aunt Ona Belle tugged at her ear and answered, "We could talk to Dubbie's grandparents. They live in Conway. If you drove there, you could make it in about four hours."

Uncle Joe looked across the room in thought and said, "I'll take Dubbie with me and go tomorrow, after the morning feeding."

The next morning, Uncle Joe was up earlier than usual. The house was cold. We had a frost during the night, and the rooms had cooled after the fire burned out in the potbelly stove. He restarted the fire, filled the coffee pot, and placed it on the burner.

I was half-awake on my bunk bed but heard him preparing the fire in the kitchen. The open porch was cold, but I was comfortable in my bed regardless of the weather. I was snuggled inside several handmade blankets and did not look forward to placing my feet on the cold wood floor. I regretted leaving my socks too far away to reach without getting up.

Action time. I sat up, grabbed my long-sleeve flannel shirt, slipped it on, and pulled on my pants. Picking up my shoes and socks, I hurried to the kitchen to sit next to the stove and finish dressing. The coffee smelled good and Uncle Joe poured two steaming cups, handing one to me. I was learning to drink coffee but didn't think it tasted very good. As far as I was concerned, its main purpose was a hot cup I could use to warm my hands.

Returning to the porch, I pulled on my jacket and started down the path to the barn. First priority was a stop at the outhouse. It was too cold to sit down, so I urinated standing up and put everything else off until the day warmed. We had what we called slop jars, but I did not have one on the porch. When it is cold enough, the toilet seat can frost over and cause you real problems. I had learned that the hard way by parking my bare butt on a frozen toilet seat early one morning. The frozen seat stuck to my behind, and I had to tear myself loose. I was sure my butt was bleeding, but I was not about to ask anyone to take a look. I chose suffering in silence over dropping my pants to anyone who wanted to take a look. From that point on, it was number two during the heat of midday. When you use an outhouse every day, you develop a time to do your business and that is always when the day has warmed.

Stepping out of the outhouse, I saw Sandy waiting close by. Both animals slept in the doghouse resting beside the path, just down from the outhouse. Each sleeping area had its own door that was covered by a hanging feed sack. The thick supply of straw inside each house had been well placed so that each dog would be warm and comfortable. The sloped roof was covered with tar paper that kept the straw dry when it rained. The outside had been painted red to match the barn. As I opened the feed room door, the livestock walked to their stalls. It's common for farm animals to stay out all night. If it is extremely cold, they may go into their stalls, but usually they just get under a tree. They have a coat that grows a bit during the fall, and cold is not a problem. Each knew which stall was theirs and after walking inside, turned to watch me while they waited for their feed.

I moved at a rapid pace. Even the mules seemed more serious this morning. The cool morning seemed to motivate us to get on with our assignments.

When I returned to the house, Uncle Joe was ready for the drive to Conway. The car had been checked and was prepared for the trip. A jack, spare tire, tire patching kit, hand pump, and assorted tools had been loaded in the trunk for use when needed.

The first part of the trip was over dirt and gravel roads that ran through thickly wooded forests. Tree branches hung over the road, shutting out the sun. This went on for miles but finally opened to farming country. We passed several farms with cows, horses, and mules wandering in large pastures beside their barns. Most of the barns were painted dark red. Some had an advertisement painted on their steeply sloped roofs. One said, "Better use Vitalis," and another said, "Days

Work," in large white letters. I believe that had to do with chewing tobacco, but I'm not sure.

The road wound around a farm with a fenced pasture that included the side of a grass-covered hill. Several cows, all facing the same direction, grazed in contentment. Uncle Joe looked out the window and with a twinkle in his eye said, "Look at those cows grazing on the side of the hill. Did you wonder why they are all facing the same direction?"

I looked out the window and answered, "No, I haven't thought about it."

"Well," he said, pausing for effect, "that's because they are high-side cows."

I watched the cows as we passed the hill and decided to ask, "What's a high-side cow?"

He looked over at me with a slight smile and said, "The cow's two legs that are on the high side of the hill are shorter than the two on the lower side. That way, the cow can stand straight on the hill." He snickered and continued, "You didn't know that?"

"No." I laughed, suspecting that he was kidding me, but decided to ask, "What happens when they turn around? Do they fall over?"

He was laughing so hard that he had to wipe his eyes while struggling to keep the car on the road. Finally, getting control, he attempted an answer. "Nope," he said, gasping for breath. "They can only walk one way until they get to the end of the hill. Then they kind of wobble back to the barn."

"Uncle Joe, I think you are putting me on."

"Nope." He snorted to keep from laughing. "Just look out the window. You don't see any of them facing the other direction, do you?"

I was having trouble believing what he said, but the cows were all facing the same direction and it made sense.

Just before reaching Conway, the road improved and wound alongside the Arkansas River. It was the most scenic part of the trip but no more than two miles long. The road wound back into farmland, and we entered Conway, a small town with only a few thousand people.

We stopped at the only service station in town to purchase gasoline and get directions. A slender man in grease-stained overalls walked toward Uncle Joe and said with a smile, "Afternoon. Do you need some gas?"

Uncle Joe answered, "Yes, sir. I'd like you to fill her up."

As the mechanic removed the gas cap from the car and reached for the pump nozzle, Uncle Joe said, "I have come to see Bill Martin. Do you happen to know where he lives?"

The mechanic said, "He has a Ford that I work on from time to time. Doesn't live far from here. I'll tell you how to get there."

As Uncle Joe paid for the fuel, the mechanic made change and gave directions. After a short drive, we arrived at a small redbrick house with a screened-in front porch that ran the width of the building. A wooden swing large enough to seat three people hung just inside the screen door and was suspended from the ceiling by chains. Three straight-back chairs with worn vinyl seats sat at odd angles beside the swing.

My grandparents did not have a telephone, and we were unable to contact them prior to our trip. They did not know we were coming. Uncle Joe stepped out of the car, walked to the screen door, and knocked. Turning, he signaled me to get out of the car and join him.

There was no answer at the door. He knocked again, harder this time. After a brief pause, my grandmother stepped through the door to the porch and said, "Yes? What do you want?"

Uncle Joe stepped back as they locked eyes, and he said, "Are you Mrs. Martin?"

She raised her chin and looking down at him said, "Yes."

"My name is Joe Corley. I need to tell you about your daughter, Alice." Clearing his throat, he continued, "I have her son with me. Can we come in?"

I stood behind my uncle and looked back at the car, wishing that we could leave. I knew about my grandmother, and none of it was good. She rose to her full height, extended her chin, frowned, and glared at Uncle Joe in silence. It was clear that she was upset by the intrusion. "I guess so," she said. "Come on in. I'll get Bill. He's out back."

Uncle Joe opened the screen door as she left the porch to get her husband. We stepped inside and remained standing just inside the door. Several minutes passed before Grandma returned with Grandpa in tow. I remained behind my uncle while the three people glared at each other in silence. Their actions clearly said "You are not welcome here." Grandpa looked at Uncle Joe with a furrowed brow and downturned mouth but said nothing. Grandma was clearly in charge and had no intention of being friendly.

Uncle Joe offered his hand to Grandpa and introduced himself. Slow to react, Grandpa held out his hand and with a cold-fish handshake, remained silent. Uncle Joe locked eyes with Grandpa and asked, "Can I come in? I need to talk to you."

Grandpa lowered his chin to his chest and answered, "Certainly. By all means, do come in."

Grandma pointed to the mat in front of the door and snapped, "Wipe your feet!"

Grandpa retreated to the parlor while we wiped our feet and followed Grandma into the room. I was reluctant but did not want to be alone on the porch, so I followed a few steps behind. I did not know what was about to happen, but I was sure it was about me. Everyone's tone and attitude had me worried.

The living room had a musty smell, and was average in size and overdecorated. The carpet was smaller than the room, showing two feet of oak floor at each wall. A couch along the back wall was worn by age and covered with a crocheted afghan that gave it a comfortable look. A rocking chair, end table, and upholstered chair lined the opposite wall, making the room look smaller than it should. A well-used fireplace with wood stacked alongside helped give the room a homey look. A black cast-iron bulldog with a white face sat in front of the door holding it open.

Grandfather was average in size but thin and bald with only a slight fringe of gray hair around his ears. Rimless glasses were perched on his nose that made his eyes look small and close together. His full cheeks and double chin gave him a humorous look that was not deserved.

As he talked, he lowered his head, making the double chin even larger. He pointed to the couch and told us to sit as he moved into the rocking chair, sat back, and rocked quietly. He did not want to be in the room and was there because his wife insisted. Grandmother sat in the only other chair in the room, while I remained standing.

Uncle Joe looked at me and said, "Dubbie, we need to talk for a minute. Why don't you go outside and give us a little time?"

I nodded and started for the door. I knew that the talk was going to be about me, so instead of leaving, I settled down on the porch swing. As they talked, I could hear everything they said. I rocked forward and could catch glimpses of them as they talked.

Uncle Joe said, "I am sorry to bring you bad news, but your daughter, Alice, is in the state asylum at Little Rock."

Grandma said, "How long has she been there?"

Uncle Joe said, "I don't know, but I think it has been about two years . Ona Belle and Dubbie went to see her, and she is in bad shape. Wesley had her committed and then took off and left Dubbie. He lived alone for a while and then showed up at my place asking for a place to live. We took him in and are going to raise him."

Grandpa listened to Uncle Joe as he talked but made no effort to respond. With no further thought about her daughter, Grandma said, "What is it you want from us?" It was obvious to all that she was the decision maker in charge of the family and did not care about her daughter. Her frozen looks and body English shouted that she wanted this meeting to end.

"We don't have the money to feed, clothe, and raise a young boy," Uncle Joe said. "I have come to ask you for some help. If you could help with a little money each month, it would be appreciated."

Grandma's eyes flashed and she paused, clenching her teeth in thought. The overstuffed chair was her throne, and she sat stiffly erect and thrust her chin at Uncle Joe, rejecting his words.

Her response was blunt and vicious. "Why should we help? Wesley is a drunk that no one wants around!" With flashing eyes and a set jaw, she continued, "Dubbie is going to be just like his old man—no damn good. We don't want any part of Alice, Wesley, or the boy."

With eyes as hard as steel, she looked at Uncle Joe and said, "We are not going to help and do not want to be involved." She continued, "There is nothing to add to that, so you can be on your way."

I rose from the swing and left the porch, quietly closing the screen door. Listening to them talk left no doubt that these people hated my family and me personally. I was shaken by what Grandma had said but quietly took a vow.

No way, old lady. Not me! I am going to grow up, get an education, and make something of myself! You will see! I am going to have a good job, and a nice family that is happy and loves me.

Tears blurred my vision and ran down my face as I ran across the yard and down the street. *I am not like my dad! Not me, old lady! You will see!* I said the words in my mind again and again as I walked along the shoulder of the road.

My uncle stepped out of the house and walked down the road in my direction. Seeing the tears on my face, he said, "Come on, son. Let's go home. We don't need these people. We can make it without them." He placed his hand on my shoulder as we walked to the car.

The car, always hard to start, was true to form in my grandparents' yard. Uncle Joe ground the starter again and again with no luck. Giving up, he said, "Sounds like it's flooded." Opening the hood and checking the carburetor, he said, "Yep, it's flooded. We'll give it a minute to dry out and then try again." He closed the hood and returned to his seat behind the wheel. Several minutes passed while I stared at the empty porch and waited. There was no movement in the house, but I thought I saw someone peeking out the living room window. They clearly wanted us out of their yard.

Time to try again. Uncle Joe pushed the starter button on the dash, and the engine roared to life. With the choke off, it settled to an easy idle and was ready to go. He backed down the drive and began the long trip home.

I sat quietly and tried to think through what had just happened. My grandparents didn't care about me. They did not care about what happened to me. The only people in the world that cared about me were Aunt Ona Belle and Uncle Joe. It sounded like they could not afford to keep me. I decided to work hard and do everything I could to make them happy. Deep in thought, I stared out the window but hardly noticed the car moving down the road beside the Arkansas River.

Uncle Joe looked at me, tousled my hair, and said, "We can make it fine without that old bitch. Don't let what she said bother you."

I looked over and said, "I am not like my dad! I am going to work hard and do my job."

"You are not at all like your dad. You're more like old Mike, our mule. Hardheaded and humorous." He chuckled and continued to watch the road.

I choked back tears and tried to laugh. "Yeah, like Mike," I said. "But he's bigger than me."

"Yes, but you have some growing to do." He dodged a pothole in the gravel road. "Someday you will be stronger than Mike. I know I will be proud of you."

I looked over at him and said, "I'll work hard. I won't let you down."

Uncle Joe answered, "I know you will. We don't need these people. We'll be fine."

I loved my aunt and uncle and knew they loved me. Without them, I would be all alone. I looked out at the fields passing by and knew I could never let them down.

Two hours later, we pulled into our drive. Uncle Joe beeped the horn, and Aunt Ona Belle stepped out on the porch and waved. As we walked to the house, she called, "I have some lemonade inside. Come in and I'll pour you a glass."

We walked into the kitchen as she poured lemonade into three glasses filled with ice and asked, "How was the trip? Tell me about it."

Uncle Joe pulled his chair back from the table, sat, and took a swallow of his drink. After some thought, he said, "Interesting." He took another swallow from his glass.

Aunt Ona Belle settled into her chair at the kitchen table, looked at Uncle Joe, and said, "Well?"

I sat quietly taking sips of my lemonade while waiting for his answer. He tugged at his left ear and said, "Mrs. Martin is one tough old lady. Her husband is totally under her control. He didn't say one word during our entire conversation—just sat there like a zombie. When I told them Alice was in the hospital, they didn't bat an eye. They don't care. It's not just Alice; it's the entire family. Mrs. Martin couldn't be worse if she was a witch. She is one coldhearted woman." Aunt Ona Belle nodded, picked up the pitcher, and filled our glasses. It was going to be a hard winter, and they needed to make plans.

I picked up my glass, opened the screen door, and walked across the porch. Sandy waited outside, wagging his tail, and came to me as I took a seat on the steps. They needed to talk, and I felt in the way. Giving Sandy a pat, I walked to the barn to begin my evening chores. While I worked, I thought to myself, *You are wrong about me, old lady. You will see.* It was a thought that would motivate me through school and well into my adult life.

Chapter Twenty-Four
A Summer Job

School was out, and I had found an opportunity for a summer job working at a ranch near Mountain Home, Arkansas. They wanted a young man who had some knowledge of what to do on a ranch that was also a working farm. Knowledge of farm animals was a must. I was qualified for the job but wanted the approval of Uncle Joe and Aunt Ona Belle.

I sat on the seat beside my uncle as he drove the loaded hay wagon alongside the barn. We jumped down together, and I started pulling the alfalfa bales off the wagon to be stacked in the storage area. Uncle Joe was inside and would move them to the back of the room and stack the pile as high as he could reach. This would continue until the wagon was empty, and it gave me an opportunity to talk as we worked. As I pushed a bale inside the door, I commented, "Did you hear about the ranch up north that hires high school students for summer help?"

Always a man of few words, he said, "Yep."

I had just completed the eighth grade but was big for my age and used to farmwork. I said, "That's a job I can do."

"I know you can, but you would have to live up there all summer. Do you think you can do that?"

"Yes, sir, I can. It would just be summer work, and I would get back here in time for school. Can I have your permission to go?"

"I think you should go. It would be good for you, but you might want to talk to your aunt about it."

The noon meal is the largest of the day on a farm. The early morning work is finished, and a hearty meal is always in order. We unhitched the animals as the dinner bell rang. I looked toward the house and led Mike into his stall to remove his harness while my uncle dealt with Cricket. That done, we walked across the barnyard and up the path to the house.

The well at the back of the house provided water to wash up. Using the hand pump, I filled a bucket with water and carried it to a weathered and peeling wooden table standing beneath an oak tree. A vise mounted on one corner was used to hold farm implements that needed sharpening. I bent over the bucket, filled both hands with water, washed my face, and ran my fingers through my hair, adding water so that it was soaked. A towel that I used for drying hung on a tree limb just above my head.

A second bucket for drinking water hung next to the pump and had a long-handled dipper for daily use. I emptied the bucket and pumped it half-full for a cool drink and poured the remainder of the dipper over my head. Freshly washed and cooled off, I was ready to answer the call of my growling stomach.

Mounting the porch steps, I could smell the food we were about to enjoy. The odor of pork chops, green beans, mashed potatoes, corn on the cob, and biscuits filled the air and made my mouth water. Large mugs of iced tea made the meal perfect.

I enjoyed the food in silence until Uncle Joe commented, "Dubbie wants to do summer work on a ranch. He would have to start next week and stay there all summer. What do you think?"

Aunt Ona Belle knew about the ranch and was prepared for the discussion. Her question was for me. "Do you think you can stay there all summer and do the work?"

I knew she was concerned about me, and I did not want her to worry. I said, "I know how to do the work. Uncle Joe taught me how. I should be able to save some money for school clothes next fall."

She hesitated, sipped her tea, and then said, "Well, it will be good for you. We will miss you around here, but I think you should go."

The next day, I used the party line to call the ranch. They had my letter, and as we talked, they agreed to hire me for the summer. Their truck would be in my area early next week and would be instructed to drive to our farm for me, my horse, and my personal effects. I was to be packed and ready to load.

Several days later, a truck pulling a thirty-five-foot horse trailer parked in front of our house as dawn was breaking. The driver was six feet tall and slender, with well-worn jeans, a western shirt, beat-up boots, and a sweat-stained straw hat. He approached me with a smile and said, "Hi, I'm Bubba. Are you the kid I'm taking to Mountain Home?"

I said, "Yes, sir. Me and my horse, Tony. Do you have enough room for him?"

Bubba said, "No problem. Let's open the back door and set up the ramp. You can lead him into his stall and tie a line to his harness."

Bubba walked to the rear of the trailer and unlatched the door. We lowered the ramp so that I could walk Tony inside to join the horse already on board. The front part of the trailer was loaded with furniture that Bubba called "camping equipment." I walked up the ramp holding a leather strap attached to Tony's harness, and he followed me into the trailer. Both horses stood quietly while I tied the strap to the trailer so that he would remain there during the trip.

Tony was small in size but, as with most cutting horses, exceptional at herding a cow so that his rider could rope and control the animal. He was quick and would dodge left or right, stopping the cow from running away. After several attempts, the cow would give up and just stand still.

The challenge for me was to stay aboard Tony as he moved to control the cow. Both my hands would be busy with the rope, and I had to control the horse and stay on him, using my knees. If I relaxed a little and Tony dodged, I was left in midair to fall to the ground. That happened more than once as I learned his moves, and the taste of dirt motivated me to improve. We had become a team that was good at cutting cows out of a herd.

With the trailer loaded and locked, I opened the passenger door and climbed in next to Bubba. The seats were much higher than in a car, and looking out the window over the long hood was exciting. The roomy cab had a sleeper bunk that was just behind the seats. Small windows at each end of the mattress could be opened for ventilation.

Bubba made several adjustments and pressed the starter, and the big engine roared to life. As we started down the road, I asked, "How long will the trip to Mountain Home take?"

"Most of the day," Bubba said. "If you get tired, climb up in the sleeper and get comfortable. We have to make one stop at the truck scale. Let me do the talking there. Our license is for hauling animals, and I may have a problem with the furniture stacked in front of the horses. We are not licensed to haul furniture, so I am calling it camping equipment. If they buy that, we are okay. If they don't, they will hold us at the scale until we have another truck drive here to take the furniture off our trailer. Cross your fingers!"

As we traveled north, the flat farming country fell behind. The hills challenged the truck, and Bubba worked at shifting gears to keep us moving. I climbed into the sleeper and noticed I could see out even better from there. Stretched out and listening to the engine, I soon went sound asleep.

One hour later, we pulled to the side of the road and slowed to a stop on the truck scale. As Bubba stepped down from the cab, I slipped out of the bunk, opened the door, and jumped to the ground. The small building beside the scale was occupied by two men in dark blue police uniforms. Both had badges on their shirts. Bubba opened the door, and I followed him inside to a counter that ran the width of the building. The closest policeman approached the counter, and Bubba handed him his paperwork. After brief hellos were exchanged, the man asked Bubba, "What do you have on board?"

Bubba replied, "A couple of horses and some camping equipment."

After a brief silence, the man stamped the paperwork, returned it to Bubba, and said, "There you go. You can be on your way."

Bubba thanked him, and we returned to our truck. The engine was still running. I slammed my door shut as he shifted the gears to start us rolling. We were on our way, with no other truck scales between us and the ranch. Bubba took a deep breath and looked relieved. I climbed back into the bunk to enjoy the ride.

After another hour, we reached Mountain Home. Bubba found a parking spot near a small café, looked back at me, and said, "Do you think you could handle a hamburger?"

"Yes, sir!" I answered. I was wide awake and wanted to get out of the truck and stretch my legs. I thought of a hamburger and patted my stomach as Bubba parked in an open space beside the hamburger stand.

Bubba said, "I'll get us two to go, and we can eat 'em in the truck. We have to keep moving because of the horses."

I stepped down from the cab of the truck to the strong smell of hamburgers and French fries. Once inside, Bubba ordered two hamburgers, French fries, and two Cokes. This was my kind of meal! The cook placed our order in two sacks, Bubba paid, and we returned to the truck. He divided our meal and handed me a Coke. I placed it between my legs and waited for the burger and fries. He passed the sack to me, and we started down the road munching away at our sandwiches.

The ranch was located five miles from town, down a gravel road off the main road, leading farther north. The ranch house was a sprawling white wood building with a screened-in front porch that ran its width. Bubba parked the truck next to the barn, and we opened the door to the trailer, set up the ramp, and unloaded the horses. I led each one to a nearby pen and removed the harnesses. As they moved to the water trough, I closed and locked the gate.

We started toward the house, and Bubba said, "After I say hello to the boss, I have to be on my way. I have another pickup scheduled in Conway tomorrow and need to get in position."

Daniel, the owner, was about six feet tall and slender. He was wearing jeans and a western shirt with sleeves rolled above his elbows. His well-worn cowboy hat covered a full head of black hair streaked with gray. He had the compact muscle of a man who had done physical work all his life. His weathered face was wrinkled and brown from hours in the sun. Straight white teeth and a crooked nose gave him a distinguished look. An oversized belt buckle with the word "Champion" on it held his jeans in place, as well as my attention. I stared at the buckle and knew this man was a rodeo champion. I had visions of him riding a bucking horse to a standstill. Even better, a brahma bull, and staying with it until the buzzer. I had some serious questions to ask when the time was right.

Daniel shook Bubba's hand and said, "Thanks for bringing Dubbie and his horse to the ranch."

Bubba looked down at his shoes and said, "You're welcome. I need to be on my way but would appreciate a glass of water first."

Daniel's wife, Ann, heard them talking and came from the kitchen with a tall glass filled to the brim and said, "Here you go, Bubba. It's nice and cool."

He accepted the glass and started to drink as Daniel turned his attention to me. "It's good to have you here, Dubbie," he said. "There's plenty to do on a ranch, and we can use your help. Your bedroom is the second one on the right. You can put your gear in there."

Imagine that! A bedroom! Is this place heaven, or what? I returned to the truck for my clothes, which were in an army surplus duffle bag. It was going to be a good summer.

The barn was a short walk from the house. Like most barns, it was painted red with doors that opened in front and back and a loft that was the same size as the main floor. The loft also had doors that opened in front, with a hoist for loading and unloading hay. The steep roof had been built that way so that snow would not build up on it and collapse the building.

The main floor had six stalls and a feed room with a locking door that kept the animals out. A ten-foot water trough sat to the right of the barn door. The pipe and spigot attached to its side provided clean, fresh water.

The circular pen to the right of the trough was used to break and train horses. A six-foot-high post in the center of the pen was needed when an animal refused to settle down. Loop the rope around the post, and a horse, no matter how strong, could not drag its trainer or tear down the post.

The fenced pigpen a few feet from the rear barn door looked used but was empty. At dinner that evening, I asked Daniel if there were any pigs on the ranch, and he replied, "There sure are, but not in pens. This is Arkansas razorback country. They run wild around here, but that's only part of the problem. During the Great Depression, farmers could no longer afford to feed their pigs. Some they slaughtered for food, but most were turned out to survive on their own. The domestic pigs mated with the razorbacks to produce some four-hundred-pound hogs that are mean and can be dangerous. They are also destructive to our crops. That's why we use hog wire on the bottom half of our barbed-wire fences. It's to keep out hogs. It doesn't always work, but it does help."

Daniel continued, "There are places where a hog can break through the fence or manage to wiggle under it to get inside the field and tear

218

up our crop. You will see them on our property from time to time, and I want you to be careful. They have been known to attack humans, so stay on your horse. Always carry your rifle. You may need it if one of them makes a run at you. One of your jobs will be to ride fence looking for holes in the wire. You can take some tools and wire with you to fix the damage. There is always damage to repair, and with the size of the ranch, it takes two days to ride the entire circuit. The line shack in the back of the ranch is a good place to stay the night if you decide to complete the circuit without returning to the house."

Riding the fence was a job no one liked, which was why the work was given to me. Repairing breaks in the fence was work, but at the end of the day my reward was the line shack. Wow! Eating beans from a can heated over an open fire. Sleeping on a bunk inside a line shack. Move over, John Wayne and Tom Mix. I'm the new cowboy in town.

Chapter Twenty-Five
Riding the Fence

Everyone at the ranch attended the evening meal. Daniel's wife, Ann, had a full-time cook but worked with her to prepare our meals. It was good food enjoyed by all. I had worked there for two weeks and knew our meals were on a set schedule. Be on time, or you don't get to eat.

I cut a slice of butter with my knife and laid it on a biscuit while Daniel watched me from across the table. He pulled at his ear with his left hand and said, "Do you know the ranch well enough to ride the fence and repair holes?"

I laid the biscuit on my plate and answered, "Yes, sir. I have been all over the ranch and know every bit of it by heart."

Daniel said, "Good. Start tomorrow. Take a pack mule with you to carry what you need. Don't forget a blanket and some food if you intend to stay at the line shack. I want to check your gear before you leave to be sure you have everything."

I hardly slept that night and was up well before dawn and went to the barn. While my horse, Tony, munched away at his oats, I brushed his red coat until it shined and then combed his mane and tail. He looked over the half-open door as I returned from the tack room with his bridle. I placed the bit in his mouth, slipped the bridle over his ears, and buckled the chinstrap in place.

The mules were kept in a corral behind the barn and were always a challenge. They knew to avoid work by not being caught. You can't just walk up to a mule; you have to rope him. My rope was ready, and I knew which one I wanted as I entered the corral. Jasper was on the far side of the pen looking at me as I approached. My throw was accurate and went over his head and around his neck. As I pulled on the rope, he came to me and lowered his head so I could scratch his ears. He was the gentlest mule in the pen, which was why I had selected him to carry my gear.

Packing took an hour, and I finally was ready to go. I saddled Tony and led both animals to the water trough for a drink. As I stood beside the trough, Daniel came out of the house and walked in my direction.

I looked up grinning and said, "Morning. Looks like it's going to be a nice day."

Daniel spat and then kicked the dirt with the toe of his boot and said, "Are you all packed and ready to go?"

"Yes, sir, I am. Do you want to check my gear?"

Daniel stepped forward to my saddle while I held Tony's reins and watched, hoping I had done everything right. Satisfied with Tony, he moved to Jasper and asked, "Did you pack grain for the animals?"

"Yes, sir. It's in a sack on the other side."

Daniel said, "Good. It looks like you are all set. We have been having problems with hogs in the big alfalfa patch. We need a big harvest there, but some hogs have gotten in and torn up a large area. Look the patch over close, and be sure to fix the holes they caused."

I answered, "I'll look it over close."

Daniel gave me a stern look and said, "If you have any trouble, come back to the house. Do you understand?"

As I mounted Tony, I looked down at him and answered, "I know the ranch and understand what needs to be done. I have my rifle and will keep my eyes open for wild hogs, so there shouldn't be a problem."

I was nervous about his questions and wanted to assure him that I could do the job. Tony shook his head as I nudged him with my heels and headed out the gate toward the north pasture with Jasper in tow. As we entered the pasture, several crows cawed and flew up in front of our path. Crows have their own language, and I imagined them alerting their friends and shouting for me to get out of their pasture.

I repaired holes in the fence for the next three hours; then I left the pasture and walked Tony to a creek running through a small valley. Jasper's lead was tied to my saddle, and he followed along. When we reached the creek, both animals had a long drink while I washed my face in the cool water. We were about to start the hillside portion of the fence, and the going would be much harder. I sat on a rock and planned the remainder of my day. I wanted to be at the line shack before dark so I could unsaddle the animals and build a small fire.

As I stood up, I noticed some movement in the brush on the other side of the creek. When I looked closely, I saw a hog standing completely still, looking at me. He had to weigh three hundred pounds and did not look friendly. Slowly and deliberately, I moved beside Tony and pulled my 22 rifle from its holster. It was my Christmas present and held seventeen long rifle shots. If the hog attacked, I might not be able to kill it, but I sure could slow it down. I was ready, but the hog still had not moved. I decided to mount Tony and try to avoid a fight by moving down the hill. The big hog grunted and then squealed but did not move. I reached Tony and climbed into the saddle, holding the rifle in my right hand. The reins were looped over the saddle horn, and I picked them up with my free hand and dug my heels into Tony, urging him to move. He pranced and then leaped forward. We were out of trouble. Now that the pig was behind us, I could return my rifle to its scabbard and settle back in the saddle.

Lake Norfolk was near our property, and I steered Tony toward a nearby cove. We started over a small hill, picking our way around moss-covered gray rocks and scrub oak trees. It was easy going, but Tony was sweating and started to breathe hard. My straw hat shielded me from the sun, but sweat was beginning to get in my eyes. I removed my hat, wiped my brow, and looked up to see several buzzards circling off to the right. That was always a sign that something was dead, and I decided to take a look. As I reached the spot below the buzzards, two more flew up from the brush. That had to be the spot where they were feeding, probably on a carcass. I moved Tony in that direction and began to smell the stink of rotting meat, further proof that something was dead behind the bushes.

I remained on Tony and moved closer. As the brush separated, I could see a half-eaten dead hog and stopped. Three hogs were feeding on the carcass; one turned to face me and grunted, showing its teeth. It was about to attack. Tony danced in place as I pulled my rifle from its sheath. Two more hogs appeared behind their leader and grunted as they looked in our direction. This was a pack, and with my arrival they felt threatened. There could be more hogs in the brush around us. The leader charged, with two more following behind. I fired a shot in the air in an attempt to stop their attack. The leader stopped and turned to chase a buzzard that had just landed on the carcass. Protecting their food became a priority as the other hogs followed their leader.

I backed Tony out, and we went on our way. As we moved out of danger, I took a deep breath and returned my rifle to its sheath. No hogs were behind us, and I relaxed in the saddle.

As Tony walked along, I remembered a jingle that we used to sing in the school yard to taunt the girls. After a minute, I remembered every line. Girls thought our song was repulsive and always ran away when we sang it. That was the fun part, and we were at our best when at least four boys sang as they imitated soaring buzzards. This was a song that eleven-year-old boys could get into:

If I had the wings of a buzzard
Over an old dead mule I would fly
I would feast on guts for supper
And have some pus for pie.

The temptation to try this on with adults came on a Saturday morning while my friends and I played catch in the front yard at the Revere house. Several ladies were in the living room having tea when I called the boys together and said, "I'll bet I can talk those old ladies into letting us sing our special song for their group."

Jimmy grinned and said, "Are you talking about our buzzard song?"

"Yep," I answered. "If you guys have guts enough to do it with me. I will tell the ladies that we are The Barnyard Quartet and have a special song to sing in their honor."

We were standing in a circle trying to decide what to do when J.C. grinned and said, "We should line up in front of the fireplace, but when we start to sing tuck our hands under our armpits and move around the room flapping our elbows like wings." Everyone laughed, and we started toward the house.

I counted nine ladies in the room as we entered and stopped near the door waiting for their attention. Mrs. Revere looked our way and said, "Do you boys want something?"

I smiled my best smile and answered, "Yes ma'am. We have taken up singing and call ourselves The Barnyard Quartet. We have written a song and would like to sing it for your group." *That should do it,* I thought.

The ladies smiled their agreement, and we lined up in front of the fireplace. It was time to have fun and shock the ladies. We stood at attention while they waited for us to begin. With all our enthusiasm, we bellowed, "If I had the wings of a buzzard."

The women watched in stunned silence as we continued, "Over an old dead mule I would fly." We moved about the room circling and flapping our elbows in imitated flight. Flap, flap, circle, circle. A lady in a print dress sat with her mouth hanging open, while an older woman in a black ankle-length dress rose for her attack.

Now for the punch line. The four of us bellowed in uncoordinated enthusiasm, "I would feast on guts for supper."

The lady in black lunged for the poker beside the fireplace and yelled, "You get out of here!" I knew the end was near, and we moved toward the door singing our closing line, "And have some pus for pie!"

The poker lady was attacking in full force as we bolted through the front door, laughing out of control. She followed us to the porch waving the poker above her head and shouting, "And don't come back."

We ran to the barn and followed James Charles up the ladder to the hayloft.

I sat on a bale of hay beside J.C. as Jimmy and James Charles laughed and collapsed on a pile of loose straw.

Jimmy chewed on a straw and said, "Did you see the glare in that old lady's eyes when she ran after us with a fireplace poker? If she could have caught us, we would have been in trouble." He scratched his head and laughed.

"It will take a while for those old gals to cool off." James Charles chuckled. "We need to stay up here until they leave the house." Two hours later, we slipped out of the loft and headed for home, leaving James Charles to face his mother.

I grinned while thinking about how much fun we had that day and stepped out of the saddle to tie Tony in the shade of an oak tree. His neck was covered with sweat, and I removed his saddle so that he would cool down. Then, stripping off my shirt, jeans, shorts, and boots, I ran toward the water. A gray moss-covered boulder at the waterline provided a perfect place to dive from. I climbed the rock and did my best cannonball.

After a brief swim, I walked out of the water to bring Tony and Jasper for a drink. They drank their fill, and I tied Jasper to a small tree close to the water. Tony followed me into waist-deep water and stopped for another drink. As he began to drink, I realized that this was a horse with no fear of water. I stepped in front of him, and taking the reins, led him deeper into the lake. He followed with no resistance.

A few feet farther, and Tony was swimming. I grabbed a handful of mane and drifted with him as he swam. We moved together, and Tony swam in an arc that would return him to shore. When my feet touched the bottom of the lake, I led him back to the tree to dry off so that we could continue our journey.

The afternoon was uneventful. Several fence repairs later, we arrived at the line shack. I unsaddled both animals and gave them a good brushing. It was still daylight, and I decided to have a look inside the shack. There was no furniture, and a woodstove sat in one corner. If needed, it would warm the room during the winter months. A small window in the center of the back wall was clouded but provided a dim light. Two well-used candles had been left on the sill for use after dark. The bunk bed along one wall had springs attached to a wire mesh and a thin mattress that was stained and wrinkled from years of use. I patted it with my hand, and dust appeared in a cloud that I had to duck.

A wooden box and a bushel basket sat beside the bed. The box was badly worn and creaked when I opened the lid. Inside was what appeared to be a very old record player. A basket beside the player was filled with round barrel-type records. With some tinkering, I realized that the records could be slipped over the holder in the box. The old machine was probably built before flat records were invented.

I placed the needle on the record and cranked the handle. Slowly, the record began to move. I cranked harder; it moved faster. The scratchy sound from the record was fiddle music played by a man who called himself "The Arkansas Traveler." After a brief turn at the fiddle, the Traveler would stop playing and tell a story. These were stories about small-town people and their problems. As darkness approached, I lit a candle and continued listening to The Arkansas Traveler late into the night. My favorite story was about Peg Leg Jones, who drank too much at the pub and stuck his peg leg in a knothole in the wooden sidewalk as he was walking home. The Traveler said, "Old Peg Leg walked around and around his peg leg for a half hour before he could get it unstuck." On to the next story, with more fiddle music.

The last half of my ride included the alfalfa patch, a ten-acre field that produced enough hay to feed the livestock through the winter. The field was surrounded by barbed wire stapled to wooden posts that stood firmly in the ground, ten yards apart. The bottom half of the fence was secured with hog wire designed to keep out wild hogs. But hogs are aggressive, and the larger animals can break through, which was why I was riding the fence making repairs.

I entered the field through a wooden gate large enough for a hay wagon. The alfalfa was almost knee-high, green and healthy. The only other growth in the pasture was a tall oak tree near the fence on the other side of the pasture. I remained on Tony, turned to the left, and began my inspection of the fence. When I couldn't see any breaks on the front side, I moved to the back and spotted an area where the alfalfa had been trampled. A hog had been there, probably sleeping in the alfalfa after eating its fill. Farther down, I spotted the break, jumped down from Tony, and started making repairs.

Finished with the repairs, I walked back toward Tony, who was tied to a fence post. As I returned the tools to my saddlebag, a hog from somewhere in the field grunted and then squealed. Scanning the field, I spotted the animal standing in the alfalfa fifty yards to my right. It was looking directly at me and began to charge.

The hog, light in color with a mat of hair down the center of its back, had to weigh four hundred pounds but did not look fat, just big. And mean. This was a wild animal that was attacking me at a run. I fired one round of my rifle in the air, hoping that the noise would scare the hog away. No luck there.

The hog continued to attack, grunting and showing its teeth. I raised my rifle and began to fire, aiming at the hog's huge head. My gun barked again and again, but the hog kept coming. When the gun was empty, my last option was to run. But could I outrun an adult hog? I sure intended to try, and I headed in the direction of the tree, with the hog following my path. The grunts were louder and the hog was closer as I approached the tree. Salvation was near! A low overhanging branch was my ticket to safety. I grabbed the branch and swung up out of the reach of the hog. I sat on the branch while the animal danced, squealed, and grunted as an invitation for me to come down and fight. I looked down at an animal, which was bleeding heavily but was still alive.

Tony and the mule were not bothered by the hog and remained tied where I had left them. I intended to stay in the tree until the hog either left or died. I straddled a large branch, leaned back against the tree trunk, and waited. My horse was okay, and I just had to wait this thing out.

An hour later, the hog was still there but was no longer standing. It appeared to be dead. I swung down from my perch on the branch, picked up my gun, and reloaded with shells from my shirt pocket. I wanted to be prepared for other hogs in the area. Walking toward Tony, I heard new squeals and grunts from farther inside the patch. Not again! The tree wasn't that comfortable.

Turning in the direction of the noise, I saw a baby pig that looked about two months old. As it walked in my direction, four others followed in line. I realized that the hog I had killed was a female that attacked me while trying to protect her young.

These young piglets would not survive without their mother. I decided to return to the ranch house to tell Daniel about the pigs.

Daniel was sitting on a stool in front of the tack room repairing a broken harness as I opened the gate and entered the yard. He could see the concerned look on my face and dropped the harness on the floor as I jumped down from my horse and said, "Hi."

He frowned as he looked at me and said, "I didn't expect you back until later today. Is everything okay?"

"I had a problem with a hog in the alfalfa patch," I said. "She charged me, and I had to kill her. After I killed her, I discovered that she had five baby pigs. They look too young to survive alone. I would like to put them in the pen out back. That is, if it's okay with you."

Daniel removed his hat, wiped his brow with a handkerchief, and said, "Are they domestic pigs? Can we raise them?"

"The mother was big but looked like a barnyard hog to me. She was living in the wild and broke into our alfalfa patch, probably for food." I kicked a small pile of dried horse dung with my boot and waited for his answer. I wanted his approval to go get the pigs and bring them back to the barn.

Daniel rubbed his chin in thought and said, "Hitch a mule to the small wagon, and go see if you can round them up. Be sure to get all of them, because any that are left behind will probably die in the woods. Put them in the empty pigpen, and we will raise them."

I grinned and said, "Yesssss, sir!" I led my horse to the barn. I unsaddled him and after a quick brush-down, released him into the yard. Jasper was in good condition and had been trained to pull a wagon. Daniel stepped into the tack room, removed his harness from a peg on the wall, and handed it to me.

Jasper stood quietly while I fitted the harness, buckled it in place, and hitched him to the wagon. Using the wheel for a step, I climbed up, sat on the seat, picked up the reins, and slapped Jasper's behind. The mule moved toward the gate behind the barn. As I passed Daniel, he laughed and said, "Have fun chasing those pigs! You've got your work cut out for you." He laughed again as I jumped down to open the gate and lead Jasper outside the yard.

One hour later, I arrived at the alfalfa patch and stopped the wagon by the oak tree that had been my perch earlier in the day. The piglets had remained in the patch and were moving around near their mother.

Hopping down from the seat of the wagon, I remembered the annual pig-chasing event at the county fair. The pig used at the fair was a little older and faster, and had been greased to make the chase a real challenge. I looked at the pigs in the field and realized that they were not about to come to me. I was going to have to chase them down, one at a time. I selected the largest one, thinking it would be the most difficult. I was right about that; it took over fifteen minutes to catch that one. Chasing pigs for the next hour became more work than fun. My clothes were soaked with sweat and dirty from many attempts to dive and catch one of these cute little live wires.

With all the pigs loaded in the wagon, I climbed on my seat, picked up the reins, and slapped them on Jasper's rump to start the trip back to the barn. Daniel was still working in the tack room but opened the gate to let us into the yard. I was sweating and covered with dirt and alfalfa, but maintained my seat with attempted dignity. Daniel looked at me and began to laugh uncontrollably. "What happened to you?" he asked. "You look like you've been in a war."

I gave him a brief smile and said, "These are baby pigs, but they are fast, and it took me over an hour to catch them and put them in the wagon."

Daniel walked to the wagon and leaned on the sideboard. He folded his arms and said, "These are domestic pigs all right. Probably related to some hogs set free during the Depression. Put them in the pen out back. It will be your job to feed them every day."

"Yes, sir," I said from my seat while Jasper pulled the wagon to the rear of the barn.

All baby animals are cute, and these piglets were as cute as they come. They pranced and squealed as I moved them from the wagon to their new home. Within the next few days, they settled down and all was well.

They adopted me as their new mother and squealed with delight when I entered their pen. That could have been because I fed them sour mash twice a day. The mash had to be mixed with water at least two hours prior to each feeding, and then poured into a trough inside the pen. All five maneuvered for position as I poured the wet mash down the trough. It looked like oatmeal but was orange in color.

Farm animals expect to be fed at the same time every day. My little pigs expected to be fed each morning at five thirty. That was my habit and their expectation. That is, until one Saturday afternoon when just about everyone on the ranch went in to town. Excited about the trip, I took a bath and even washed and combed my hair. Wearing a clean shirt and freshly washed jeans, I headed for the truck. As the engine started, I climbed into the back of the pickup and took a seat on the spare tire. After a short drive, Daniel parked the truck at the town square. Everyone had plans and went their separate ways; I headed toward the drugstore for a double-dip strawberry ice cream cone. With that treat in hand, I returned to the town square. Several wooden picnic tables rested on the lawn in front of the post office. All were sturdy but worn from years of use and outdoor weather. I counted six tables, all occupied by men playing checkers. Two tables were surrounded by men watching the games; the others played alone. Several of the men had half pints of whiskey in their hip pockets that they would nip at from time to time. This was checker-playing country, and the players were serious. Tired of watching checkers, I walked to the only movie house in town to see what was playing. The theater always played a western on Saturday, but I wanted to know who starred and the name of the movie. To my delight, the star was Wild Bill Elliott, a two-gun-totin' good guy who always beat the bad guys. The theater was packed, but I found a seat halfway down the center aisle and settled in to enjoy my "lickerish" and watch Wild Bill catch the bad guys.

It was midnight when the truck pulled to a stop in front of the ranch house. I jumped down from my spare-tire seat and headed to my room. It had been a full day, and I was ready for bed. Stripping to my shorts, I slipped under the covers and fell sound asleep. Tired from the late night out, I broke my schedule and slept through feeding time. As dawn broke, I heard strange noises in my room plus an occasional squealing sound. I rolled over and opened my eyes to see five piglets dancing around my room and squealing for me to wake up. It was feeding time, and they had pushed their way through the screen door and found my room, and were insisting that I get up and feed them breakfast. The biggest pig, which I had named Hugo, was the leader, and he had his platoon in tow. Sleeping was impossible. As I sat up and dressed, I thought, *What would two-gun-toting Wild Bill Elliott do with a situation like this? Probably pull his guns and fire a couple of shots in the air to clear the room!* After several weeks, the pigs managed to get out of their pen. I could see that the pen was empty as I approached for their morning feeding. They were gone, and I did not expect to see them again. I felt bad, but there was work to be done so I put it out of my mind. They were cute little pigs, each with its own personality, and I missed not having them in the barnyard.

One day, I roped and saddled two horses for a couple who were planning to go for a ride. They lived in town but showed up at the barn every Tuesday morning to ride the horses they owned and boarded at the ranch. I always had them saddled and ready unless it was raining.

Tuesday was also my day to clean out the stalls inside the barn. It was a weekly chore that required a wheelbarrow, a large shovel, and a strong back. I provided the strong back and started on the far stall. Hard work and a warm day combined to dampen my shirt and jeans. The job would take most of the day, and I needed some water from the spigot just outside at the water trough. After a long drink, I ran the water over my head. Cool water on a hot day is one of the pleasures of life on a ranch.

Turning to go back inside the barn, I saw one little pig come around the far side of the building and walk toward me. It was the biggest pig, leader of the pack. The second pig rounded the corner, followed by the other three. All trotted in my direction with squeals to get my attention.

My babies were back! They were hungry and wanted to be fed. They surrounded me with oinks and squeals as I bent down to give each a pat and scratch their ears. They followed me while I retrieved their food pail and led them back to their pen. When I dumped the wet mash in their trough, they bumped and pushed each other for position and started noisily smacking their food.

It was no longer necessary to keep them in a pen. The barnyard was their home. I left the gate to their pen open so that I could feed them at their trough. They always followed me into the pen when I was carrying a bucket with their food. Hugo soon learned to respond to his name when I called him and would follow me around the yard. You may not be able to teach a pig to sing opera, but Hugo did just fine with "oink, oink.".

With summer coming to an end, it was time for me to return to Peaceful Valley and go back to school. I sat on the step to the tack room and thought about how much I would miss the ranch and my baby pigs. It had been a fun summer, one that I would always remember with a smile.

Chapter Twenty-Six
The Roach Tablet Factory

The two-story redbrick mansion sat on three acres of lawn, surrounded by flowering magnolia trees. A circular gravel driveway attached to the road on both sides of the property made for easy access to the front entrance. Six white pillars rested on the forty-foot-long concrete porch and extended to the roof just above the second floor. It was a stately mansion with an impressive entry. A narrow gravel road ran down the right side of the property, winding its way to a brick two-car garage. The path continued to a small barn at the back of the property that was surrounded by an enclosed barnyard. A lone milk cow chewing her cud stood near the water trough next to the building. She was the only animal in the barnyard.

Unk (pronounced like uncle but without the *-le*) was the owner and had lived there most of his adult life with his wife, who passed away two years before. On warm days, he would spend his afternoons sitting in a two-person wooden swing that hung from a tree in the backyard. I rode my bike toward his house and could see him sitting in the swing, rocking gently back and forth. I laid my bike down in the tall grass beside the swing, smiled, and said, "Hi, Mr. Harmon."

He raised his head to look at me and said, "Hi, Dubbie." He then motioned for me to sit by his side. A well-worn cushion extended the length of the seat and made swinging more comfortable. I tossed my safari hat on the ground and slipped in beside him as the swing continued its slow move forward. Unk continued to move the swing while we enjoyed a moment of quiet. I leaned back and listened to a blue jay sound its alarm in the tree above our heads.

The repeated call was the aggressive bird's way of saying it would defend its nest if we came closer. I looked up out of respect; I had been flogged by one and knew they would not hesitate to dive at my head.

Unk saw my concern and said, "That bird has a nest in the top of this tree and thinks the entire backyard is off-limits to humans." He chuckled and continued, "So far it hasn't flogged anybody, but I don't think the eggs have hatched. It will get even more aggressive when its babies are in the nest crying for food."

"Does it nest there every year?" I asked.

"This tree has been home to a pair of blue jays for at least three years, maybe even more." He looked across the yard in thought and then continued, "When I bought this property and built the house over thirty years ago, the tree this swing is hanging from was just a few feet tall."

The swing continued to move as I looked over at the massive tree trunk and said, "Wow, did you plant it when you built the house?"

"Nope," he answered. "It was already here when my wife, Lynn, and I built the house and decided to leave the little sapling right where it was. That was about the time I thought up the idea of making a powder that would kill roaches. People living in the south have an ongoing battle with roaches in their homes, and it seemed like a good idea to produce something that would help them get rid of the pests." With a small grin he continued, "Have I ever told you about how it happened?"

"No, sir, you haven't," I answered and tilted my head expecting him to continue.

"It took me almost a year to develop the formula for a powder that would do the job. I worked in my garage using trash cans and buckets to mix the chemicals for a powder. I needed live roaches for my test and had to buy them from a bait store down at the river. Lynn thought it was an impossible idea and kept after me to give it up, but I refused. It finally came together, and I rented a small building in North Little Rock and started selling small packages of the powder to stores in the area. The product was effective, but a loose powder in a house was dangerous, especially if there were children around. That's when I came up with the idea of pressing the powder into pills and selling them in small packages. My wife and I ran the business and worked there every day until she died two years ago. I couldn't run the business without her and got our daughter, Ann, to take it over. She had never married and shared a small home with another girl. I talked them into moving into my house, and they have been here ever since. Both work at the plant every day. Ann manages the business, and Betty is in charge of the operation."

I watched as he packed his pipe and lit it with a match. He inhaled deeply and blew out a cloud of smoke while I sniffed the air, enjoying the smell of tobacco, and looked down at the grass growing out of control in the yard.

"Mr. Harmon—" I said.

He interrupted to say, "Call me Unk. That's what everybody calls me."

I turned, faced him and said, "Unk, your yard needs mowing. Can I do it for you?"

He puffed his pipe in thought and looked at the yard before answering, "You're right; it needs mowing, but it's a big yard. Do you think you can handle the job?"

"Yes, sir, I do," I answered. "I can mow it for you this Saturday."

He pursed his lips looking at me and said, "Okay, and if you do a good job, you can mow it every two weeks. I'll pay you one dollar an hour. Do we have a deal?"

"Yes, sir." I smiled. "I'll come here right after I finish feeding the livestock."

I awoke Saturday morning as dawn peeked above the trees and slipped into my clothes before entering the kitchen in search of my shoes. The fire in our stove crackled, and the room was warm and comfortable. Uncle Joe walked in from the back room and said, "Morning. Coffee's ready. Do you have time for a cup, or do you have to go?"

"Yes, sir," I answered. "I told Mr. Harmon that I would mow his yard after I fed our livestock. He told me I could mow it every two weeks if I do a good job, so today is important."

Uncle Joe handed me a steaming cup of coffee and said, "I know you will do a good job. When you finish mowing, be sure to ask him if he needs anything else. Unk is easy to get along with, so you should not have a problem."

I sat in a chair beside our stove and sipped my coffee thinking about my day. Anxious to get started, I placed my half-full cup in the sink and headed to the barn, fed the livestock, and then mounted my bike for the ride to Mr. Harmon's house.

I had been mowing for two hours when Unk walked out the kitchen door and settled in his seat on the swing. The hard-shell safari hat I wore kept the sun out of my eyes but was good for little else. My shirt was soaked with sweat and sticking to my back. I pushed the mower along a flower bed beside the house. Unk waved, and I decided that it was time to take a break and join him in the swing. I shut down the mower and walked in his direction. He smiled and said, "There is a pitcher of cold iced tea on the kitchen counter. Pour yourself a glass and join me."

I bounded up the porch steps and opened the screen door to the kitchen. I licked my lips, thinking of a cool drink of tea. Several tall glasses sat beside a sweating pitcher filled with ice and tea. I filled a glass half-full, took several gulps of the cool liquid, and then filled it to the brim and walked outside to join Unk on the swing. I sat beside him sipping my tea as the swing moved slowly back and forth, not much more than a foot each way. Unk produced a pipe and packed it with tobacco from a pouch; then he clenched it between false teeth. The rich tobacco smell drifted to me as he held a lit match to the bowl and made a sucking sound.

We sat together in silence while he enjoyed his pipe, and I thought about telling him about my mom. I needed to talk to someone, and trusted Unk. We continued to enjoy the silence until I looked over at him and said, "My mom is sick and in the hospital. I went to see her, and she had changed so much I didn't know who she was."

He continued to move the swing and in a low voice said, "Your aunt told me about your mother. I know a little about her condition."

I watched him repack his pipe and reach in his shirt pocket for a match. He lit the match on the swing's armrest, held it above the tobacco, and inhaled deeply. I watched and enjoyed the sweet tobacco smell as he blew several clouds of smoke.

I looked up and asked, "Do you think she will get well?"

He puffed on his pipe, blew out smoke, and said, "Most people eventually get well, and I'll bet your mother is one that will do just that. Just give it some time."

I wanted to believe Unk but was worried. My mother had been gone a long time, and I wondered if she would ever come back. I looked over at Unk and said, "Do you really think she will be all right?'

He blinked several times, and then removed his pipe and answered, "I have heard that your mom is a strong person. I'm willing to bet she will be okay and you will have her home soon."

I believed Unk and said thanks as I returned to my lawnmower. With Sandy at my side, I gave the starter a rapid pull. It turned over but failed to catch. Sandy moved away as I made another pull. Several pulls later, I opened the choke all the way and gave the cord another pull, and the engine sputtered to a rough start. It coughed, sputtered, and settled into a smooth idle after I shut off the choke. Sandy retreated to the shade of a magnolia tree while I moved back and forth, cutting grass.

I was concentrating on mowing and did not notice the black pit bull standing at the edge of the lawn in the scrub bushes beneath a tall oak. His broad head, wide mouth, and muscular frame were those of a fighter. He stood quietly as I moved to the far side of the lawn. The big dog looked at Sandy, lowered his head, and growled, showing sharp teeth in a mouth that was strong enough to break bones. While I was at the far side of the lawn, he decided it was time to attack.

Sandy, unaware of impending danger, sat quietly watching me with his tongue hanging from the side of his mouth. The big pit bull growled and moved across the yard at a gallop, using his head to knock Sandy onto his back. A trained fighter, the dog bit down on Sandy's throat. Unable to breathe, Sandy kicked his feet in the air in a futile attempt to escape. With each movement, the black dog tightened his grip.

As I turned at the end of the yard, I could see that the two dogs were in a fight. The black demon, with a constant growl, was trying to kill Sandy. I ran to the dogs and kicked the black dog in the stomach with all my strength. With a yelp he released Sandy, snarled, and turned on me. As the dog charged, Sandy rolled over and attacked, knocking him off his feet, and bit at his flank while I landed another kick, this time to his chest. The big dog turned to bite Sandy, and I landed my strongest kick of the day to his stomach, lifting him into the air. He yelped and landed on his side in the fresh-cut grass. Our attack worked, and the dog rolled to his feet and ran. I chased him out of the yard and returned to see that Sandy was not hurt. The teeth marks on his neck oozed blood but were not serious. I smoothed his coat and found no other damage. Unk had been watching from his seat on the swing. Still breathing hard, I sat beside him, took a deep breath, and puffed out the air. The swing moved gently back and forth for several minutes, and he said, "You saved Sandy's life. That dog had him by the throat and would have choked him to death. He gave you a good fight, and you could have been hurt. I'm glad you ran him off. Good job."

I nodded and said, "The Collins farm breeds pit bulls for fighting. I have been over there and seen the place where they fight. I'll bet that was one that got out."

I looked across the lawn and realized that the lawnmower was still running. Sandy wagged his tail and followed me as I returned to work.

Summer was approaching, and the grass had to be mowed more often. I could complete the job in one day, and worked on Saturday after feeding our livestock. After a short bike ride to the mansion, I opened the shed door and rolled the mower outside to the gravel path. It needed fuel, and I returned to the shed for the gas can, screwed on the spout, and filled the tank. As I pushed it toward the lawn, Ann stepped through the kitchen door and waved. She walked in my direction as I waved back and said, "Good morning."

She answered, "Good morning. Our lawn looks good. You are doing a good job."

"Thanks."

"School is just about over for this year, isn't it?"

"Yes, ma'am. We are out for the summer in two weeks."

"Summer is our busy season at the plant," Ann said. "We could use an extra box boy for the summer. How would you like to come to work for me?"

It was exciting and I was too stunned to answer, but I nodded a yes.

Ann said, "Good. Can you start the Monday after school lets out?"

My voice returned. "Yes, ma'am. What time do you want me there?"

"We start at eight every day. Your shift will be for eight hours with a half hour for lunch."

The Roach Tablet Company was located in a concrete block building on the outskirts of town. The long, narrow building had ample parking in front with two small offices inside a glass front door that had windows on each side. The remainder of the building, over two hundred feet long, was where the tablets were made, boxed, and shipped to distributors and retailers throughout the south. A large door at the back of the building was used for shipping and receiving, and remained open every afternoon for easy access to trucks as they backed to the dock.

Sacks of flour lined one wall alongside a commercial mixer with a metal bowl that could hold one hundred pounds of flour and the ingredients needed to make the pills successfully. Two six-foot-high tablet machines stood in the center of the room, bolted to the concrete floor. A two-foot-high metal funnel attached to the top of each machine supplied powder that flowed down to a flat, round wheel lined with holes. The wheel rotated at high speed as the powder filled the holes and was pressed into tablets; then the tablets were dumped into a tray at the bottom of the unit.

The final step was to load the tablets into small boxes so they could be displayed on shelves in stores. This was done by three women who filled the boxes by hand. I was the only male employee in the building. All of the mixing, boxing, crating, and shipping was done by women, with me as a floating helper.

Rebecca was in charge of the tablet machines. It was a sensitive job, as the mixture had to be correct to produce firm tablets. I had been assigned to be her helper. She was a stout woman almost six feet tall with square shoulders, a mop of unruly red hair, and wrinkles around her eyes that made her look older than her thirty-four years. The high-top shoes and coveralls she wore were white with blotches of flour. With a spot on one cheek and flour in her hair, she looked like a baker having a bad day.

We were introduced, and Rebecca said, "Hi. We can use some help. I hope you don't mind hard work!"

"I live on a farm," I answered. "I'm used to work and know how to keep up."

"Good. I need about ten sacks of flour brought over to the mixer. Load them on the cart, and stack 'em beside the machine."

I soon learned that mixing was always done at the start of the day. The machines would make tablets until the day's mixture was used up and were quiet the rest of the day. The afternoon was for folding and packing boxes. The building was quiet, and the women could talk while they worked. I folded boxes and quietly listened to the chatter.

Rebecca looked at Judy and said, "I heard that you had a hot date Saturday. How did it go?"

Judy answered, "It was okay. We didn't do much. Had a drink at the South Street Club and danced some; then he drove me home."

We lived in a dry county, but there were private clubs that you could join for a lifetime fee of five dollars. South Street was known for strong drinks and its lively band. I continued folding boxes and listened as they talked.

"Sounds like a down evening," Rebecca said. "No backseat fun there!"

"You got that right. I was home by ten thirty."

Shirley said, "I had more fun than that staying at home with the children."

I was not sure what they were talking about but blushed and continued to fold boxes.

The following Friday was my first payday. Ann handed envelopes to each lady and gave one to me. I looked inside to see more cash than I had seen in my lifetime. I folded the envelope, placed it deep in my pants pocket, and continued folding boxes. I was planning a surprise for my uncle Joe that night.

Our farm was a five-mile bike ride from the plant. The trip seemed to fly by as I thought about how to give Uncle Joe the money I had earned. I leaned my bike against the porch and bounded into the kitchen with a loud, "I'm home!"

Aunt Ona Belle was stirring a pot on the stove and looked up, saying with a smile, "I'm cooking a stew for dinner with cobbler pie for desert. Joe is at the barn. Ring the bell and wash up."

I did as I was told and was the first one at the table. While Aunt Ona Belle worked at the stove, I dug the envelope out of my pocket, smoothed out the wrinkles, and slipped it under the knife and fork beside Uncle Joe's plate.

Once everyone was seated at the table, Uncle Joe said a brief blessing and the food was passed around. I was too excited to eat and watched as he picked up his fork and noticed the envelope for the first time.

"What's this?" he said, picking it up. I suppressed a smile as he opened the wrinkled package and looked at the cash inside.

With a stunned look, he asked, "Where did this come from?"

I could no longer contain myself and said with a smile, "It's my pay for working at the pill factory. It's for the family."

He nodded and said, "Thanks. It will help."

I spooned sugar into my tea and stirred but noticed that my aunt was smiling as she blinked back tears.

I loved them both and knew that I was a burden. This was the way I could help. I planned to work at the factory for the remainder of the summer and intended to give all the money to Uncle Joe.

Summer seemed to pass in a flash. I stopped working and started back to school. Fall was approaching, and we had crops to harvest. The alfalfa fields had to be cut, cured, and baled into hay to feed the livestock for the winter. Timing was important because the alfalfa had to lie in the field for three days before it dried enough to be baled. A rain on one of those days would ruin the entire crop.

Uncle Joe watched the weather closely and said, "We'll cut the big field on Tuesday, let the sun dry it out, and bale on Saturday."

"Can we do it all in one day?" I asked. "Or will we have to finish it Sunday?"

Uncle Joe said, "The baler will drop the bales on the ground, and we will pick them up on Sunday. It will be a busy day."

It was two days of hard work, but as the sun set Sunday afternoon, the last bale of hay was safely stored in the barn. As we were finishing our work at the barn, Aunt Ona Belle rang the bell for supper. Uncle Joe closed the feed room door, and we walked across the barnyard together. As I stepped through the gate, he said, "Take a look in the rain barrel. There's a watermelon cooling in the water. Bring it in, and we'll cut it tonight."

The cool water in the rain barrel always brought a watermelon to the right temperature for eating. I looked in the barrel, and a twenty-pound melon was floating right on top. I lifted it out and started around the back of the house toward the porch. The wet melon slipped from my grasp and fell to the ground, bursting into several pieces.

As the watermelon broke open, I yelled, "I broke the watermelon!"

Uncle Joe rounded the corner of the house and could not help but laugh after seeing the look on my face. The melon was on the ground in five big pieces.

Uncle Joe said, "It's all right. There's still plenty there to eat. Let's pick up the pieces and take them inside." I made several trips taking the watermelon to the kitchen. It was in pieces, but we had watermelon that night.

Chapter Twenty-Seven
The Hess Dairy Farm

The narrow gravel road wound its way around a hill beside the main road as it passed our farm. It could be thought of as a driveway but was almost a half mile long and ended at a dairy farm owned by the Hess family.

The Hess family had a history of dairy farming in Germany, where Adolph Hess grew up.

At sixteen, he was the tallest of his four brothers and three sisters. His slender frame was complemented with broad shoulders, strong muscular arms, and a thick neck below a melon head covered with an unruly mop of dark brown hair. His piercing blue/gray eyes and square chin commanded attention, but a quick smile and easy laugh put people at ease. As the second of four brothers and three sisters, he was responsible for feeding and milking the cows early each morning and again at dusk. This was accomplished with the help of his brothers and one sister who participated in the milking.

Their farm was far enough from Stuttgart to avoid damage in the war and continued to provide milk to the area during the fighting. The family breathed a sigh of relief when Germany surrendered and peace prevailed once again.

Adolph had heard stories about America and the many opportunities available to men of all nationalities. He dreamed of moving to America, and he worked at other farms trying to save enough money to move to New York. He was a hard worker that farmers contacted when they needed extra help. Fields needed plowing in the spring, and he was always available during the day. Crops needed tending during the summer months, and hay had to be cut and baled in the fall. It was work he was good at and provided money that he intended to use for his trip to New York City.

It took two years' hard work to save enough money to purchase a ticket on a rusty, weather-beaten transport ship that would take him to Ellis Island in New York.

He used his first week in the city to locate a place to live and hunt for a job. A boardinghouse near the docks rented rooms by the week. The rent included one meal a day, served at six o'clock. A dining room on the first floor had three tables that could seat thirty boarders. Several men were long-term tenants who worked on the docks as stevedores and knew how to find work. Adolph followed their advice and found a job loading freight on one of several docks in the area. It was hard work, but he was young, had a strong back, was willing to work, and was well liked by his supervisor.

Each day, men in search of work gathered at the entrance gate to the dock to wait for their name to be called. Adolph learned that hard workers were always called first and made sure his supervisor knew how fast he was on the job. His efforts paid off, and he became a daily "call-out" at the company.

It took two years for Adolph to save enough money to start his dairy farm. During that time, he learned English and became a regular at the local library. Because southern states had the mildest weather, they became the focus of his study.

Evenings and weekends were almost always spent at the library. One librarian, a nice young lady, spoke both German and English and offered to help with his search.

Betty was tall and slim with shoulder-length blond hair, blue eyes, and a large mouth that produced a warm smile. Her ample bosom was well hidden by a starched white print dress that buttoned at the neck and had full-length sleeves. A silver chain around her neck held a broach given to her by her grandmother.

She was devoted to her work and could see the frustration on Adolph's face as he moved about the bookshelves. She had seen him before and decided to try to help.

"Hello. I have seen you here before. Is there a particular type of book that you are searching for?"

"I am trying to learn about the southern states," said Adolph. He did not know this lady and was afraid of how she would react to his plan to start a dairy.

"Which states do you have in mind?"

"Arkansas and Missouri are the two I want to know about."

Betty led him through the stacks of books to a shelf along the back wall and said, "These are historical and should give you the information you need." Glancing down the row of books, she pulled two containing information on both states.

Handing the books to him, she said, "Take a look through these and see if you find what you want. If you need more information, let me know and I will help."

Adolph thanked her as she walked away, tucked both books under one arm, and started toward the reading area. Once there, he flipped through the books looking for information about climate, cost of land, and living conditions. Both books fell short of the information that would help him decide where to locate his farm. With limited knowledge of how the library works, he decided to tell his plan to Betty and ask for her help.

Betty proved easy to work with. She listened with wide-eyed concentration as Adolph shared his dream of opening a dairy farm in America. They began to search as a team. Betty collected information during the day, and Adolph returned to the library each night after work to read the documents she produced. Several weeks passed, and they became friends. Betty's shift ended at eight each night. Adolph invited her for tea at a nearby café. It was their time to talk about dreams of a better life. With the information she provided, he selected Arkansas for his location and contacted Greyhound to arrange a bus trip to the state capital, Little Rock.

As he discussed his plans with Betty in their favorite café near the library, he could see the sadness in her eyes. Adolph ordered a draft beer while Betty drank tea and talked in German. "I am going to miss you, Adolph. I like you a lot. It's been fun working with you in the library."

"I could not have done my research without you. You have been a great help that I will not forget. Can I write to you from Arkansas?" Adolph asked.

"Yes, please do. I will look forward to reading about your search for property."

They walked to the front door of her flat and stopped under the lighted entrance. The silence became uncomfortable. Adolph pulled her to him; she rested her head on his shoulder and said in a whisper, "I am really going to miss you, Adolph."

Adolph said, "I am going to miss you, too. I promise to write and tell you about everything I find in Arkansas."

He reached down and gave her a tender kiss that sent a shudder through her entire body. She stepped back and watched as he walked down the street without looking back.

The following day, Betty arrived at the library one hour before her usual start time. Hard work was the answer to an aching heart, and she intended to put in long hours every day. One month passed, and she wondered if she would ever hear from Adolph again. The letter arrived one month later and was on the floor inside her apartment as she opened the door.

Adolph had purchased twenty-five acres of land and started building a dairy barn while living in a tent on his property. He described the fertile pastures surrounded by trees with a stream running through the back section. The front pasture was fenced and now contained five cows he had purchased at the stockyard auction.

Betty read every word, but the last paragraph caused her to sit on her couch and gasp for breath.

"I miss you so much and know you will love it here. Together we can build our farm and raise a family. I want you to come to Arkansas so that we can be married and live together the rest of our lives. I will call you at the library next week for your answer. If it is yes, we can make arrangements for you to depart New York City."

She worked long hours at the library the following week, intending to be there when Adolph called. The telephone was mounted on the wall just behind the receptionist's desk, with the earpiece resting on a hook just above the hand crank. It had been installed several months before Adolph left and was rarely used, but he had the number tucked away in his wallet.

The phone rang on Wednesday afternoon; Betty answered but could barely hear Adolph, the static was so bad. Adolph shouted, "Betty, will you come to Arkansas and marry me?"

Betty answered so loudly people at the reading tables looked up. "Yes, Adolph, yes!" It was love over Ma Bell, and people nearby smiled.

They planned for her to depart New York the following Saturday. She resigned her position at the library and returned to her furnished apartment to pack for the trip. She intended to take two suitcases of clothing and personal items, discarding everything else.

The Greyhound bus terminal was close by, and she decided to talk with the ticket agent about the trip. The heavyset man had a round face and broad nose, and was bald with a fringe of gray hair around his ears. His kind eyes and friendly smile put her at ease as he asked, "May I help you?"

"Yes, I need some information about how to get to Little Rock, Arkansas. I need to go next Saturday if a bus leaves on that day."

"Yes, it leaves at ten thirty," the agent answered. "The trip takes two days, and you will have to change buses three times."

"Should I purchase my ticket now or wait until Saturday?" she asked.

"I recommend you buy it now, as it can get pretty busy in here on Saturday."

She purchased her ticket and tucked it safely in the purse hanging from a strap on her shoulder. After thanking the agent, she left the terminal and returned to her apartment. Packing was going to take time as she eliminated things that would overflow her cases.

The following Saturday, Betty arrived at the bus terminal at nine thirty, checked her two suitcases, and walked to the waiting area for a seat until loading was announced. She had planned the trip and dressed for comfort by wearing jeans, high-top shoes, a flannel shirt, and a gray wool coat for warmth at night.

With boarding announced, passengers lined up beside the bus facing the open door. A porter pushed a cart to the rear of the line, opened a large door, and began loading baggage into a compartment below the passenger seating area. The driver stood beside the door looking very official in a gray uniform with shined shoes and a cap that covered his streaked hair. Loading started with the driver punching each ticket and authorizing boarding. There was room for thirty-five people, but only twelve boarded. More people would be added as the bus wound its way through New York to the open road.

The seat next to Betty remained empty. She was exhausted and had slept poorly for several days as she thought about the trip. To be on the bus was a relief, and she relaxed and soon fell sound asleep.

At each stop passengers got off and others boarded. The bus began to fill, and a portly middle-aged lady filled the seat beside Betty. The movement awakened her, and the lady smiled and said, "Hi, my name is Bea. I'm going to St Louis. Where are you headed?"

"I'm going to Little Rock," she answered.

"Do you have relatives there?"

"No, I'm going there to get married and live on a farm."

"That's interesting," Bea said with a twinkle in her eye and a friendly smile. She began asking questions, and they talked well into the night.

Before departing the bus in St. Louis, Bea gave Betty her address and made her promise to write and tell her all about the wedding and the farm. It was the start of a pen pal relationship that would last for years.

Adolph worked from dawn until well after dark each day to complete the barn. He designed it to feed and milk cows. One side of the barn had a sliding back door that was the entrance for the cows. They could enter through the door, walk down the aisle, and turn into one of the many empty stalls. The front wall of each stall was a slatted V-shaped rack that could be loaded from the back with hay. The rack held the hay, but the boards were far enough apart to allow easy access by the hungry animal. The cow could eat while being milked.

Feeding was timed so that the hay would run out about the time the milking was done. With nothing more to eat, the cow would return to the pasture. Cows were fed and milked early each morning and again in the late afternoon. It was a schedule they were trained to follow, and milking had to be done at the same time every day.

With Betty on the way, Adolph worked to make their temporary home as nice as possible. The tent was twenty feet long and ten feet wide, mounted on a hardwood floor. Living alone, Adolph had given no thought to furniture. A straight-back chair and bedroll were the only two things inside the tent. He stood in the center of the room and realized the need for a table and chairs.

A trip to Sammy's Supply House and Used Furniture Store was needed to solve the problem. He raised the hood on his three-year-old truck and checked the water and oil. After closing and latching the hood, he climbed into the cab and cranked the engine, which started and settled into a quiet idle.

The trip to town would take over one hour over a gravel road that crossed two creeks without bridges. Adolph knew that the key to crossing even a shallow creek was to do it slowly. Water splashed up on the engine would cause it to die, and he would be stuck.

He approached the first creek and braked the truck to a stop just before entering the water. Placing the transmission in first gear, he slowly released the clutch, easing the front wheels into the water. The truck crossed the creek and crept up the bank on the other side. All went well, and Adolph proceeded down the road to his next challenge.

Ten minutes later, he arrived at the larger creek. The water was deeper and could be a problem, but Adolph decided to take a chance. He eased the truck into the water, but at midstream the engine died and he was stuck.

The Revere farm was close by, and Adolph knew they had a tractor. The water was just below the running boards on the truck. The engine would not start until the truck had been pulled ashore and dried out. Opening the cab door, he jumped down into the knee-high water and waded to the bank, stamped his feet, and started toward the Revere farm. Adolph could see Ben Revere in the barnyard as he crossed the field in front of the house. Ben looked up and waved as Adolph approached.

Ben said, "Hey, Adolph. How come you are afoot? Did your truck break down?"

"Morning, Ben," Adolph said. "No, I am stuck in the creek and need a hand. Can you take a minute and pull me out?"

"Sure. Let me get a chain for the tractor, and we can get you out of there."

Ben walked to the barn and unhooked a chain hanging on the back wall of the feed room. The tractor was parked alongside the barn. He climbed onto the seat, started the engine, and said, "Stand on the rail behind me, hold on, and I'll drive us there."

Adolph stepped on the rail and said, "Thanks."

Five minutes later, Ben backed the tractor to the front of the truck while Adolph hooked the chain to the bumper strut. Ben slowly pulled forward while Adolph climbed into the cab and waited for the pull to start. The chain tightened, and Ben revved the engine and slowly let out the clutch. The big rear wheels of the tractor spun in the loose gravel on the bank and then caught traction and began to move. He continued until the truck was completely out of the water; then he stopped and let the tractor roll back to loosen the chain.

Adolph got out of the truck, unhooked the chain, and passed it up to Ben while thanking him for the help.

Adolph said, "I am going to town to get some furniture. The lady I am going to marry will arrive here in two days, and I want to be ready. I will be coming back through here later today. I hope the creek will be a little lower so I can make it home."

"I'll be here all day," Ben said. "If you get stuck on the way back, let me know and I will give you a pull."

"Thanks, Ben!" Adolph said as the tractor slowly pulled away.

Adolph opened the hood of the truck and removed the distributor cap to make sure it was clean and dry. Replacing the cap, he decided to give the engine a try. Applying full choke and pressing the starter brought the engine to life with a roar. As he reduced the choke, it settled into a quiet idle. Adolph waited for the engine temperature to reach its normal level, and then put the truck in gear and continued his trip.

One hour later, he braked to a stop in front of an industrial warehouse that was badly in need of repair. The sign announcing "Sammy's Supply House" looked as old as the cracked and peeling building.

With no other customers around, Sammy was standing at the door smoking an oversized cigar. As Adolph stepped out of the truck, he said, "Good morning. Welcome to Sammy's."

Adolph nodded while moving toward the entrance. Sammy was in his early forties, average in height, and slight of build, with gray hair, a heavily pockmarked face, and a broad nose that made his eyes look too close together. His badly worn jeans and heavily soiled white T-shirt had been worn several days and were in need of changing.

He stepped back as Adolph passed through the door and said, "You're welcome to have a look through the warehouse. Is there anything I can help you with?"

Adolph stopped, thought for a minute, and said, "I am looking for a table and two chairs that will fit into a kitchen. Do you have anything like that?"

"I sure do. They are in the back. Follow me."

The warehouse was cluttered with narrow aisles that limited movement, but Sammy moved at a rapid clip that challenged Adolph. The floor was loaded with farm equipment, spare parts, office furniture, and household items covered with dust. All looked well used but were now available for sale.

As they reached the back of the warehouse, Adolph could see tables and chairs stacked in a pile well over six feet high. Several tables were upside down on top of others, and none were covered. The corner of the building had leaked during a rain. Some of the furniture was damaged beyond repair. While Adolph watched, Sammy began moving tables out of the way in search of one that was presentable.

As he pulled a dust-covered table into the aisle, he said, "This one looks solid and doesn't have any water damage."

Adolph began to look the table over closely. The oak circular top was three feet across and covered with dirt and grime. He wiped the surface with his hand, and the wood underneath was solid. It stood on a single wood base with four feet at the bottom, giving it stability on the floor. It was acceptable, and Adolph helped carry it to the rear door of the warehouse.

He turned back to the pile to look for chairs as Sammy climbed on furniture, moving deeper into the stack. Sorting through the chairs, he found two straight-back wood chairs that went well with the table. As he handed them out to Adolph, he said, "These will match your table. Look them over, and tell me what you think."

Adolph sat on one chair and wiggled his behind, and there was no creaking or movement. It was a solid chair, and the other one also passed his inspection. As they carried them to the door, Sammy said, "That's a sturdy set. It will clean up real nice."

As he moved the chair under the table, Adolph said, "I'm getting married next week and need enough furniture to make my wife comfortable. She is coming in from New York this Saturday."

Sammy listened to Adolph talk and saw this as an opportunity to sell more furniture. They stopped in front of a stack of bedroom furniture, and he said, "Son, you are going to need more than a table and chairs to make your new wife happy. You should have at least two chests and a washstand. Do you have a bed?"

"No, but I do have a sleeping bag and some blankets."

"Well, that's not gonna do. Your wife is going to expect a bed to sleep in. Let me show you what I've got."

An hour later, with Sammy's help, Adolph had added two chests, a washstand, and a bed to his purchases. The trip home flew by as he dreamed of meeting Betty at the bus station on Saturday.

The gate to his farm was secured by a rope that looped over the fence post, holding it in a closed position. Adolph stepped out of the truck, removed the loop, and walked the gate around to its open position. Cows stood nearby looking on, and one bellowed its irritation at the intrusion of a truck into the pasture. Adolph drove through, locked the gate, and parked in front of the tent. As he positioned the furniture in its new home, he worried if Betty would like what he had bought. He hardly slept the next two nights. During the day, he repositioned the pieces several times trying to find the right locations inside the tent. After several attempts, he finally gave up and decided to leave those decisions to Betty.

When Saturday arrived, Adolph was awake an hour before daylight. The bus was scheduled to arrive at noon, but he had the morning chores to complete before driving into town. There was always the creek to worry about. He wanted to allow enough time to still be early in case crossing it was a problem.

The Greyhound bus terminal was located in downtown Little Rock. The pale blue building was designed for passenger use, with rows of high-back wooden pews in a waiting room just inside the front door. The left wall had two doors, one marked "Women," the other "Men." Both had signs that said "White only." The back wall had two glass-enclosed ticket windows with agents sitting on stools to answer questions and sell tickets. The double doors to the right opened to the bus loading area. Two Greyhound buses were parked at an angle with their doors open ready to accept passengers. The parking slots directly in front of the doors were marked "arriving buses only."

Adolph parked in front of the terminal at ten o'clock. It was his first trip to Little Rock, but he was too excited to look around. He wanted to be alongside the bus when it pulled into the terminal and had arrived early to be there for Betty as she stepped onto the loading ramp.

Time seemed to stand still. Noon came, and the bus was nowhere in sight. Adolph paced back and forth on the dock waiting for Betty to arrive. Finally, at twelve thirty, the bus rounded the corner, slowed, and eased into the slot directly in front of the waiting room. The bus door opened, and the driver stepped down to assist with unloading passengers. Adolph stood close by as passengers stepped off the bus and moved into the terminal. Then Betty took the driver's hand and stepped

251

down. The bright sunlight hurt her eyes as she squinted and looked for Adolph. He stood to her right with a big smile on his face. It was an awkward moment as they stood frozen, looking into each other's eyes. Adolph moved forward, opened his arms, and embraced Betty in a hug that he hoped would never end. The gentle rub of Betty's arms on his back felt good, and he grinned as he continued to hold her close.

The driver opened the baggage compartment and placed the luggage on the sidewalk in front of the bus. Betty selected her two bags, and Adolph carried both to the truck. Still smiling, he opened the door as she stepped on the running board and slipped into the seat.

As the truck chugged toward the farm, they planned their wedding. Adolph had learned that the justice at the courthouse in North Little Rock could perform the ceremony but required two witnesses. He intended to ask Joe and Ona Belle to attend the ceremony on Monday.

Adolph stopped on the bank of the creek bed and stepped out of the truck for a closer look. While Betty watched, he located a tree branch and waded into the water to measure for maximum depth. The water level was down, and if he was careful the truck should be able to make it.

As he eased the truck into the water, Betty squealed with delight and laughed as they crossed. Both were laughing as the truck pulled out of the water to complete the crossing. As they continued down the rough dirt road, Adolph thought, *Her laugh is as beautiful as she is!*

Later that day, as the sun set over the trees, Betty and Adolph walked to the barn for the evening chores. Betty knew nothing about cows but was eager to learn, and Adolph talked as he worked. She used a pitchfork and threw hay into the V-shaped racks while Adolph did the milking.

With hay in all the stalls, she decided to try milking. Sitting on a short stool at the rear of the cow, she placed the bucket directly under its swollen udder and leaned forward, resting her head on the cow's stomach. As she grabbed a teat and pulled, the cow seemed to tighten up, and no milk came out. Again and again she tried, but no milk. Adolph, milking the cow alongside hers, saw her frustration and said, "It's okay. Don't worry. You will get the hang of it. You have to make the cow comfortable before she will give you milk."

Adolph finished the milking, and they returned to the tent to enjoy the evening. He sat in a chair at the table and watched while Betty unpacked her suitcases and arranged clothing in the chests. It was their first night together, and he could see that she was nervous. He intended to wait until they were married to consummate the relationship. When they went to bed, he held her close and they fell asleep in each other's arms.

Tent living is as close as you can get to open-air camping. Every sound around the tent can be heard. Chirping birds and squirrels in trees all sound as if they are only a few feet away. Adolph awoke early but remained in bed listening to the activity around the tent, along with the occasional crowing of a rooster.

Dawn had been announced, and it was time for the morning chores. He pulled on his coveralls as Betty sat on the bed and reached for her jeans and flannel shirt. Buttoning the shirt, she stood and gave Adolph a warm hug along with a tender kiss on his lips. As they separated, he glanced longingly toward the bed but realized there was work to be done.

The morning was cool, and both of them pulled on light jackets as they walked to the barn. The cows were already in their stalls waiting for their morning ration of hay. Betty pitched hay into the racks while Adolph started milking.

As they finished, the sun was above the trees and the day began to warm. Adolph reached for Betty's hand and said, "Let's go for a walk. I want you to see our land. There is a creek and a small pond at the back of our property, and I want you to see them."

Uncle Joe and Aunt Ona Belle always attended church on Sunday. As the newest member of the family, my attendance was required, and I dressed in clean jeans, high-top shoes, and a flannel shirt for the occasion.

There was one church in the area, attended by all who had a spiritual need. Services started at ten thirty every Sunday under the leadership of the Reverend Billy Willard. He was a tall, thin man in his midforties, bald with a fringe of gray hair, a large round nose, and barn door ears that were too large for his head. The look was a requirement for the hellfire and brimstone sermons the reverend laid on us every Sunday. He was a showman with a message. When he was on a roll, his sermon could last two hours, followed by a call to the altar for all who wanted to be saved from their evil ways.

The sermon ended with the reverend walking down the aisle and stopping at the entrance doors to receive the positive comments of the membership as the parish emptied. He shook each person's hand as they thanked him for his motivational talk.

Uncle Joe, always quiet, shook his hand and said, "Thank you, Reverend."

Aunt Ona Belle, more outspoken and with a sense of humor, said, "Keep it up, and you are going to lead us out of our evil ways."

Her relationship with the reverend was strained because of her unusual belief about donating money to the church. The reverend believed that his membership should tithe, but Aunt Ona Belle would have no part of it. She met with the reverend and explained that she would donate based on the quality of the sermon. She would put money in the collection plate based on her opinion of the prior week's sermon. The reverend, looking stunned and at a loss for words, said, "Thank you for coming."

Aunt Ona Belle, with a slight smile and a twinkle in her eye, said, "Based on what you had to say, I think you are going to owe me two dollars next week."

The reverend blinked rapidly and clenched his jaw as the next member approached to offer his hand, with a positive response.

Sunday afternoon was a day of rest from farming and a time to have an enjoyable afternoon meal. I sat on the steps, played with the dogs, and enjoyed the delicious smells wafting through the screen door onto the porch.

Looking up, I saw Adolph and Betty walking down the path to our house. Calling through the screen door, I announced, "Company is coming!"

Aunt Ona Belle walked across the porch as they approached and said, "Hi, Adolph."

"Good afternoon," he responded. "I want you to meet Betty. She arrived here from New York yesterday, and we are getting married tomorrow."

Aunt Ona Belle held out her hand to Betty and said, "Congratulations. Welcome to Arkansas. Adolph has worked on his farm for over a year but it needs a womans touch."

Betty, with her head bowed, mumbled, "Thank you."

Adolph said, "I have come to ask you and Joe to stand up for us at the courthouse. Can you do it?"

"I'm sure we can," Aunt Ona Belle said. "But I need to ask Joe if he can take the time off."

Uncle Joe was at the barn. Aunt Ona Belle stepped off the porch, walked to the tree, and rang the bell that would bring him to the house. A glider and two metal chairs sat next to the tree, and she said, "Have a seat. He will be here in a minute. We have some time to talk."

The couple took seats on the glider and began gently rocking back and forth. Aunt Ona Belle slipped into a metal chair, and I continued to sit on the steps scratching Sandy's ears with his head in my lap. Star sat in front of me waiting her turn. I could see my uncle walking across the barnyard toward the house.

Aunt Ona Belle's easy manner soon had Betty talking about New York and her bus ride to Little Rock. Adolph sat quietly as they talked and waited for Uncle Joe to arrive. They had become friends when he had helped him build his barn, and Adolph looked forward to introducing Betty.

As Uncle Joe arrived, Aunt Ona Belle returned from the kitchen carrying a tray with five glasses of iced tea and placed it on the table in front of the glider. He sat next to his wife as she passed out the tea and said, "Help yourselves to the sugar and lemon."

Adolph spooned sugar into his tea, stirred, and took a long drink. Looking at Uncle Joe, he said, "Betty and I plan to get married at the courthouse tomorrow and would like to have you and Ona Belle stand up for us."

Uncle Joe, with a twinkle in his eye, said, "Sure. What time do you want to leave tomorrow?"

Aldoph pursed his lips and thought out loud. "We have to get the milking and chores out of the way first. We could be here around nine. Can you be ready by then?"

"I will be ready anytime after eight," Uncle Joe said. "When you finish your work, come here and we can go in my car."

As they talked, Aunt Ona Belle invited Betty to come inside and discuss details for the wedding. They were excited, and laughter could be heard through the open kitchen door.

The next morning, Uncle Joe poured coffee as we warmed our hands around the stove. The morning was cool, and a fire took the chill off the room. He looked at Aunt Ona Belle and said, "As excited as they are, I expect them here before ten o'clock. We need to be ready."

Aunt Ona Belle said, "Dubbie, do you want to go to the wedding?"

I was relieved at being given the option and said, "No, ma'am. I have some things to do here."

Adolph and Betty approached our house shortly after nine with smiles on their faces. Adolph did not own a suit and had dressed in clean jeans, work boots, and a pressed denim shirt. His well-oiled hair had been combed straight back and stuck close to his head.

Betty was wearing a white ankle-length dress that buttoned at the neck and had full-length sleeves. Her grandmother's broach hung from a chain around her neck. Adolph had polished her high-top lace shoes to look almost new.

They were married at the county courthouse that afternoon, with Uncle Joe and Aunt Ona Belle witnessing the event. The demands of farm life eliminated any thought of a honeymoon. They returned to their farm for the evening chores and to prepare for their wedding night.

Chapter Twenty-Eight
A Letter from Mother

With school out for the day, I gathered my books and left the classroom to catch the bus that would take me home. The buses were parked in a line around the circular driveway in front of the school. I found my bus, climbed aboard, and took a seat halfway back. I was early, and most of the seats were empty. Mr. Todd sat in his seat and waited for everyone to load.

The trip to my stop took about twenty minutes. We were the third stop along the way. The brakes screeched as the bus slowed to a stop and Mr. Todd opened the door. I walked down the aisle and could see Sandy standing outside wagging his tail. My arrival was the highlight of his day.

I stepped off the bus, crossed the yard, and headed for the house. With Sandy at my side, I said, "Go get the paper, boy." It was on the far side of the lawn, and he galloped in that direction. While he picked up the newspaper, I ran toward the house. The race was on! The winner would be first at the porch. Just twenty feet from the porch, Sandy galloped past me to win the day.

I dropped my books on the chair beside my bed and entered the kitchen to see if a snack could be sitting out. My aunt looked up from the sink and said, "A letter came in the mail for you today."

"A letter? Who from?"

"Here it is. Why don't you open it and see?" She handed me the envelope.

It was sealed but badly wrinkled from its trip to our house. The return address said A. Black with a street address in Phoenix, Arizona. I knew my mother was no longer in the hospital but had lost contact and did not know where she was or how she could be reached. I was fourteen and had lived on the farm for over three years, and I loved my new family. Dad had disappeared, and this letter was the first contact by my mother.

I walked through the kitchen door to the porch, sat down on my bed, and dug a small pocketknife out of my jeans. I laid the envelope gently on the blanket and smoothed out the wrinkles. With my hands folded in my lap, I looked out across the yard in a daze. I worried that the letter would end my time on the farm living with the family I had grown to love. Minutes passed as I tried to gather the strength to read what was on the bed near my leg. I took a deep breath, blew it out, and decided it was time. Picking it up, I turned it over wondering what mysteries it contained.

I was afraid of tearing the envelope and wanted to open it gently. My hands were shaking as I worked the knife down the side of the envelope and removed two folded pages. I opened the wrinkled pages, smoothed them on the bed, and began to read.

Dear Dubbie:

I am no longer in the hospital. Wesley got me out and we took a Greyhound bus all the way to Phoenix. The trip took four days and we had to change buses several times. The trip across Texas took almost two days.
It was a long hot trip but Phoenix is a nice town. We have rented a small one bedroom place at a tourist court and your dad has a job at a repair shop. We like it here and if all goes well, plan to stay.
I love you very much and want you to come and visit either over the Christmas holidays or during summer. If you can come, I will send you the money for the trip through Western Union.
Please write and let me know if you can come.

Love, Mother

I read the letter again and dropped it on the bed as if it were alive. With my elbows on my knees, I rocked forward and held my face in my hands. I took a deep breath and batted back tears, trying to regain control.

I stood, picked up the letter, and walked into the kitchen with it in my hand. Aunt Ona Belle looked at me and said, "Is it from your mother?"

"Yes," I answered and held it out for her to read.

She took the letter, pulled a chair away from the table, sat down, and began reading. I stood with my hand on the back of her chair and waited until she finished.

She folded the pages, dropped them on the table, and continued to sit in her chair without moving. I stood quietly by as she looked out the window without making a sound. Minutes passed.

I avoided eye contact by looking out the front window. The screen was covered with vines, and a small tree frog was slowly making his way to the top of the window. The suction cups on his feet kept him from falling, and he was in no hurry.

The letter remained on the table. She rubbed the side of her nose with her finger, and then pushed the chair back and stood. Looking at me, she said just above a whisper, "It sounds like your mother is doing much better." I gave a slight nod as I walked to the couch and plopped down, stretched, and crossed my legs. She looked uncomfortable but finally said, "Well, what do you think?"

"I don't know what to think. What do you think I should do?"

"Joe will be back in about an hour," she said. "After he has read the letter, we can ask him what he thinks."

That was fine with me. I needed time to think and said, "I have to take care of the feeding." I started across the room toward the porch. Sandy and Star were waiting beside my bed. I crossed the porch, bounded down the steps, and walked to the barn with the dogs close behind.

I opened the feed room door as Sandy placed his nose to the ground and slipped under the floor of the feed room through a small opening. He was after a rabbit, and I suspected that the floppy-eared guy would be leaving the safety of the barn shortly. Sure enough, out popped the rabbit at a run on its way to a neighboring barn, with Sandy close behind.

Sandy yipped as he ran, and the rabbit used a zigzag pattern in an effort to confuse the dog. It was working, and Sandy could not react fast enough to catch the young bunny. He was losing the race, but I gave him encouragement and in between belly laughs said, "Go get him, boy! Go get him!" The rabbit raced across our barnyard to the safety of the neighbor's barn and slipped through a small hole in the ground beneath the floor. Sandy slid to a stop and stood barking in front of the hole in a wasted effort to scare the rabbit.

The chase was over, and I shouted to Sandy, "Here, Sandy. Come here, boy!" The big dog turned and trotted to me, wagging his tail. I reached down, patted his head, and said, "You did good, but he got a jump start on you. Better luck next time." He licked my hand as I stroked his head and gently scratched his ears. He sat on his haunches as I rubbed his back with a final pat and turned to begin feeding the livestock.

I stepped outside the feed room with a pail of grain while Sandy perked his ears up and watched. I looked down at the gentle, sweet dog and said, "You're my best friend, Sandy. I wish you could talk and tell me what to do. Aunt Ona Belle is upset, and when Uncle Joe reads the letter, I don't know what will happen."

The sun dropped behind the trees, casting long shadows across the fields. It had started to cool, and I expected a light frost during the night. As I stepped out the feed room door, I heard my uncle's Plymouth turn into our drive and stop in front of the house.

I continued feeding the livestock as Uncle Joe crossed the yard and entered the house. I knew that Aunt Ona Belle would tell him about the letter, and that would help. I dreaded going to the house and decided to brush down Cricket while she continued to eat. Her coat glowed as I brushed out her tail and then moved to Mike's stall. His coat was clotted with dirt from a recent roll that he had enjoyed in the barnyard. Using a curry comb, I made sweeping strokes, creating a cloud of dust. His coat required more work, but I was in no hurry. I finished with a brush that would make his coat glow. Mike stood quietly enjoying the attention as I moved forward to scratch his ears. I wrapped my arms around his neck and pulled him close in a hug. The big animal turned his head toward me in a show of affection. I inhaled his musty smell and thought, *If you could talk, I know you would say something nice.*

I stepped out of the stall as Aunt Ona Belle rang the bell for supper. My uncle was washing his hands in a bucket of water on the cleaning table as I reached the house. I said hi to him as he ducked his face over the bucket and splashed on water. His eyes were closed, and he patted the table searching for his towel. I decided to help and placed it in his hand. He wiped his face, looked at me, and said, "Is everything okay at the barn?"

"Yes, sir," I answered. "I just finished feeding and brushed down Cricket and Mike. They look good, and their coats are getting thick for winter."

"A good brushing always helps," he said. "Are you ready for supper?"

I smiled and answered, "Yes, sir." We turned and walked to the porch.

I had left the letter on my bed and scooped it up as we entered the kitchen. I slipped into my chair at the table and placed the letter beside my plate while watching Uncle Joe sugar and stir his iced tea. Food was passed around, and I began to eat with my head down over the plate. I could not think of what to say and made eating the answer.

Aunt Ona Belle sipped her tea while looking at Uncle Joe and said, "Dubbie got a letter from his mother today."

Uncle Joe swallowed a mouthful of food and said, "Is she still in the hospital?"

"No," she answered. "The letter has a return address in Phoenix, Arizona. I think Wesley got her out of the hospital and moved there."

"Phoenix," he said. "That's a long way from here."

I picked up the envelope and handed it across the table. He stopped eating, dropped his fork beside his plate, and reached for the letter. Reading was difficult for my uncle because of his limited schooling, and he did it slowly. I sat in a chair at the end of the kitchen table and watched his lips move silently as he read. Aunt Ona Belle stirred a pot of beans on the stove while we waited for his reaction.

As he folded and laid the letter on the table, he looked at me and said, "That's quite a letter. What do you think, Dubbie?"

I was not prepared for his question and said, "I don't know. What do you think I should do?"

Uncle Joe made a fist and placed his thumb against his lips in thought. "Phoenix is a long way off. If you decide to go for a visit, it will take four days on a bus to get there. You will have to go alone, but

Greyhound allows fourteen-year-old boys to travel by themselves, so that shouldn't be a problem." He continued, "It's up to you to decide if you want to do it."

Aunt Ona Belle saw the strained look on my face and tried to relieve the pressure. "You don't have to decide now. Take some time to think about it. I'll bet that you have some questions. Let's talk about it tomorrow after you come home from school."

The sun had set, and the evening was starting to cool. Uncle Joe added wood to the fire in our stove, and we gathered around enjoying the warmth. The radio was turned on, and we prepared to listen to our favorite program, *One Man's Family*. The theme song started to play as we placed our chairs around the stove to keep warm and listen. This was a ritual we followed every night during the fall and winter months.

Cool evenings always made for a quick trip to bed. I undressed, placed my clothes on the chair beside it, and slipped between the covers. The bed was cool but would warm from my body heat and be comfortable. The night was quiet, with only two owls calling in the nearby woods. Their calls back and forth in a language all their own would continue for several hours, stopping long after I fell asleep.

As I listened to them, my thoughts returned to the letter. Was my mother well? It was a good letter, but I was afraid for her. Had my father changed and gotten a job? I loved them both but had so many questions. It was impossible to sleep, and I lay awake well into the night thinking about what I should do.

The next morning, I put the letter out of my mind, did my chores, and caught the bus to school. In class, I drifted away from my studies and back to the letter. It seemed that the best thing to do would be to visit my parents in Phoenix. Christmas break was just over a month away, and school would be closed for two weeks. I could make the trip out and back and still have some time with my mother and father.

I decided to tell Aunt Ona Belle and Uncle Joe that I wanted to visit my parents over the Christmas holidays. I loved them very much and knew that my decision would hurt. They had become a mother and father to me, and I valued their love and loved them back. I was in a situation that would upset them, and the pain I felt would not go away.

I sat quietly on the bus waiting for Mr. Todd to reach my stop. Sandy, always reliable, was waiting beside the door as I stepped down beside the mailboxes. He licked my hand as I gave him a gentle rub on his head and started for the house.

I wanted to talk about my decision at supper and decided to avoid the kitchen and go directly to the barn. I dropped my books on the bed and started to turn as Aunt Ona Belle called out, "I have some apple pie in here. Do you want a piece?"

"Yes, ma'am," I answered and returned to the kitchen. The dogs waited on the porch as I stepped through the door and made an effort to smile. Aunt Ona Belle placed the pie and a glass of milk in front of me and said, "How was school today?"

"Fine."

"Have you thought some more about your mother's letter?" I could see the concern in her eyes; the letter had everyone upset.

I took a bite of pie, sipped my milk, and said, "I've tried not to but can't get it off my mind."

"Me, too," Aunt Ona Belle said. "There are so many unanswered questions."

"I had trouble going to sleep last night," I said. "My mind was going around in circles. All questions, no answers."

I paused for another bite of pie, gulped my milk, and said, "What do you think I should do, Aunt Ona Belle?"

She turned and placed a cover over the pie plate on the counter, looked at me, and said, "We love you very much. You are the son that we never had, and we want you to stay here with us. Joe and I have talked about enclosing the porch soon, and you will have a room. That said, I know you love your mother, and if you want to visit your parents over the Christmas holiday, we will understand."

I did not look up, finished eating my pie, stood, and carried the plate to the sink. As I turned away from the sink, Aunt Ona Belle stood beside me, put her arms around me, and gave me a long hug. With my head on her shoulder, tears began to run down my face. I moaned, and she said, "It's going to be all right, Dubbie. We will get through this." She knew I was hurting and was trying to help.

"Thanks," I said, and I turned away so that she would not see me crying. I left the kitchen, crossed the porch, and started down the path to the barn. Sandy and Star seemed to sense a problem and walked close to me the entire way.

I opened the feed room door and sat down on the step. Sandy sat beside me and placed his head in my lap. I stroked his broad head and said, "I'm in a mess and don't know what to do. Everybody is upset, and it's because of me. I wish you could talk and tell me how to get out of this." Having Sandy close made me feel a little better.

I finished the feeding and was locking the feed room door as I heard my uncle's car turn off the road toward our house. I wanted him to have some time with my aunt and was deliberately slow in finishing my work. Aunt Ona Belle rang the dinner bell, and I took my time walking to the house. I gathered the empty dog dishes and carried them to the kitchen to fix their food. Uncle Joe was in the back room as Aunt Ona Belle carried dishes to the table for our meal. We were avoiding each other, and I could feel the pressure.

Aunt Ona Belle motioned for me to take a seat and said, "It's ready. Let's eat."

I slid my chair away from the table, sat down, and waited. Uncle Joe walked in from the back room, took his seat, looked at me, and said, "Hi, Dubbie. How was your day?" He passed a bowl of steaming mashed potatoes in my direction.

I said, "Fine." I took the bowl and placed a large scoop of the creamy dish on my plate. Everyone was quiet as other dishes were passed around and eating began. I ate in silence, taking small bites, followed by gulps of tea. With my head down, I avoided talking with Uncle Joe. I didn't know what to do, so nothing seemed to be the answer.

When the meal was finished, Aunt Ona Belle began clearing the table and placing the dishes in the sink. The time to talk could no longer be avoided. I looked at Uncle Joe and said, "I have thought a lot about the letter since it came yesterday."

Uncle Joe said, "Me, too. We love you, and you are a part of our family. A young boy like you should not have to make such difficult decisions, but this is unavoidable. No matter what you do, someone is going to be upset. Take your time, think it through, and do what you think is right. I will support your decision even if it makes me unhappy." He pushed his chair away from the table, stood, and walked to the stove to stoke the smoldering fire.

The stove door clanged shut as I said, "I've been thinking about going to Phoenix over the Christmas holidays. What do you think?"

"It's a long trip. Across Arkansas and all the way through Texas before you even get to Arizona." He continued, "The trip will take about four days. You will have to go by yourself. On a trip like that, you will have to change buses just about every time they change drivers. Do you think you can handle all of that?"

"It's the only way I can find out how my mother is," I said. "I think I can do it." I waited for his answer.

We made eye contact, and Uncle Joe said, "I don't like the idea, but if you don't go, you will always be sorry. I think you should make the trip."

"Yes, sir," I said. "I'll write Mother and ask for the money I need for tickets."

I wrote the letter the next day during study hall at the school library. Not knowing what to say worked to my advantage, so I wrote one short page telling her the date I could leave and time of arrival in Phoenix. I folded and placed the single page in my math book.

The final bell rang as I gathered my books for the ride home. With school out, the yard was in a state of mass confusion as kids walked the long row of parked buses in search of their ride. I remained in my room but knew I had to load soon or miss my ride. I tucked the books under my arm and started for the bus. I located the bus and climbed the steps while Mr. Todd sat behind the wheel and said, "I was about to leave. You almost got left behind."

I gave him a shy grin, nodded, and said, "Thanks for waiting."

The bus was full, with no empty seats. I walked down the aisle expecting to remain standing, and the bus started to move. I moved to the back of the bus and spotted an open seat on the back row next to the wall. I stepped over two kids and plopped into the empty seat with my books on my lap.

Sandy waited beside the bus as I stepped out and started for the house. I dropped my books on the steps to the porch and continued walking to the barn. I needed some time alone, and the barnyard was my favorite place. Talking to the animals always helped, and I needed some time to think.

I opened the feed room door, sat on the step, and gave Sandy a pat. Cricket looked at me with her big brown eyes, swished her tail, and walked in my direction. I rubbed her nose as she lowered her head, waiting to have her ears scratched. Sandy watched as the big horse nuzzled my shoulder in search of a tidbit. Aunt Ona Belle rang the supper bell as I finished the evening feeding and filled the water trough. I started for the house with both dogs close behind.

As I entered the kitchen, Aunt Ona Belle said, "I made some cornbread for dinner, and it's still warm. Do you want a piece?"

I nodded and said, "Yes, ma'am." I eagerly pulled my chair back from the table as Uncle Joe stepped in from the back room and took his seat. We waited as Aunt Ona Belle placed dishes on the table and took her seat. Uncle Joe said the blessing, and we passed plates of potatoes, fried chicken, and cornbread after taking a generous helping of each.

Between bites of chicken, I said, "I gave Cricket a good brushing, and her coat looks a lot better."

"Good. How do the mules look?" Uncle Joe asked.

"They look okay, but I plan to give both a good brushing tomorrow."

Several minutes passed as we ate in silence. The quiet became uncomfortable, so Aunt Ona Belle looked at me and said, "Do you need some help with your letter to Alice?"

"I wrote it today in study hall but didn't mail it because I need an envelope and stamp."

"I have both in a box under the bed," she said. "When we finish supper, I'll get them for you."

"Thanks," I said and continued eating.

As I waited for the bus the next morning, I placed the letter in our mailbox and raised the flag that would alert the postman about outgoing mail.

I did not understand what made my mother and father move so far away. Why Arizona? I studied a map in the school library but found no answers. Memories of my visit to the hospital were on my mind. Maybe that was why Dad took her so far away—to get a new start. I had not lived with my parents for over four years and was nervous about our meeting.

I did not know how to prepare for the trip and asked my aunt to help. I was sitting on my bed as she opened the screen door, stepped onto the porch, and said, "Are you getting ready for your trip?"

"I don't know what to take," I said. "Can you help me get ready?"

"Yes," she answered. "You will need something to carry your clothes in. I have an army duffle bag that should do it. Look in the bedroom closet. It should be on the floor."

I crossed the porch and moved through the kitchen into the bedroom. I found the crumpled bag in the corner of the closet. It had room for more clothes than I would need.

Aunt Ona Belle looked at me and said, "Wear your jacket. You will need it during the trip."

I nodded and reached for my jacket to place it on the bed next to my duffle bag. Three shelves attached to the wall at the far end of the porch served as a chest for my clothes. Socks and shorts occupied one shelf, with shirts in the middle and pants on the top shelf. Aunt Ona Belle selected a supply of each, brought them to my bed, and said, "These should do. It's more than you will need for the trip."

"Thanks." I nodded and began stuffing clothes in the bag.

The time had come, and I was excited. The trip was frightening. I had doubts about boarding a bus that would take me away from the people I loved and a life that I had enjoyed for four years. The strain in our house was a tension that would not go away. With packing done, I undressed, slipped into bed, and tried to go to sleep. I wanted to go but was sad about leaving my aunt and uncle. Filled with thoughts of things to come, I lay there wide awake. Hours passed before I finally drifted off to sleep.

Dawn was starting to break as I slipped out of my warm bed, dressed, and crossed the porch. Sandy joined me as I started down the path to the barn. The mules stood quietly near the gate; Cricket remained in her stall waiting to be fed. Jack nudged me as I closed the gate and stroked his nose. He lowered his head and playfully nipped my shoulder. Mike moved beside Jack and crowded the older mule for some attention. It was as if the animals knew I was leaving and were waiting at the gate to say good-bye. I patted Mike's neck and turned away as my eyes filled with tears. I loved them and did not want to leave, but I had no choice.

They followed as I walked to the barn and waited while I opened the feed room door. They stood at the door looking inside as I filled a pail with grain, turned to the door, and said, "You guys aren't making this any easier. You should be in your stalls instead of looking at me." Mike seemed to understand and turned and walked to his stall. Jack swished his tail but did not move. I emptied the pail in Mike's trough and walked back to the feed room while Jack watched. The big guy turned his head toward me and swished his tail as I approached. He looked as sad as I felt. I dropped the pail, wrapped my arms around his neck, and pulled him to me in a big hug. I leaned my head against his neck and inhaled the musty smell that only mules have. Jack stood quietly while we enjoyed the time together.

The next morning, I could hear movement in the kitchen as I crossed the porch, opened the door, and stepped inside. Aunt Ona Belle believed in breakfast and made a good one every day. Heat from the woodstove had made the room warm and comfortable. I stepped to the stove, rubbed my hands together, and held them out to warm.

Aunt Ona Belle turned away from the cookstove, looked at me, and said, "You should have something to eat before we drive to the bus station. I'm making sausage and eggs with skillet toast."

"Thanks," I said. "I'll get out the milk and set the table." I was too excited to eat but did not want to let my aunt down, so I planned to try.

Uncle Joe entered the kitchen fully dressed as Aunt Ona Belle placed generous helpings of her breakfast on each of our plates and set them on the table. A plate piled high with toast rested in the center of the table, and Uncle Joe reached for the top piece and handed one to me. I started to eat and realized that breakfast was a good idea.

The trip to the bus station seemed to pass in a blur. Uncle Joe and Aunt Ona Belle sat in the front seat, and I was in the backseat beside my duffle bag. When we reached the station, I stepped out with my bag while my aunt went through her checklist, making sure everything was right.

"Do you have your ticket?" she asked.

"Yes, ma'am," I answered. "It's in my pocket."

"Do you have your spending money?"

"Yes, it's in my shoe so that I won't lose it."

"The driver will store your bag," she said. "Keep your jacket with you on the bus. You probably will need it at night and in the high country."

I folded the jacket over my right arm and gave her a nervous smile.

My uncle stepped forward, gave me a bear hug, and said, "Take care of yourself."

Aunt Ona Belle turned to me, and I could see the tears in her eyes. My eyes watered as I blinked to keep tears from running down my cheeks. With a warm hug, she said, "You be careful. As soon as you get there, work out your schedule and let us know the time you will arrive back here so we can pick you up."

"I will," I said and turned away toward the bus. The driver was standing beside the door taking tickets, and I had to board. I climbed the steps into the bus without looking back. I didn't want them to see the tears running down my face.

I waved to my family as the bus backed out of its slip. I was too nervous to sit back and continued to look out the window as the bus moved forward. I looked over my shoulder at my aunt as she buried her head on my uncle's chest, sobbing.

The strange feeling in my stomach was giving me doubts about the wisdom of making this trip. I had a consistent, reliable life with my aunt and uncle, but that now seemed to be in doubt. The big diesel engine purred as the bus rumbled down the road through tree-covered hills that blocked the sun. I folded my jacket into a makeshift pillow but could not sleep.

I watched the countryside go by with memories of sitting on my grandparents' porch listening to Grandma tell my uncle that I would be "no damn good" just like my old man. Tears filled my eyes, and my throat became too tight to swallow. The sting of what she had said burned into my brain to remain there for life. I railed at her comment and committed my entire being to succeeding in life. The negative statement became a positive motivator to remain with me forever. I was driven to succeed; failure was not an option.

Four days of watching the countryside roll by through the window of a bus was a time to consider the future. My life was about to change, and I worried that it would not be good.

Chapter Twenty-Nine
Trip to a New Life

I listened to the diesel engine purr and gazed out the window as the bus made its way down the road. My aunt and uncle had become my parents, and I loved them dearly. The picture of them standing beside the bus as it pulled away would remain in my mind forever.

The sun dropped behind the trees and the bus was quiet with only the hum of the engine as it continued its push toward Texas. I looked out the window at miles of trees and small clapboard houses. I opened the window and smelled the cool air as it flowed into the bus. I took a deep breath, puffed it out, and sat back in my seat. The half-empty bus was quiet, giving me plenty of time to think.

Sleeping on a cot on an open porch had become my home. The blankets my aunt made kept me warm and comfortable even in winter with an occasional snow. Two owls in the nearby woods continued their calls into the night well after I had drifted off to sleep. The whip-poor-wills down by the creek called every night unless it rained. Maybe they didn't like the water, because all was quiet when rain was falling.

When morning light turned the horizon to gray, I remained under the covers until Sandy padded across the porch and touched my face with his cold nose and licked my forehead. It was the best wake-up call a guy could have, and I knew to expect Uncle Joe to have coffee on the stove. He would pour me a cup as soon as I was seated beside the fire.

Cricket, Mike, and Jack would be at the barnyard gate waiting for me tomorrow morning, but I would not come. I would miss feeding them and silently wished I could be there with Sandy and Star at my side.

Jack was a mature mule, the grandfatherly type. Nothing excited Jack. At ten years old I could swing on his tail and he would only look back to watch. I learned to ride bareback on that mule but was too small then and had to get him to stand beside a stump so I could climb up and jump on his back. He did not always stand still and would time his slight movement away from the stump as I began my leap for his back. That was when I learned that a mule is blessed with a sense of humor. After three or four attempts, each followed with a fall to the ground, he would stand still and accept me as his passenger.

With a sly grin I remembered Halloween night with my three friends. Putting a cow in the belfry of a church would be talked about for years by farmers living in the area. Who would have thought that the cow would get stuck up there and take the following day to remove, while most of the community gathered to watch? My friends and I took a silent oath, and to this day no one knows who put the cow up there. It was a great Halloween trick.

I dozed as the big bus drifted across Texas but sat up when we stopped at a station for a bathroom break. It would take us two days to cross the state, and the barren land seemed endless.

I thought about my mother and hoped that she would be well. I knew that she almost died in the hospital and was glad that was over. I wished the bus would hurry so I could see that she was all right. My father? Always a problem, and I doubted that he had changed. I could only hope and fidget in my seat as we moved toward Dallas.

I loved my aunt and uncle and wanted to be with them, but I knew that I had to go see my parents. At fourteen, I was forced to make adult decisions that were painful. I choked back tears, thinking, *This is more than just a visit. I may not see Aunt Ona Belle and Uncle Joe for a long, long time. Like it or not, my mother is going to want me to stay in Phoenix, and that's what I am going to have to do. I will do that but will dream of someday returning to the farm.*

I decided to write to Aunt Ona Belle from Phoenix and ask her to leave my cot on the porch because I would be back.